BORN TO EAT

"*Born to Eat* answered all my questions about baby-led weaning. Leslie and Wendy Jo will help parents raise children who feel good about food and their bodies, which is preventative medicine at its best. I wish this book had been around when my daughter was a baby! Highly recommended for new parents."
—Katja Rowell, MD, author of *Helping Your Child with Extreme Picky Eating*

"A phenomenal read for those interested in starting solids with real food!"
—Jenny Best, founder of Solid Starts

"What comes over in this easy-to-read book is that moving on to solid foods should be a positive experience, and that we can trust our babies to know their own bodies. By choosing healthy foods and being present and purposeful at shared family mealtimes, we can feel confident to sit back and let our children make their own discoveries and decisions—because we are all *Born to Eat*."
—Gill Rapley, PhD, coauthor of *Baby-Led Weaning*

"*Born to Eat* emphasizes two of the most important aspects of child feeding that also happen to be lacking in our society today: connection and trust. Leslie and Wendy Jo combine their professional experience with their parenting wisdom to remind us that feeding our children is supposed to be a simple, fun, and nurturing experience, rather than one of stress, guilt, and worry. *Born to Eat* protects a child's ability to self-regulate their intake and nurtures their innate curiosity of food. For any parents considering the baby-led weaning approach or an approach that fosters a healthy relationship with food for the entire family, *Born to Eat* is a must!"
—Lindsay Stenovec, MS, RD, CEDRD, owner of Nutrition Instincts & founder of The Nurtured Mama Club

"Problem solved! *Born to Eat* is like a trustworthy friend showing you the ropes of feeding your infant with love and compassion. As new parents, we care deeply about doing what's best for baby, but food can be especially overwhelming. Read this book and experience the joys of watching your child explore eating with curiosity and engagement. Leslie and Wendy Jo give you the information you need and the permission to make it work for your family through the years."
—Rebecca Scritchfield, author of *Body Kindness*

"*Born To Eat* is a must-read for anyone thinking about trying baby-led weaning. It's a practical guide that provides simple, actionable steps for each stage of the process and addresses all of the common questions and fears that many parents have."
—Lindsay Livingston, RD, founder of *The Lean Green Bean* blog

"The bottom line is that parents are working too hard to feed their babies. It should be fun! Not intimidating. Let your baby explore and learn from experience on their own time. And if you think about it . . . the healthiest foods—foods in their whole, unprocessed form—are actually the easiest to self-feed! *Born to Eat* is a resource that every parent needs on their shelves."
—Sidney Fry, MS, RD, James Beard award–winning
food writer and nutrition expert

BORN TO EAT

A BABY-LED WEANING GUIDE THAT SUPPORTS INTUITIVE EATING FOR THE WHOLE FAMILY

SECOND EDITION

LESLIE SCHILLING, MA, RDN, CEDS-S & WENDY JO PETERSON, MS, RDN

Skyhorse Publishing

Disclaimer

This book contains suggestions and advice for starting solid foods with your infant. It is not a substitute for medical care or medical advice. All infants and families are different, so please discuss this process with your pediatrician and other members of your support team.

To CC and Anya:

Because of you, we've embraced our own good-enoughness knowing that is the surest way for you to claim your own. Never forget that you are fearfully and wonderfully made, our loves. You two brought *Born to Eat* to life, and we pray that you will confidently enjoy each bite this life has to offer.

and

To B and B:

You're the most supportive and loving copilots two rule-breaker women could ever ask for. Thank you for not only trusting us on this journey with your favorite baby girls, but also showing the world there are *Born to Eat* dads, too.

CONTENTS

INTRODUCTION

The simple act of eating has become so overly complicated. It can be nerve-racking simply to attempt to feed ourselves well, much less our children. It doesn't have to be that way.

Parents are some of the most talented, selfless, and overwhelmed people out there. We're parents; we know! What mom, dad, or caregiver wouldn't want to reduce anxiety around feeding and increase our confidence in nourishing our kids? As nutrition experts (and moms) who've worked in the dietetics field from pediatrics to pro sports, we're cutting through the hype and fads to make feeding easier for baby and, hopefully, less stressful for parents. We believe that infants (and adults) are *Born to Eat*.

Born to Eat is a philosophy that we feel supports a lifelong, healthy relationship with food and body that begins with a self-feeding approach as an infant. This is the process that we use with our own kids, not just because it makes sense and has been around since the dawn of man, but because it has a growing body of research to support it, as well. Infants supported in this approach are eating foods of the family and becoming natural eaters, hopefully with incredible feeding confidence and self-regulation skills. We believe that self-feeding is a successful method. Our entire population wouldn't exist if it wasn't.

In our society, people are constantly bombarded with confusing and conflicting messages from social media, the Internet, well-meaning friends, and even health professionals. We, Wendy Jo and Leslie, have taken the research and coupled it with our professional and personal experiences to start clearing up the nutritional mumbo-jumbo that can make us overthink food, feeding, and trusting our bodies for a lifetime. This is one of the main reasons we decided to write *Born to Eat*. That, and the fact that we are *Born to Eat*.

Our Journeys to Self-Feeding

Leslie's daughter was five days old when friends came to visit. They didn't come empty-handed, either—they came with food, really good food, and the book *Baby-Led Weaning* by Gill Rapley and Tracey Murkett. They spoke of how they were using baby-led weaning with their son, and right away Leslie was interested—partly because the thought of making baby food was absolutely daunting and partly because serving foods of family seemed like a really nice option.

Leslie and her husband being the geeks they are, they studied the emerging research on baby-led weaning and interviewed experienced professionals before starting their daughter, CC, with her first piece of steak, egg, avocado, etc. It just made sense: no pricey pastel blenders or purées in ice cube trays while baby learns about taste, texture, and develops fine motor skills by eating foods of the family. . . . Where do we sign up?

It's not easy; learning a new skill never is. Leslie's family is one that likes to cook most meals and sit down to eat together. This was a very helpful habit already in place. Regardless, it takes time and it's messy, but oh so worth it. We'll provide plenty of tips to help with that, don't worry!

Leslie and her husband were so grateful their friends brought them that book; it ignited a spark in Leslie because she knew it wasn't just about the food, but about the family attitude and behaviors around food that can shape a child for lifetime. And, that shaping happens mostly at home in the family environment very early in life. Leslie has spent more than twenty years working with children and adults who never got to develop (or have lost) their own body trust. We feel that this approach can help change that. It starts with self-feeding and supporting your child's autonomy, but the *Born to Eat* approach is so much more.

After watching Leslie embark on this journey with CC, other friends and colleagues joined in. When our buddy Rebecca Scritchfield joined in with her two little ones (you may know her—she's the author of *Body Kindness*), Wendy Jo was convinced this journey was the journey for her family, as well. Like many parents, she was eager to get started, champing at the bit for all the signs of readiness. When her daughter turned five and a half months old, they began the journey of self-feeding. Without giving too much away just yet, Wendy Jo shares that this has been the most rewarding part of parenthood for her family. As a nutrition professional, food ranks pretty high up there in her household, and they look forward to mealtimes as a family. Now Wendy Jo's daughter, Miss A, shares in the joys of eating with the family; whether dinner is Thai, Indian, Mexican, or Italian (her favorite) food, she's all in. With this approach, parents can become far more relaxed and baby can take the lead with self-feeding. It was apparent to Wendy Jo and her husband that Miss A was also *Born to Eat.*

> **"There is no such thing as a perfect parent. So just be a real one."**
> —Sue Atkins

Perfectly Imperfect

First off, let's get something straight: this isn't a perfect parenting book. Nor is this book a perfect nutrition book. We are not perfect parents, and even though we are nutrition experts, we don't eat perfectly. Like you, we're parents doing the best we can. What we do promise is to share the best information we have (thankfully not always conventional), comforting steps, nutrition tips, stories, and our own journeys. We want your family to feel great about the family plate without overthinking food.

Join us as we walk the perfectly imperfect path to parenthood while living in a very nutritionally confusing world. We'll start with our no-nonsense guide to self-feeding beginning at about six months of age, then we'll carry you through the late infant and toddler stages. We'll take the tenets of baby-led weaning and self-feeding and guide you through feeding your little one. Our hope is that this process will not only be a liberating experience for you and your family but also help you promote body confidence in your child (and hopefully yourself). You might just get more meals seated at the family table while you're at it. It won't be perfect (there's really no such thing), but it will be real and that's okay!

It's hard out there as a parent. We live in a culture of misinformation and shaming; food shaming, body shaming, parent shaming, you name it! If it's not *eat this to be healthy*, it's *here's the path to a perfect body* (which is only an illusion of photo editing that's perpetuates the thin-idea: also not real). We even hear things like *if you're not eating this* (insert fad of the week) *or doing this diet, you should be ashamed*. Let's face it, we live in a culture that thinks shaming is a sport (it's sad and sick). If you're not doing what others are doing, then you're wrong, a hippie, lazy, or just crazy. We absolutely do not want shaming of any kind to be a part of the *Born to Eat* philosophy or community.

How to Use This Book

Born to Eat is divided into four parts. Part 1 will take you through the background of a *Born to Eat* approach, including the background on baby food, the science behind a self-feeding or baby-led approach, and tools for preparing for your journey. Part 2 has five chapters, each devoted to eater stages from the pre-eating beginner to the advanced eater. If your little one is six months or sixteen months, there's a place to jump right in! Part 3 truly brings the *Born to Eat* approach full-circle. It's not just about feeding a baby; it's about a healthy environment for the whole family that fosters body confidence and trust. We'll guide you toward a *Born to Eat* mentality for the adults in the household, help you plan meals, and learn to savor taste and textures as a family. In Part 4, we share our favorite first foods, how to cook and serve them, along with breakfast, lunch, and dinner favorites. We're so excited you're on this journey with us!

What's New?

This is our second edition. We're so honored to share it with you and your family. We've made quite a few revisions and additions. In this edition, you'll find additional references to new books and social accounts that align with the Born To Eat approach. Since our first edition, the focus on baby self-feeding and preserving a baby's natural intuitive eating instincts has exploded. Many of our peers and colleagues have created social platforms, developed courses, and written books to help parents on their journeys. We can't wait to share them with you!

You'll find more recipes the whole family can enjoy in part 4. Our colleagues have contributed some of their favorites as well. In chapter 10, we've added more resources for parents and self-care. In general, we've added more flexibility and, hopefully, have reinforced the message that this process can be flexible, based on your family's and child's needs.

We've also taken a lot out of the book. In our first edition, we wrote things that could be read as diet culture, and in some cases, were diet culture phrases without us realizing it. The first place you'll notice this is our subtitle—it's new! In this edition, we've removed the phrases, slogans, and sentences that may show up as diet culture with surgical precision. You'll find more information about weight inclusivity and the Health at Every Size® (HAES®) approach. And, if you're wondering, what the heck is diet culture? We've defined it as well.

Diet culture will not be our legacy!

Journal Notes

Thoughts about Starting Your Journey

_____

_____

_____

_____

_____

_____

_____

_____

_____

_____

_____

_____

_____

_____

PART 1

THE *BORN TO EAT* FOUNDATION

CHAPTER 1

WE ARE *BORN TO EAT*

> "To trust children we must first learn to trust ourselves...and most of us were taught as children that we could not be trusted."
>
> —John Holt

Leslie and her husband were nervous walking into the pediatric specialist's office. The last time they were there, their little one, CC, was four months old and getting her upper lip tie evaluated. But at this visit, they were preparing for a lecture on common feeding practices. They were breaking the mold, going against the grain, and not following the conventional norms of introducing solids to an infant. Their daughter was about seven months old now and eating solid foods at the family table. She was trying and eating the same foods that Leslie and her husband were eating. They both expected to be scolded as they waited to tell the doctor how they were feeding CC without purées or baby food. Instead of a lecture about purées and textures, he said, "Why would I have a problem with that? That's how most of the world feeds their children." Leslie and her husband just looked at each other in disbelief and excitement.

Nothing has ever made so much sense to us. Humans have been around for thousands of years. We've not only thrived, but we've flourished. All without baby food. Think about it: the human race has made it this far, largely on foods of the family. Only in recent decades have we begun overthinking our foods, which has led to chronic dieting, chronic disease, and epic confusion about the best way to feed ourselves and our families. We, as humans, are *Born to Eat*. It's an innate skill that has simply been overcomplicated and underappreciated. It seems only natural to start at the beginning—with our babies. For the most part, when developmentally ready, they can eat what we eat and hopefully become healthy, happy eaters, enjoying foods of the family in the process.

> Only in recent decades have we begun overthinking our foods, which has led to chronic dieting, chronic disease, and epic confusion about the best way to feed ourselves and our families.

Many countries, aside from the United States, feed their babies this way once they're physically and developmentally ready. From birth, babies around the globe are fed in a variety of manners, whether it be the breast, a bottle, pre-masticated food (pre-chewed and fed to baby), food from the hands of a caregiver, or using a spoon. Many cultures around the world feed their babies what the family is eating and in the same manner. There are also places in the world where families don't make or have access to baby foods, yet their children are still fed and grow.

The use and production (or invention) of commercial baby food became popular during the late 1920s. There had been no major need for special foods for infants, since recommendations in those times were not to give solids until around one year of age. As women entered the workforce, there was a greater demand for a convenient way to feed their children. The age recommendations to introduce solids became younger and younger, some even just weeks after birth. By the 1950s, commercial baby food was mainstream and touted to be a more contemporary way of feeding. It was often marketed as a superior food to what parents could make at home. Ultimately, commercial baby food became a convenience item marketed to the modern woman. What parent wouldn't want to do the best by their baby? The creation and existence of baby food today makes sense to us, and we understand why people chose to use certain baby food products. Parents and caregivers are busy and want what's best for their children.

But what if we were to hit rewind? What if we returned to an era of no baby food, where the foods our infants ate were just the same foods that were a part of the whole family's diet? What if we, the parents, provided foods to the family without fussing over the freezer trays or expensive pastel blenders? What if this meant the possibility of better body trust and a healthy relationship with food for a lifetime? That time is now. This is the *Born to Eat* approach. We believe that it's less confusing, possibly more nutritious, and even—get ready—easier in the long run than contemporary and conventional advice.

> **We're aren't saying that people who've used baby food did something wrong. We're saying there's another way.**

We believe there's really no such thing as baby food, or kid food for that matter. Clever marketing and restaurant menus try their best to convince us as parents that certain foods are more exciting and acceptable to kids. It's also convinced us that kids just don't like so-called adult food or foods of the family. Many believe it's normal for kids to live on chicken fingers, French fries, and mac-n-cheese since they simply don't have the taste for vegetables. While we find those foods appealing for all ages, this is very far from the truth, and we're excited to correct that notion. Don't get us wrong—there are some great, baby-friendly convenience foods that we use while on the go or traveling, but for most of our everyday meals, our little ones eat what we eat. It's the *Born to Eat* way. There are ways we have modified our food preparation to be more baby-friendly. But, on the whole, what we make for dinner is what the family eats. And our clients have been very happy to learn that there are no short-order cooks in *Born to Eat* homes.

> "What I realized is that the approach was very natural for both my girls. I believe it was the best for my family because it saves time and money, and it enhances our interest in our baby's eating—saying 'This is Grandma's tuna salad' meant more to me than 'Here's the puréed chicken.'"
> —Rebecca Scritchfield, registered dietitian, food and fitness expert, and author of *Body Kindness*

Simply put, once developmentally appropriate, baby is allowed to self-feed the foods of the family while still using on-demand breast or formula feedings. This leaves the need for being spoon-fed purées completely out of the process since baby is self-feeding. We, Leslie and Wendy Jo, often use the terms *baby-led weaning* and *self-feeding* interchangeably. There's some debate about the terms, but let's not get hung up on that. The *Born to Eat* approach starts with baby self-feeding with safety precautions and nutrition advice along the way. Although self-feeding is considered nontraditional, it isn't a new way of feeding. It's been used for thousands of years.

The term *baby-led weaning* (BLW) was first coined by Gill Rapley and Tracey Murkett in their book *Baby-Led Weaning: The Essential Guide to Introducing Solid Foods*. We both found this book very helpful and were glad to have had it for a resource. Dr. Rapley has paved the way for a innate approach to feeding that focuses on foods of the family table. Their book has spurred an emerging body of research, as well. Being the foodies and nutrition therapists we are, we knew we wanted to add to these amazing feeding resources and demonstrate how a feeding approach can impact not just what babies are eating, but *their relationship with food and body for a lifetime.*

Like we mentioned, *Born to Eat* isn't just an approach to feeding using a baby-led style or self-feeding techniques—it's a philosophy. As you've gathered by now, we believe humans are *Born to Eat*. There's a drive to eat as soon as a baby is born. Just watch how a newborn will bob for the breast or bottle within minutes of birth. We are born with innate skills that guide our desire for nourishment. In the early years of life, we can take something so beautifully designed in nature and support it through nurture likely leading to a healthy, lifelong relationship with food and our bodies.

The *Born to Eat* philosophy starts with a self-feeding baby but encompasses so much more. We feel that any parent, adult, or child can embrace the *Born to Eat* key values:

1. Eat foods of the family as often as possible, from the developmentally appropriate infant through adulthood
2. Honor and support self-regulation of body nourishment through intuitive eating
3. When possible, eat as a family to foster connection
4. Support lifelong body confidence, trust, and gratitude while embracing body diversity

Let's break these down a bit . . .

But, First, Let's Talk about Diet Culture

We think it's important to be clear about diet culture from the beginning. It includes an almost $260 billion weight-loss industry and is the reason we question our food choices and how we define health. There is no better definition than the one created by our colleague, Christy Harrison, in her book *Anti-Diet: Reclaim Your Time, Money, Well-Being, and Happiness Through Intuitive Eating.*

"Diet Culture—a system of beliefs that equates thinness, muscularity, and particular body shapes with health and moral virtue; promotes weight loss and body reshaping as a means of attaining higher status; demonizes certain foods and food groups while elevating others; and oppresses people who don't match its supposed picture of 'health.'"

Diet culture is so wrapped up in "health" and medical communities that it can be hard to see. But, like we tell our clients, if you can start to see diet culture, you can't unsee it. Then you can help free your family from it.

Diet culture will not be our legacy. It is not welcome at the Born To Eat table.

Eat Foods of the Family as Often as Possible

We believe that families know how to feed their children the best way possible. By including foods of the family (without the input of diet culture), the family culture, beliefs, and values can be supported. We want you to determine the foods that fit your family's traditions, heritage, and budget. Our job is to help you make it feel safe and simple while including key nutrients for growth and development.

Honor and Support Self-Regulation of Body Nourishment through Intuitive Eating

We've all experienced feelings of physical hunger. Our stomach may growl, we may feel a bit off, or we may have this gentle sensation of emptiness. It's also safe to say that most people have experienced being satisfied, or getting just enough at a meal and feeling the need for more food a couple hours later. On the flip side, many, if not all of us, have probably experienced that overly, almost sick, full feeling—like after a Thanksgiving feast.

Watching an infant turn away from food, push food away, or purse her lips to refuse food is a visual sign of this amazing, innate self-regulation skill. They are demonstrating that they're tuning into their bodies, and we are honoring their fullness. Supporting a child with self-feeding, or allowing the infant to honor their own hunger and fullness cues, is called *responsive feeding*. We feel it can support lifelong trust in one's body along with feeding competence.

> Intuitive Eating is a self-care eating framework, which integrates instinct, emotion, and rational thought and was created by two dietitians, Evelyn Tribole and Elyse Resch in 1995. Intuitive Eating is a weight-inclusive, evidence-based model with a validated assessment scale and over 100 studies to date.
> —Evelyn Tribole, https://www.intuitiveeating.org/definition-of-intuitive-eating/

This approach also supports intuitive eating for the whole family. In their book *Intuitive Eating: A Revolutionary Anti-Diet Approach*, authors and fellow dietitians Evelyn Tribole and Elyse Resch suggest baby-led weaning as a way to support raising an intuitive eater by protecting their inner wisdom about eating.

In our fast-paced and, unfortunately, dieting-obsessed society, we often ignore and distrust our own intuitive cues to feed ourselves. We believe in fostering self-regulation in our children and as adults even if we have to relearn it. There's no room for dieting or restrictive behaviors in a *Born to Eat* home.

When Possible, Eat as a Family to Foster Connection

In this busy world of ours, it can be a struggle to sit down and share a meal with loved ones. Family meals model for our children how to eat, how to behave at the table, and how to try new foods. At an early age, babies watch parents hold silverware, chew food, and savor (and dislike) what they're eating. It's important for babies to watch their caregivers chew, drink from a cup, use a fork, and enjoy flavors and to listen to them describe their foods. We understand the busy life, especially if you have multiple children or work multiple jobs. When possible, take a seat at the table, savor each bite, share your memories and connection to the food, and enjoy the blessings of a family meal. There are numerous reasons to make family meals a priority, and many of them are far greater than just eating food. We'll talk more about that in chapter 10.

We believe the food we choose to eat is worth our full attention. When we're present with our food, we can appreciate how it makes us feel. Giving our food our attention can help us experience pleasure with taste or texture and then and then acknowledge the feeling of satisfaction when we've had enough. If we're present, which means no distractions like the television, emailing, social media, games, etc., it allows us to truly enjoy food, both physiologically and psychologically. We also believe that part of the satisfaction component of eating is to experience pleasure, whether it is to satisfy hunger or excite our taste buds. Being purposeful with food means spending some time to plan eating experiences like meals and snacks. You don't have to get all spreadsheet on us, but it's a good idea to know what's on the menu for dinner. It can impact eating and feeding choices all day long.

A little planning can allow for learning the many aspects of food, such as the nourishment certain foods provide, as well as appreciating and accepting a variety of flavors. Is the food spicy, sweet, smoky, bitter, or tart? So often, we go through a meal and never give a moment's thought as to what we're really tasting—not just eating, but truly tasting the food in front of us. *This* is presence with food. We're consistently coaching our clients to tune out of their jobs when possible and actually take a lunch. We frequently recommend moving away from the television or

computer screen to tune into the food so we can experience and taste the food in front of us. On the flip side, it's just as important that we give ourselves permission to step away from a food if it really isn't that satisfying. That can only be accomplished when we're present with our food and the eating experience.

The earlier babies begin to experience flavors and textures, the greater the likelihood they'll try new foods in the future. And we don't believe that *gross* and *yucky* are food descriptors, but they do offer insight into our child's eating experience. Our presence and purpose with foods help model and empower our little ones to trust their own self-regulation skills and seek the pleasure of food to satisfy physiological hunger.

Support Lifelong Body Confidence, Trust, and Gratitude while Embracing Body Diversity

Like we've mentioned, we're born with skills we need to regulate our bodies. Not feeling able to self-regulate, either as a result of dieting or simply not paying attention to our food, can undermine our body confidence over time. This is the ultimate setup for a very unhealthy relationship with food and our bodies. We want to make every effort to nip that from infant feeding going forward, and that's why we think the *Born to Eat* approach, which includes the entire family, can make such an impact. When we have confidence that our bodies have what it takes to self-regulate things like the need for food (hunger), the cue to stop eating (satiety), or the need for sleep (getting tired), we don't look for external ways to control our bodies. Having this type of body confidence early in life lays the foundation of body trust. When we trust that our bodies can guide us, we aren't as likely to seek external means of control (like dieting and dieting behaviors) because we've had years of experience of our bodies doing just what they were meant to do—self-regulate.

As parents and caregivers, it's important to foster that inner trust in our infants and children, whether that means letting them stop eating after only a couple bites of food or being up front about what's in front of them. We also have an honesty policy when it comes to eating and food. Trust is crucial to any relationship, and that includes the ones we have with food and our bodies. We're not going to tell you to hide foods or be deceptive about what you're putting on the plate; this doesn't allow for a trusting relationship with food and can sabotage the child-caregiver relationship down the road. We don't have to assume they're not going to like something (like vegetables) and sneak them into a recipe. That's not what we'd consider a win and it sure won't earn their trust in feeding.

When we begin to understand what the food in front of us can do for our bodies, we have an opportunity to also teach and express gratitude. Gratitude for what we have in front of us—like a warm meal, family and friends, a table to eat at, or a variety of foods—can give us and our kids a positive perspective around food. Gratitude doesn't stop at the dinner table, but it's a wonderful place for it to start. Practicing gratitude helps us appreciate our amazing bodies. The energy we gain from food is what fuels our lives. It supports our play, going down a slide, jumping up and down, helping others, learning, reading a bedtime story, or giving a giant hug. Practicing gratitude is a part of the *Born to Eat* approach.

As we practice gratitude and moving away from diet culture, it's essential that we help our children understand that bodies are different on purpose. Bodies come in all shapes, sizes, colors, and abilities—and all of them are good. What a wonderful world it will be when all bodies are accepted as they are.

Both of us are grateful. So very grateful. We're grateful that we've used, curated, and reaped the benefits of the *Born to Eat* approach in our own lives. And we're grateful that you are holding *Born to Eat* in your hands right now. It's our hope you'll share in the joys of the *Born to Eat* approach.

Journal Notes

How does Diet Culture show up in your family? How can the Born to Eat philosophy help?

_____

_____

_____

_____

_____

_____

_____

_____

_____

_____

_____

_____

_____

_____

_____

_____

CHAPTER 2

BENEFITS OF THE SELF-FEEDING APPROACH

> "Everything you have likely been told about how babies learn to eat is the result of a century of marketing, not evidence or physiology."
>
> —Jenny Best, Founder & CEO, Solid Starts

Wendy Jo watched her little girl, beneath a yogurt-smothered face, work on chewing, eating, and gagging on a cooked pear wedge. Talk about nerve-racking! Little A made some gagging noises (thank goodness), had a full gag effect, spit out the pear, and then proceeded to grab her next piece. Meanwhile, Wendy Jo was sitting on her hands with her eyes glued to Little A, trying to demonstrate to *chew, chew, chew.* Even as a trained professional in food and nutrition, Wendy Jo still had to calm her nerves, hide her own fear, and give her daughter the opportunity to learn on her own. This would not be the last time in life she'd have to watch her daughter navigate challenges on her own, so perhaps it was a good thing Wendy Jo started training herself right away. The good news is that with every meal and every bite, Little A gained confidence and skill, and so did her mama.

Feeding ourselves can be tricky at times. Feeding our kids the right food, at the right time, with the right texture—that can be downright overwhelming. We'd be lying if we said it wasn't scary for us, even with our nutrition backgrounds. They're our little ones—our beautiful and amazing kids. We want them to be healthy, safe, and well. That's why we both decided to study and use the baby-led style or self-feeding approach with our infants. In our study, we found that not only can this approach be an appropriate feeding method for most infants, but it may also be associated with lower maternal anxiety about the feeding process.[1] Yes, please! We both signed up for less anxiety!

Babies take their time. They're watching you eat, and learning with every bite. If a person is constantly in a rush or finds themselves distracted during mealtimes, it could spell trouble down the road. If your skin crawls when a mess occurs, or you jump with every piece of dropped food, you may want to either rescue a dog (the best food vacuum cleaners on the planet) or perhaps choose a different feeding approach. Of course we're kidding, but the truth is this approach is messy at first. In our own experiences, we've found that kids who've used this approach have better use and control of their spoons and forks at an early age. The mess is huge, but short-lived, and our dogs sure enjoy the treats their two-legged siblings drop their way.

Beyond the mess potential, you can find some information out there that scares parents and discourages starting the baby-led or self-feeding process. We discovered some of these warnings in the midst of self-feeding with our own kids. It was important for us to remember that change isn't necessarily wrong, but it's almost always scary.

> Research suggests that most healthy full-term infants do not need the addition of complementary foods until about six months of age.[2] When developmentally appropriate, most infants appear to be ready for self-feeding, or baby-led weaning.

Benefits of the Self-Feeding Approach

Whether we're talking to parents or professionals or reading the research, the main fears for using this approach are choking, the potential to miss the key nutrient iron, and slower growth patterns.[3] Let's face it, there are some challenges when it comes to baby-led weaning, just like with any type of feeding. We feel the benefits far outweigh the potential risks, or concerns, and we're going to address each of those concerns using the emerging research on this feeding method. It's also important to note that emerging research has *not validated* those possible risks. They're simply concerns or fears, albeit valid ones, that we will address.

The potential benefits don't just end at food for the family (and the family pet). We feel that using a self-feeding approach is more economical and could even have a positive societal impact, as well. If you're like us, you probably like to save money, you want to buy foods that feed the family (not just baby), you'd absolutely want to skip out on being a short-order cook, and you want to foster feeding skills and body confidence in your child. And, if you're like us, baby-led weaning or a self-feeding approach may be the perfect fit for you and your family.

> It's not just that a self-feeding, or baby-led, approach makes incredible sense to us; it's that emerging levels of research suggest that an approach like this has the potential for lifelong benefits around eating and food acceptance.[4]

At first, some of the benefits seem superficial: less time in the kitchen, not spending money on commercial baby food products, or having a less selective, or picky, eater. However, self-fed babies stand to have even greater benefits when it comes to health and wellness. Having a child who is confident in trying new foods and textures or who is more in tune to hunger and fullness cues means that child is less likely to overeat. We believe this feeding method supports the self-regulating eater by allowing the development of body trust with responsive feeding. Because of this, there is the potential for fewer body concerns in the future. Let's dive in with the benefits of the approach, and we'll weave in addressing those concerns as we go.

Improved Feeding Skills and Confidence

The self-feeding approach can promote the learning of chewing before swallowing. From the start, babies who self-feed chew or gum food first, then swallow. By doing so, they learn to recognize their gag reflex and continue chewing before swallowing. A baby who is being spoon-fed and starts with purées is likely learning to swallow first without the opportunity to practice managing foods or textures at their own pace. Additionally, the spoon-feeding process doesn't allow for exploration of baby's own normal and maturing gag reflex, particularly if the caregiver is in control of the spoon.

> "There is neither rational nor research to support the use of purées or spoon-feeding for normal, healthy six-month-old babies. Babies of this age are keen to be independent and to use the skills that they are developing. Six-month-olds who resist being spoon-fed are displaying normal behavior and following their instincts, not being difficult."
>
> —Gill Rapley, PhD, *Community Practitioner*, June 2011, volume 84, number 6

Dr. Gill Rapley, coauthor of the book *Baby-Led Weaning,* suggests that the critical phase for chewing development is from six to nine months of age.[5] This is when many babies are still eating fully puréed foods. If the baby is not introduced to more solid textures during that critical chewing development stage, they may become toddlers who are more difficult to feed. We also interviewed pediatric speech therapist and feeding specialist Jacqueline Henry, MA, CCC-SLP, about this approach. Not only does she use aspects of baby-led weaning with her feeding clients, especially self-feeding and food exploration, but she used it with her daughter, as well. Jacqueline suggests that using a self-feeding approach has many benefits when baby is developing oral-motor function, like increased exposure to a variety of textures and self-management of those textures for a more efficient and safe swallow in the future. She also proposes that this approach to feeding allows a more natural progression and maturation of the gag reflex that normally shifts from the front of the tongue toward the back of the tongue. Jacqueline has used self-feeding and baby-led weaning methods with many infants and even those who have some feeding difficulties and developmental delays. She suggests, and we support, that it's important to be open-minded about the feeding approach for every child, even if that means using self-feeding strategies, spoon-feeding strategies, or a combination of both to meet the needs of the child.

Benefits of the Self-Feeding Approach

One of the primary concerns with the baby-led weaning method (or any feeding method, really) is choking. Choking is not something we, or any health professional, take lightly. And across the board, this is the most common fear we hear from fellow parents and health professionals. It's important to note that many parents are unsure of the difference between a normal gag reflex and a choking event. We get how scary it can be just to watch your child gag the first couple of times. We both had to sit on our hands as our babies learned to navigate through a gag. However, it's critical as a parent of a newborn, toddler, or child to know the difference between choking and gagging. We'll clear up those differences in the next chapter. In cases where choking was reported, regardless of the feeding strategy, it was almost always related to specific foods. In chapter 5, we'll list foods that have been noted to increase the risk for choking and textures that may pose a problem. As we progress, we'll even suggest when to introduce them. Feeding our little ones requires time and presence, no matter the feeding method.

It's not just parents who are cautious about this approach. In one study assessing the attitudes of healthcare professionals and mothers toward baby-led weaning, researchers found that some healthcare professionals believed there may be benefits of baby-led weaning, such as supporting self-regulation, yet they still had an attitude of concern about the potential increased risk of choking, iron deficiency, and lower intakes.[6] However, few of those healthcare professionals had actual involvement or experience with the baby-led weaning approach. On the other hand, the parents who successfully used this method reported no major concerns and suggested that they would highly recommend it to other parents. A negative attitude toward, or inexperience with, the method doesn't make it an invalid option. Like the parents in the study, we felt it was worth exploring and using with our own children. Thank goodness, all of the pediatricians and pediatric specialists we encountered through our journeys did, as well.

Emerging research is helping calm some of these fears. A new study published in *Pediatrics*, the official journal of the American Academy of Pediatrics, suggests that infants using a supported baby-led weaning approach were *no more likely* to choke than infants using more traditional feeding methods.[7] Any feeding method can result in choking, but parents can be educated to help reduce the risk. We acknowledge as parents and nutrition professionals that every child is different, temperamentally and developmentally, and will learn and grow at a different pace. As a parent, it will be up to you and those in your circle of trust to make that call for your little one. Both of us started with whole foods where our babies self-fed; however, we also allowed our babies to self-feed purée-like foods such as yogurt, cream of wheat, oatmeal, and applesauce. We also watched our babies work through gags, luckily, without incidents of choking while using this feeding approach.

The Potential for Growth Concerns

As we mentioned earlier, one concern about the baby-led style or self-feeding approach is a slowed growth pattern or lower weight-gain progression. We're not compelled to believe this is necessarily a bad or good thing. While baby is being allowed to self-regulate and learning to eat, we believe that the growth pattern could be exactly on course for that particular child (providing they're developmentally appropriate for self-feeding). Just like adults, babies come in all shapes and sizes, and that's normal. So we're not sold on this particular concern.

While we don't believe that weight is a good indicator of health or healthy behaviors in adults or children, we understand the necessity of weight as a benchmark for measuring growth and development in infants and children. One study that noted the concern that babies using the baby-led weaning style of feeding had slower weight gain or lower body mass indexes (BMI) also reported that the infants who were spoon-fed gained weight at an above-average rate.[8] Just like we don't use the number on the scale as a predictor of one's health, the BMI is not a proxy or predictor of health. The BMI is a measure of one's height in relation to weight. It may be a useful tool for studying certain populations, but not useful for making individual recommendations, whether for an adult, a child, or an infant.

The American Academy of Pediatrics and the World Health Organization recommend to start complementary feeding *around* six months of age when the infant is developmentally appropriate and the gut is mature enough to accept solids. We recommend starting a self-feeding approach at the same time using the same developmental markers that we'll cover in chapter 5.

According to the Feeding Infants and Toddlers Study (FITS, 2002), developmentally appropriate infants given the opportunity to self-regulate their energy intake will do so.[9] We feel that infants using this approach not only typically excel in food variety, eating skill confidence, and self-regulation,[10] but they may also be less susceptible to weight dysregulation later in life. As nutrition therapists and registered dietitians, we've seen what not having the ability to self-regulate or trust one's body can do to a person. We feel using this approach can help foster lifelong body trust—a key *Born to Eat* value.

The Possibility for Better Nutritional Quality

Using another *Born to Eat* key value, eating foods of the family as often as possible, from the developmentally appropriate infant through adulthood, may allow for better overall nutrition quality. Although some convenience foods have been demonized by diet culture, we believe there is a place for all foods at the family table. Some of our favorite convenience foods include frozen vegetables, canned vegetables, pre-chopped vegetables, premade dough, rotisserie chicken, and so forth. We like to make or buy many fun sauces, and snacks, too. We are busy working parents, and live in the real world too. That's why we recommend and use some great food products that help all of us get dinner on the table.

One of the main concerns with the baby-led weaning method is potential for iron deficiency when beginning complementary foods. According to the World Health Organization's official website, "the transition from exclusive breastfeeding to family foods—referred to as complementary feeding—typically covers the period from 6–24 months of age."[11] Generally, approximately six month of age is when a breastfed baby has possibly depleted their available iron stores deposited in the last trimester of pregnancy and must add iron-rich foods into their diet. The amount of actual milk feedings shouldn't decrease when solid foods are introduced around six months of age. This is why the term is *complementary* feedings. While formula-fed babies still get iron from their formula, starting complementary foods with iron-rich options provides other key nutrients, as well. Regardless of the milk source, we believe this is the next step. And, don't fret! We'll arm you with a list of foods in chapter 5 along with easy recipes that will help you get iron-rich foods in front of the whole family.

> For years, many have recommended giving infants iron-fortified infant cereal as a first food. This is based on tradition *and* not medical evidence.

For years, many have recommended giving infants iron-fortified infant cereal as a first food. This is based on tradition and *not* medical evidence. Many of these recommendations have lingered from previous guidelines that included feeding infants at approximately four months old when a purée (which isn't a solid) was needed due to the lack of chewing and feeding skills. Given that developmentally appropriate six-month-olds can accept prepared solid foods, there's no reason they can't have foods naturally high in iron like beef and egg yolks. Parents embracing this approach can provide these foods as daily options.

Nutrient quality isn't just an iron issue. For example, if a family struggles to get in ample protein or a nutrient-dense diet, it's likely the vitamins and minerals those missing foods provide are being left out of baby's diet, as well. If a family doesn't have time to plan meals, convenience foods can play a role in providing key nutrients. The simple act of planning and preparing to add these complementary foods may assist the whole family in eating better with more balanced meals.

As moms, and nutrition professionals, we want what's best for our children and clients. We feel that the *Born to Eat* approach allows for feeding skill development more quickly than beginning with a puréed-only phase and that the infants who are self-feeding are likely to have greater eating confidence and trust. When eating based on their own internal regulation systems, they learn to eat just enough for their bodies. Overall, we feel this approach can help ward off dieting behavior for the whole family, which could help prevent a lifetime of body and food concerns. By honoring self-regulation, an innate skill,

and focusing on a foods of the family foundation from the developmentally appropriate infant through adulthood, we can foster healthier children and families using the *Born to Eat* philosophy.

The *Born to Eat* team wants this for your baby, your family, and our own families. We want this for our society. Body trust and confidence shouldn't be uncommon. This is why *Born to Eat* is not just about self-feeding; it's a movement toward a future of body confident adults and children.

Chapter 2 References

1. Ellen Townsend and Nicola J. Pitchford. "Baby knows best? The impact of weaning style on food preferences and body mass index in early childhood in a case-controlled sample," *BMJ Open* 2012;2:e000298, DOI:10.1136/bmjopen-2011-000298.

2. Sonya L. Cameron, Anne-Louise M. Heath, and Rachael W. Taylor. "How Feasible Is Baby-Led Weaning as an Approach to Infant Feeding? A Review of the Evidence," *Nutrients* 4(11) (2012): 1575–1609, DOI:10.3390/nu4111575.

3. Lisa Daniels, Anne-Louise M. Heath, Sheila M. Williams, Sonya L. Cameron, Elizabeth A. Fleming, Barry J. Taylor, Ben J. Wheeler, Rosalind S. Gibson, and Rachael W. Taylor. "Baby-Led Introduction to SolidS (BLISS) study: a randomised controlled trial of a baby-led approach to complementary feeding," *BMC Pediatrics* 15 (2015): 179, DOI:10.1186/s12887-015-0491-8.

4. See Reference 1.

5. Gill Rapley, "Baby-led weaning: transitioning to solid foods at the baby's own pace," *Community Practitioner* 84 (2011): 20–3, accessed October 4, 2016.

6. Sonya L. Cameron, Anne-Louise M. Heath, and Rachael W. Taylor. "How Feasible Is Baby-Led Weaning as an Approach to Infant Feeding? A Review of the Evidence," *Nutrients* 4(11) (2012): 1575–1609, DOI:10.3390/nu4111575.

7. Louise J. Fangupo, Anne-Louise M. Heath, Sheila M. Williams, Liz W. Erickson Williams, Brittany J. Morison, Elizabeth A. Fleming, Barry J. Taylor, Benjamin J. Wheeler, and Rachael W. Taylor. "A Baby-Led Approach to Eating Solids and Risk of Choking," *Pediatrics* (September 2016): e20160772, DOI: 10.1542/peds.2016-0772.

8. See Reference 1.

9. Mary Kay Fox, Barbara Devaney, Kathleen Reidy, Carol Razafindrakoto, and Paula Ziegler. "Relationship between Portion Size and Energy Intake among Infants and Toddlers: Evidence of Self-Regulation," *Journal of the Academy of Nutrition and Dietetics* Volume 106 , Issue 1 (January 2006): 77–83, DOI: 10.1016/j.jada.2005.09.039

10. Amy Brown and Michelle D. Lee, "Early influences on child satiety-responsiveness: the role of weaning style," *Pediatric Obesity* 10 (2015): 57–66, DOI:10.1111/j.2047-6310.2013.00207.x

11. "Appropriate complementary feeding," *e-Library of Evidence for Nutrition Actions (e-LENA)* http://www.who.int/elena/titles/complementary_feeding/en/, accessed October 4, 2016.

CHAPTER 3

BORN TO EAT BUILDING BLOCKS

> "It's not what you do for your children, but what you have taught them to do for themselves, that will make them successful human beings."
>
> —Ann Landers

Our friend, Julie, said that her experience with self-feeding was one of fear and chickening out. She wished she had a better story to share. With baby number two on the way, she's planning to do things differently. At the time she was beginning to feed her first daughter, the pediatrician she was seeing was very negative about the baby-led weaning process (they've since changed). And she didn't know many people who had any experience with it. The first time her daughter gagged, Julie and her husband got scared and immediately threw in the towel. She says that she wishes she would have kept going now, as feeding her daughter and getting her to eat a variety of foods has been a challenge. She says her daughter isn't the worst eater and that she accepts a variety of foods, but she does run into problems when textures are mixed together, or part of a family meal or dish, or foods that are seasoned. Her daughter prefers to eat most of her foods separately, making cooking for the family more stressful and challenging. Now she wonders if sticking with the baby-led weaning process would have made a difference for her daughter and her cooking times.

Julie says it's her hope that baby number two will be different now that she has more confidence with the process. She's watched many friends embrace the approach with so much success. The first time around, she had so many fears and unanswered questions. All those little details kept her worried and prevented her from fully trying the process. She wonders if she would have been able to make it work if she knew the answers to her questions back then. Fear is such a terrible and paralyzing feeling!

Julie, along with many other moms and nutrition professionals, did us the tremendous favor of sharing all of their concerns, fears, and questions. Even though we've counseled parents of young children for years, both before and after having our own kids, we had our own questions through the process, as well. There were no answers in textbooks and many people, both friends and professionals, just passed off the baby-led or self-feeding approach as a fad. We realized that it wasn't a fad or a new thing, given that the whole human race made it this far without baby food.

In the beginning, we were eager for answers, too, just like all the parents we interviewed. We are grateful that these parents, friends, and professionals shared their experiences—the good ones and the not-so-good ones—because, when we looked at the fears and questions they shared, we realized that the same questions kept coming up over and over again. We knew we had to address them, and we knew that we could.

The As to the Qs

As promised, we've got the answers to these questions. We'll tackle them briefly here. We've got a lot to share with you, so we're going to tell you where to find more answers throughout the chapters of the book as we go.

> "I never would have even thought about skipping puréed baby food and starting with food the family eats if it was not for a friend I trusted who was doing it with her own daughter. I needed someone else's confidence and knowledge to spark my own interest, and my confidence came later–with experience."
> —Rebecca Scritchfield, registered dietitian, food and fitness expert, and author of *Body Kindness*

Top 10 Questions about a Self-Feeding Approach

1. What is the difference between gagging and choking?
2. How often should baby get breast milk or formula? Several moms I know started eliminating nursing sessions and replaced them with solid feeding sessions.
3. How many meals a day should baby get at first?
4. Should we worry about food allergies?
5. Should we introduce only one food at a time? Is there a timeline? When can we start doing little pieces of chopped grapes? How about a forkful of lasagna? When are crackers okay? Toast?
6. Can baby be served mixed-food meals?
7. How long should we cook veggies and how soft should they be? For instance, how long should we boil or steam carrots?
8. How do we serve baby portions? Wide/narrow to cut the strips/chunks? How thick should I slice a little piece of steak? How big should the toast slices be?
9. How long should baby sit at a meal to explore, play, or eat her food? I knew I needed to let her be the one to explore and feed herself, but how long should I give her to explore? Sometimes I sat there and no food would actually be eaten. I didn't know how long I should give her for each meal.
10. What if my pediatrician has never heard of, or is unsupportive of, baby-led weaning?

Q1: What is the difference between gagging and choking?

We admit this didn't come naturally to us, either. It's important to realize the difference between gagging and choking. Knowing this can give you peace of mind and information to determine if your child needs your patience through a gag or immediate assistance in the event of choking. Gagging, whether a silent movement of food or coughing, is a normal and reflexive safety mechanism that pushes food that hasn't been fully chewed or mashed toward the front of the mouth so that it can continue to be chewed and then swallowed. If baby is gagging, her eyes may water, she may cough, sputter, make gagging sounds, be silent yet intently moving food toward the front of her mouth, or may look afraid. Choking, though, is when an object or substance becomes stuck in the throat or windpipe, causing the blockage of airflow. If baby is choking, it's unlikely she'll be able to make sounds and will not be able to effectively move air. When infants are eating while reclined, they're at greater risk for choking. It's unlikely baby will have a choking episode if safe self-feeding practices are in place; however, it's imperative that parents are trained in infant CPR procedures. Most hospitals offer this as a part of their prenatal classes. There are also certain foods that tend to be common culprits in a choking event regardless of the feeding method. We'll address those foods in chapter 5.

Q2: How often should baby get breast milk or formula?

When you and baby start the self-feeding process, the foods that you provide are more for skill development than nutrition. While it's important to select foods that provide a nutritional benefit, like being iron- and energy-rich, the sole source of nutrition for baby is still breast milk or formula. Foods added during this time are only supplemental to a milk-based diet, and for this reason, they're called complementary foods. On-demand breast milk or formula feedings should continue until baby reaches one year along with their self-fed foods from the family diet.

Q3: How many meals a day should baby get at first?

We recommend starting with one meal per day. You can decide which meal of the day that is. It depends on the times of day your baby is most alert and eager to eat. Wendy Jo started Miss A with breakfast while Leslie started CC with lunch. Once your baby seems eager to eat more, add another meal with the family and increase as needed. Around eight months old, baby could be having three meals per day, and by ten months, your infant may be moving on to three meals and two to three snacks per day. Their stomachs are very small, so we have to adjust our idea of portions. One to three tablespoons of food may be an appropriate amount for each meal. Some babies may eat more, some babies eat less. Let baby be the guide.

Q4: Should we worry about food allergies?

 The baby-led weaning approach can still be followed if there's a concern about food allergies. If you have a family history of food allergies, it's a good idea to discuss introducing solid foods with your pediatrician. Emerging research and recommendations from the American Academy of Pediatrics suggest that even with a family history of food allergies, high-allergen foods be introduced just like other foods when the child is developmentally appropriate to start solids (around six months old). High-allergen foods include eggs, nuts, dairy, soy, shellfish, and wheat. Some researchers theorize that previous recommendations to withhold high-allergen foods to later in the food introduction process may have contributed to a boom in pediatric food allergies, but there is no clear reason for the rise in allergies. Food allergies are a serious and potentially life-threatening condition. Regardless of whether your child has a food allergy, all parents should consider this given that it's estimated that 1 in every 13 children has a food allergy.[1] We'll dive deeper in chapter 5.

Q5: Should we introduce one food at time? Is there a timeline?

This is a recommendation that came about when it was suggested to start puréed complementary feedings at four months of age—a time when baby's gastrointestinal tract may not have been ready for complementary foods at all. The practice of only giving a baby one food at a time was thought to help spot an intolerance or identify an allergic reaction. Many still recommend this practice, but it does not, however, reduce the risk of an infant developing a food allergy. If there's no family history of allergies and you're aware of the ingredients in the foods your family eats, we feel there is no reason to offer only one or two foods over a couple of days. We literally dove right in. If you're concerned about allergies for your little one, there's no reason you can't slow the process.

Our recommendations are to start the self-feeding journey with appropriately prepared single foods like avocados, steak, eggs, sweet potatoes, carrots, and broccoli. These single-ingredient whole foods can take the guesswork out if your child happens to not tolerate a food well. In general, we recommend starting with these foods at home so you know what's on the plate in front of you. Your meals will take shape based on your baby's ability to eat and your typical family menu, but introducing two to three foods at a meal should not be an issue. If you feel like baby has a reaction to a food, call your pediatrician immediately to evaluate. You may decide together to back off on food introductions while trying to isolate the food in question. There really is no timeline unless you've worked with your pediatrician to create one.

Q6: Can baby be served mixed-food meals?

Using this approach, your baby can be served foods of the family. We hope those foods will deliver nourishment for the whole household. Given that the first month or so of offering solid foods is more for skill development with chewing, texture, and swallowing, it's a good idea to stick with more individual foods versus mixed-food meals. We both provided our little ones with individual components of the family meal and then progressed to mixed meals like lasagna, beef stir-fry, chicken pot pie, or spaghetti and meatballs. Once you feel like your baby is starting to eat more than play or skill build, by all means, serve up your family's favorite mixed dish.

Q7: How long should we cook veggies and how soft should they be?

Steaming harder fruits and vegetables initially is best. The addition of water softens the food without making the skin or outer portion of the fruit and vegetable tough. Roasting, which is a great way to cook vegetables, will be best introduced just a bit later, as it can toughen the outer portion of some vegetables. When your baby is self-feeding and exploring the different textures of food, he will learn pretty quickly how to work around the skin of most veggies. Our rule of thumb is to steam until the vegetables or fruits are soft enough to gently press with your fingers or the food smashes easily with your tongue pressed to the roof of your mouth. We'll share our preparation tips for these foods in chapter 14.

Q8: How do we serve baby portions?

Too much on a plate is overwhelming for anyone, let alone your baby, who is trying to analyze and assess everything placed in front of him. It's a good idea to have a nonskid plate that is smaller, just for baby. Keep it simple. We recommend serving no more than three foods or three finger-shaped pieces of food at a time. When baby shows interest in having more food—like reaching for your plate, becoming upset when food is gone, or mouthing for more—it may be time to offer another piece.

Q9: How long should baby sit at a meal to explore, play, or eat her food?

However long your meal takes to enjoy and savor. There's no need to rush, and remember, they're observing and learning from you. It could take baby much longer to explore her food items than it took you to complete your whole meal. Take your time. When they appear to have lost interest, then it's time to change activities. Don't be discouraged if their attention span wanes after only ten minutes. That will get better over time as their feeding skills improve and their interest in solid food grows.

Q10: What if my pediatrician has never heard of it?

Several parents we talked to had this experience. Not knowing of baby-led weaning or self-feeding doesn't make it an inappropriate choice; it's simply not known to them at the time. Just like nutrition professionals (us), doctors have to keep up with a tremendous amount of information and may not have had the opportunity to look further into baby-led weaning and responsive eating. With that said, as parents, we must advocate for our child and do what we feel is best. One study surveying Canadian mothers about their experiences with BLW determined that most mothers relied on other parents and their own instincts for guidance on the process.[2] This is likely because the health professionals they encountered weren't supportive of or knowledgeable about the process.

This information also may be helpful to note: The American Academy of Pediatrics' desired behavior resource for physicians is a part of the AAP Health Initiatives. In this resource, the infant food and feeding desired behaviors include fostering self-feeding, which encourages the babies to feed themselves using their hands and spoons along with using a cup.[3] Helping parents understand and recognize hunger and satiety cues are also suggested desired behaviors of the initiative. These key points of baby-led weaning, written by 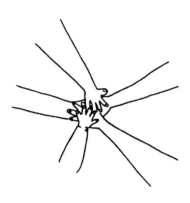 Dr. Gill Rapley, may help sum up the approach for anyone on baby's support team.

Key Points of Baby-Led Weaning

- ❏   Baby-led weaning refers to the introduction of solid foods using a self-feeding approach, and it is developmentally and nutritionally appropriate for most infants

- ❏   Breastmilk (or formula) should continue to be the main source of nutrition up to one year

- ❏   From six months, babies need to practice the skills involved in self-feeding

- ❏   Provided basic safety rules are followed, self-feeding does not present any greater risk of choking than spoon-feeding

- ❏   This method of feeding during the weaning period has the potential to influence the infant's dietary choices and relationship with food for the remainder of their life

---

Used with permission from Gill Rapley, PhD & Community Practitioner, *Baby-Led Weaning: Transition to Solid Foods at the Baby's Own Pace* in the *Community Practitioner*, June 2011.

We feel strongly that starting baby with the self-feeding approach can have lifelong benefits. These ideas, or what we term *the building blocks of self-feeding*, are not unique to just the *Born to Eat* team. Fellow parents, friends, professionals, and researchers have shaped the foundation of the *Born to Eat* approach. It's not just about eating. The *Born to Eat* approach is about how this strategy of self-feeding can foster a healthy relationship with foods and a body for a lifetime—and not just for baby.

> We feel that families who use and support the Division of Responsibility in feeding and eating foster body-confident children that grow into adults capable of eating intuitively. Just remember that frameworks are starting points. You can use this framework with the unique flexibility your family needs.

If you're embracing the self-feeding style completely, or using some spoon-feeding along with it, we believe you can cultivate a self-regulating, or responsive, feeder if you follow Ellyn Satter's Division of Responsibility. Ellyn Satter is a renowned dietitian and clinical social worker known for her eating and feeding philosophies, the Satter Feeding Dynamics Model, and the Division of Responsibility in Feeding. The Satter Feeding Dynamics Model is a well-known and well-supported feeding model in the medical and health community. It's considered a best practice by the Academy of Nutrition and Dietetics and the American Academy of Pediatrics among others.[4] The Division of Responsibility in Feeding suggests that there are roles for the parent to support the child's natural ability to eat and self-regulate by providing the foods while allowing the child to decide how much and if they will eat.

"I had to learn about feeding dynamics, the research on feeding styles, responsive feeding, and eating competence as a parent, and I am grateful that I did. Seeing the transformation in my own home, as well as the growing literature on the health and wellness benefits of eating well, guided by internal cues of hunger and fullness, convinced me that helping children grow up to be competent eaters is preventive medicine."

—Katja Rowell, MD, childhood feeding specialist and author

Chapter 3 References

1. "Resources for Kids," *Food Allergy Research and Education*, accessed September 20, 2016, http://www.foodallergy.org/resources/kids.

2. D'Andrea, Elisa, Kielyn Jenkins, Maria Mathews, and Barbara Roebothan. "Baby-led Weaning: A Preliminary Investigation," *Canadian Journal of Dietetic Practice and Research* 77(2) (2016 June): 72–7, DOI: 10.3148/cjdpr-2015-045. Epub 2016 Jan 15.

3. "Infant Food and Feeding," *American Academy of Pediatrics*, accessed August 19, 2016, https://www.aap.org/en-us/advocacy-and-policy/aap-health-initiatives/HALF -Implementation-Guide/Age-Specific-Content/Pages/Infant-Food-and-Feeding.aspx

4. "The Satter Feeding Dynamics Model," *Ellyn Satter Institute*, accessed August 5, 2016, http://ellynsatterinstitute.org/other/fdsatter.php

CHAPTER 4

SUPPORT AND THE *BORN TO EAT* PHILOSOPHY

> "Fed is best! This mantra can apply way past the infant stage; it works for kids, teens, and parents."
>
> —Oona Hanson, Educator & Parent Coach

Our friend, Nikki, was headed back to work in the midst of her baby-led weaning process. Her daughter was seven months old and exploring a variety of family foods. When she dropped off her daughter at daycare the first day, she found herself explaining the baby-led weaning process along with many justifications. As she jokingly says, "The CWGs (conventional wisdom grannies) just didn't get it, and I felt like they told me they'd support the process, but when I turned and walked out, I just knew they were going to shove a spoon in her mouth."

She was frustrated but knew that spoon-feeding wouldn't ruin her daughter. Many parents and caregivers allow the child to lead by watching the subtle cues babies

37

display when they've had enough—like turning their heads, pursing their lips, or even swatting the spoon away. In her situation, she got the feeling that wouldn't be the case, that the CWGs were going to have her daughter finishing the baby food, down to the last bite, not allowing her to self-regulate. She'd seen it with other infants there. Instead of getting totally frustrated, Nikki reached out to friends and trusted professionals to help her find a balance between her daughter being spoon-fed at preschool and allowed to self-feed using a baby-led approach at home. And, after she discussed her wishes with the staff, and educated them on using spoon-feeding while letting her daughter be the guide of if she ate and how much, it worked. So many of who've gone before us are committed to lifelong learning and are excited to support us in this journey. All you have to do is start the conversation.

> There is no perfect way to do this. It can be done all the way, halfway, or any combination in between. As long as baby leads the way, there are no flops!

It's a Messy (but Amazing) Process

We've mentioned it before—the *Born to Eat* approach is a tad messy. Okay, really messy. We've gotten a lot of laughs out of the friends and grandmas that have said there's no way they'd let their babies feed themselves in such a messy manner. We, on the other hand, gave it a shot, embraced the mess (which honestly is short-lived), and have reaped the benefits. These benefits could last a lifetime, which to us, far outweighs the mess. Let's face it—whenever one chooses to allow a baby to self-feed, whether at six months old or one year old, there's going to be discovery, and ultimately a mess. So, either way you get the mess, it's just now or later. At least starting earlier, there's a little less food on the plate to paint the wall.

We embraced the mess and bought stock in paper towels (well maybe not, but perhaps we should have), because of all the flying pasta. All joking aside, we want to give you an idea of how we handle mealtimes with some great feeding tools and tricks. Even between the two of us, we entered the process of baby-led weaning differently. Leslie's little one is older than Wendy Jo's, so there were different tools of the trade at the different times. We've worked together to come up with a list of items that made the messy process less of an issue.

Wendy Jo invested in silicone plates and placemats, which (on some surfaces) sticks to the table, and the Stokke Tripp Trapp high chair that scoots directly up to the table. She has a box of burp cloths and little towels she keeps handy for after-dinner wipe downs, and a bottle of cleaning spray for the table and high chair post meals. Miss A wore an IKEA smock (and, technically, she was doing a bit of painting). Additionally, Miss A started her eating adventures with Num Nums spoons and Think cups. As for floor cleanup, Wendy Jo skipped the vinyl tablecloth, because she has tile beneath her table and two dogs on cleanup duty.

> Miss A had a Bolognese sauce-painted face, red-streaked hair, and pasta flung across the tile, but she was flanked by two very happy Labradors. Wendy Jo would say that her dogs fell in love with Miss A as soon as she began eating. Love at first bite.

Leslie used a round mat to go under the high chair (with a footrest) at the dining room table since she had a pretty new rug and fresh paint. The avocado slice that hit the dining room wall blended right in. Luckily, having a box of baby wipes by the high chair made cleaning up CC, and her surroundings, much easier. Even the fresh paint survived without touchups. We had a variety of nonskid plates and great gripping spoons. Our favorite spoons were made by Nuk and even IKEA. Leslie wishes she would have had silicone plates and placemats with her little one.

> Our feeding experts suggest using a high chair with appropriate foot support or a footrest. Little dangling feet can be quite distracting!

OUR QUICK START TOOL LIST
Ten years have passed since we started feeding our littles. These are the tools we wish we would have had ready for baby's first bite.

- Bumkims or IKEA Smock Bibs
- Num Nums Gootensils
- EZPZMini Mat & Tiny Cup
- A high chair that fits your budget with a footrest and adjustable straps.
- A plastic tablecloth or shower liner for under your high chair.

If you're on Instagram, these accounts are our favorites for getting started with solids.
- @Solidstarts
- @Feedlinglittles
- @Natalia.Stasenko
- @kids.nutritionist

The tools we feel that can help minimize the mess may reduce the mess-induced critics. We have some very clean and tidy family members who really did not enjoy seeing the mess. We had some friends who scoffed that our babies got a daily bath. Then we had some strangers comment what adventurous eaters we had when they watched our little ones dive into their plate of Mexican food while eating out. You've probably already gotten some really great (or not) unsolicited advice. It seems everyone's a critic, whether positive or negative. Regardless, don't forget that this is your family, your baby, and your choice. What you chew (and baby chews), is up to you! We are here to empower you with the real deal, the low-down, the emerging research, and easy recipes to support you and the feeding path you pick for your child. We're on this imperfect journey together!

> The goal is getting baby exposed to self-feeding as soon as developmentally appropriate, and if it takes a few other supportive methods for baby to succeed, then so be it.

One thing is clear—there's definitely enough shaming in our culture. One of the greatest examples of mommy or parent shaming around food starts from day one, breast milk or formula. If you choose to breastfeed, formula feed, combo feed, or whatever, someone thinks something isn't right. The same is true for how you're feeding foods to your baby. We feel like you and only you can make the best choice for your baby, using the best information you have. Like we mentioned, you can do this halfway, partially, half-time, or however you need to in your life, just like Nikki did with her daughter. And it's never all unicorns and lollipops. Leslie had serious issues while breastfeeding along with guilt and shame about not feeling like she could provide enough for her daughter. Luckily for Leslie, her husband, and her little one, she had an amazing breastfeeding medicine pediatrician on her team. And Dr. Julie always said, "Leslie, don't forget this: rule number one is feed the baby." We also believe that you, the parent, needs to be fed. And that's what we're going to help you do.

The goal is getting baby exposed to self-feeding as soon as developmentally appropriate, and if it takes a few other supportive methods for baby to succeed, then so be it. You know what is best for your baby and what your baby is capable of achieving, because you see the small changes (or not) in developmental readiness daily. Trust your instincts and go with your gut and mind. When you find yourself in a position where you need support or you feel the need to explain the process to caregivers, we can help. The *Born to Eat* approach starts with a focus on baby self-feeding. We have you covered with two samples advocating for support for you and baby. One addresses a caretaker outside of the home and the other addresses a close friend or family member. You'll find these at the end of this chapter. Please take the liberty to tweak as needed. We've also included a fantastic handout called *Born to Eat* Basics, which is influenced by the *Baby-Led Introduction to Solids (BLISS) Study: A Randomized Controlled Trial of a Baby-Led Approach to Complementary Feeding*. We're positive you'll want to keep it close and copy for caregivers. **You can find the *Born to Eat* Basics Handout in the back of the book.**

It's Time for the *Born to Eat* Approach

This philosophy could change so many things in your baby's life, in your entire family's life, your life, and in our society. The *Born to Eat* approach is based on the *Born to Eat* values that we've broken down into everyday activities. It's not just a feeding approach; it's a philosophy that can foster body trust, decrease the impact of our diet-crazed culture, cultivate more supportive micro-communities, and help us have peace with our bodies and food. Who doesn't want that?

Let's do this!

I am ready:

- To not feel the need to be legalistic or perfect with any feeding method.
- To recognize that what I (and baby) chew is up to me.
- To embrace creativity with food and feeding as a learning tool.
- To realize that my family and I get to decide what foods are best.
- To make my own definition of what foods of the family will look like for us.
- To not push food on, or restrict food, from my child (or myself).

- To embrace the messy and challenging adventure together.
- To advocate for myself and my child throughout the process.

Cheers to:

- An endless supply of clean towels.
- Excellent stain-removing detergents.
- Babies who self-regulate.
- Babies who turn into children who know how to savor foods.
- Children who listen to their hunger and fullness cues.
- Children who grow into adults who love and honor their bodies who can then teach their children to do the same.

Welcome to the *Born to Eat* Community. We are so happy you're on this journey with us!

Sincerely,
L & WJ

Dear Care Team Member,

Thank you so much for caring for my baby. I have entrusted you with their care because I know you care about them, too. In the care of **(insert child's name)**, we have a request in regards to feeding styles and approaches. Based on current research, we won't be introducing foods to them until about six months old, as there are clear signs of readiness our health professionals want to see before they can eat solid foods. We'd love for you to help us take note of these signs of readiness, as we know you are around **(insert child's name)** quite often. These are the signs we are looking for:

- Sits up independently without the use of a high chair or pillow
- No longer thrusts tongue
- Shows interest in eating foods
- Reaches for foods with palm of hand or scooping motion

In addition to waiting a bit longer to start complementary foods, we are using the *Born to Eat* approach, which embraces self-feeding, where **(insert child's name)** is given graspable foods and allowed to play with, chew on, and self-feed these foods. We understand this may be a unique approach and would gladly provide more information for you.   >>

Please know that choosing this approach is in no way a criticism of traditional feeding practices. Instead, it's our hope that our child will accept a variety of flavors and textures quickly, trust innate hunger and fullness cues, and be able to self-regulate their eating for years to come.

These tips have helped us implement this approach:

- At first, only serve the solid foods I have provided, which may include sliced steak, sliced boiled eggs, avocado wedges, roasted carrots, steamed asparagus, raspberries
- Foods are soft enough to smash gently between two fingers or with the tongue to the top of the mouth
- In the beginning, very few foods are given at one time (for example, a piece of avocado wedge, 1 steamed soft carrot finger, 3 raspberries, 1 slice of boiled egg) and more is given as needed. This is so they are not overwhelmed by too much food on the plate.

If you're willing to support us in this approach, we would love your help and encouragement. We know that choking is a concern for all of us no matter the feeding method. We've recently learned to watch and coach through a normal (yet scary) gagging episode without responding with fear. Yet, choking is a life-threatening event that blocks all airflow and sounds. We're confident that in the unlikely event of choking, you would follow the safety procedures to help our child.

If this approach cannot be carried out or safely monitored under your supervision, we ask that our child could be allowed to self-feed traditional baby foods or purées. We have provided a smock to help minimize the mess and will wash this daily for you. Please let us know how we can further help you in the care and support of our child. We appreciate your care, understanding, and support.

Sincerely,

_____ (sign)

Dear Aunt Betty (or Mom, Mother-in-law, family member, friend),

First off, thank you so much for watching **(insert child's name)**. We know how much you enjoy this time with them, and we appreciate the help tremendously. We wanted to let you know how we are choosing to introduce food to **(insert child's name)**. Based on current research, we won't be introducing foods to them until about six months old, as there are clear signs of readiness our health professionals want to see before they can eat whole foods. We'd love for you to help us take note of these signs of readiness, as we know you are around **(insert child's name)** quite often.

Here are the signs we are looking for:

- Sits up independently without the use of a high chair or pillow
- No longer thrusts tongue
- Shows interest in eating foods
- Reaches for foods with palm of hand or scooping motion

In addition to waiting a bit longer to start complementary foods, we are using the *Born to Eat* approach, which embraces a self-feeding style, where **(insert child's name)** is given graspable whole foods and allowed to play with, chew on, and self-feed these foods. We understand this may be a unique approach, and we are excited to talk to you more about it and provide you with the *Born to Eat* book.

Please know that choosing this approach is in no way a criticism of traditional feeding practices. Instead, it's our hope that our child will accept a variety of flavors and textures quickly, trust innate hunger and fullness cues, and be able to self-regulate their eating for years to come.

These tips have helped us implement this approach:

- At first, only serve the solid foods I have provided (for example, sliced steak, sliced boiled eggs, avocado wedges, roasted carrots, steamed asparagus, raspberries)
- Foods are soft enough to smash gently between two fingers or with the tongue to the top of the mouth
- In the beginning, very few foods are given at one time (for example, a piece of avocado wedge, 1 steamed soft carrot finger, 3 raspberries, 1 slice of boiled egg) and more is given as needed. This is so she/he is not overwhelmed by too much food on the plate.

These behaviors have been really helpful for us to practice as well: >>

- refraining from panicking when they work through a gag
- not putting your fingers in their mouth when they are working through gagging
- helping to test foods to ensure they are the right texture
- modeling how to chew by eating the same foods with them

Another benefit to this approach is that we do not have to purchase traditional jarred baby foods. **(insert child's name)** can eat whatever we are eating as long as the food is cut in a manageable size and provided in the appropriate texture. As we go through this process of introducing foods, we have helpful lists of age-appropriate foods, textures, recipes, and those that are not appropriate for this stage.

When you are watching **(insert child's name)**, you can choose what you feel comfortable with and we will support you. If you'd like to practice this approach with us, we'd love the extra support.

Love,

_____ (sign)

PART 2

THE *BORN TO EAT* BABY AND CHILD

Feeding our little ones can be nerve-racking at first, particularly if you're using a method some consider *nontraditional*. As parents who've embarked on this journey, we divided this part of the book into chapters based on your little one's age and readiness. This is the *start here with this food* part of the book. If you're like us, you like a starting point. We've also classified ages as different levels of eaters like this:

Chapter 5: Begins with your 6-month-old or the Pre-Eating Beginner

Chapter 6: Moves onto your 7- to 8-month-old or the Beginner Eater

Chapter 7: Jumps to your 9- to 12-month-old or the Novice Eater

Chapter 8: Talks toddling with your 12- to 24-month-old or the Pre-Advanced Eater

Chapter 9: Covers the ever-changing 24- to 36-month-old or the Advanced Eater

In each chapter, we discuss readiness based on the skills generally achieved during this time. We also discuss priority nutrients. While the nutrients are important through all stages, there's no need to be overwhelmed by focusing on all of them right at the start. We get you started with necessary nutrients from the first bite with ease. Let's start the self-feeding process!

CHAPTER 5

IT'S GO TIME
(6 MONTHS—THE PRE-EATING
BEGINNER)

> "The proverb warns that 'You should not bite the hand that feeds you.' But maybe you should, if it prevents you from feeding yourself."
> —Thomas Szasz

At just four months old, Wendy Jo had a little yogi on her hands. Miss A was starting to sit up and getting ready to move out on all fours. At five months to the day, she took her first crawl. She was incredibly interested in food, watching everything Wendy Jo was eating. When Miss A napped, Wendy Jo enjoyed some of her larger meals without the little eyes and hands. Although she wanted to share that first bite of food together very soon, Wendy Jo knew Miss A was not developmentally ready. She had to remind herself that Miss A had her whole life to eat and so she needed to be patient. Wendy Jo decided to sit back and let Miss A's development take place without rushing into anything. Just a few more weeks . . .

Leslie got home from seeing clients one day to hear that six-month CC had smashed some sliced steak and avocado right into her mouth. She sucked all the nutritious juices out of the steak and smashed the avocado—some in her mouth and the rest on her face.

CC had been sitting upright independently and putting items to her mouth with control for a week or two. Her first food explorations with Dad were exciting and opened the door for many food adventures. Just before CC turned six months old, Leslie and her husband had discussed the signs for readiness and the safety steps they were going to put in place to support her self-feeding process. And she couldn't even wait for Mom to get home from work!

Both of us were excited to start this journey of feasting with our little ones. But before we jumped on the wagon, we too had to get ready for the ride. There are key things to focus on during this time, and there's no need to rush feeding baby table foods. She's got her whole life to eat. Let's make sure she's ready.

The *Born To Eat* Approach Can Look Different for Everyone

Keep in mind that if your infant was born early, or was premature, he may need more time to catch up on growth and development prior to starting solids. For example, if baby was born at thirty-two weeks (instead of forty), he *may* need about eight more weeks to catch up developmentally. Some children who are born early, or that have special healthcare needs, may have low muscle tone and need a little extra help with the process. This could look like a combination of self-feeding and spoon-feeding along with some gentle support in sitting. Children who have higher energy demands, like those with some lung and heart conditions, may need to have a focus on higher-energy foods and formulas. Some children may have issues with feeding right away and may have oral aversions related to feeding or medical traumas. This could lead to significant feeding difficulties and or the use of a feeding tube.

An incredible group of feeding professionals believe kids with special healthcare needs can still self-regulate and listen to their bodies. They, and their parents, just need the right support and tools to engage in a responsive feeding therapy program. (For more information about Responsive Feeding Therapy, visit https://www.responsivefeedingtherapy.com.) With support of feeding specialists–like many speech language pathologists, occupational therapists, physical therapists, pediatricians, and registered dietitians–a child with special health needs can also embrace the *Born to Eat* approach. It may just look different–and that's okay.

Although the American Academy of Pediatrics once recommended the introduction of solid foods beginning at four months of age, they have since updated the recommendation to a more physically and developmentally appropriate six months old. Six months is not a magical age; however, it's a great guide. Parents must consider baby's gastrointestinal system, physical development, dexterity, and oral readiness when starting solid foods.

We feel that baby should be at or around six months of age and developmentally appropriate to start solid foods. It's important to note that biological age and developmental age are not the same thing. Every baby progresses at their own pace. And, regardless of whether your child is breastfed, formula fed, or a combination of both, around six months is the general recommendation for adding complementary foods.[1] Ultimately, it's up to you and your physician to determine whether your little one is developmentally ready to start table foods. Developmental signs of readiness would include, but aren't limited to, sitting unassisted, absence of tongue thrust, grasping items with more hand control, and putting toys to his or her mouth.

Developmental signs of feeding readiness can include:

❑ Independently sitting up

❑ Absence of tongue thrust

❑ Grasping items with more hand control

❑ Putting toys to his or her mouth

❑ Demonstrating an interest in table foods

Not only do we have to look at baby's readiness, but we must also examine our own. This is the time to evaluate the family's food and eating patterns along with potential risks. Eating is a family affair. If the family's primary intake lacks variety, iron-rich foods, or meal structure, it may be time to explore new recipes and grocery items. If family meals happen in front of a favorite television show, it's most definitely time to move it to the table. This isn't just for a family meal experience and increased mindfulness; it's also for baby's safety.

Baby Jill was six months old. She'd been sitting upright for a week or two, and her parents were eager to start her on solids. Jill had been watching Mom and Dad eat for weeks. While she was playing with toys, she dropped them often and did not move them toward her mouth.

Baby Alex was almost six months old. He'd been chewing his favorite block toys and handing them to Mom and Dad. At dinnertime, he'd sit in his high chair and play while Mom and Dad ate. He kept reaching for their food.

❑ Ready
✔ Not Ready. Baby Jill is not that interested in food just yet. She must first shows signs of mouthing objects or reaching for foods. Hold off introducing foods so frustration is avoided.

✔ Ready. Baby Alex is showing signs of readiness to try eating. Sit him down for his first meal.

❑ Not Ready

If you and baby are ready, securely fasten her into a high chair and start with foods finger-sized and -shaped. Remember, baby's sole nutrition source is still breast milk or infant formula during this time. It's about skill-building with the bonus of added nutrition, which is why we call this stage the pre-feeding beginner. Baby needs to hold the food, explore the texture in her hands, and get used to how it feels in her mouth. Our first foods included bananas, ripe or cooked pears, steamed sweet potatoes, scrambled eggs, avocados, and sliced steak. These are the foods we eat, and so the family meal begins. Now is the time to consider the types of foods that your family likes to eat regularly.

Let's make sure we're off to a safe start. A randomized controlled trial (one of the best types of studies) in New Zealand, called *Baby-Led Introduction to Solids Study (BLISS)*, provided safety points to participants using this feeding method with their infants.[2] The BLISS protocol was designed as a modified version of BLW that addresses the common concerns of choking risk, potential for low iron intake, and poor growth due to a possibility of lower energy intakes by parental education. As nutrition professionals, we had these items in mind as we practiced the approach with our own children and found the educational tips and advice in the BLISS protocol very useful. We realized that our methods for keeping baby safe were right on track with their study protocol, so we've combined them here.

Pre-Feeding Beginner Safety List

1. Secure baby upright in a high chair or feeding seat. Baby should never be reclined or eating in someone's lap. As tempting as it is to hold that sweet baby in your lap, don't do it. Sitting in a high chair allows the parent or caregiver to evaluate how baby is doing at all times and respond to their cues.

2. **Never** leave baby alone when eating.

3. Let baby put food in his mouth. He needs to be in control of how fast the food enters his mouth or how much he eats at all times. As tempting as it is, you don't have to help.

4. If the food has been cooked, test the temperature of the food to ensure it has cooled enough for baby to test. Even something perceived as warm by the caregiver may be felt as hot by a baby. Lukewarm is a good introductory temperature. There's no need to have everything cold, and it is best to introduce a variety of temperatures at each meal.

5. Test the texture of the food by mashing between your fingers gently or pressing between your lips to make sure the food can be mashed with baby's gums. If not, it's not the right texture. Consider cooking the food longer or picking a different food.

6. Offer foods that have been cut or are in the form of a finger so baby can pick it up. This should a bit longer than baby's fist.

7. Don't offer foods that easily break off into small pieces or crumbs that could potentially block the airway of baby, as they can pose a choking risk. Foods we recommend avoiding at *this stage* due to increased risk of choking include raw apples, whole grapes, whole cherry tomatoes, other raw fruits or vegetables with tough skins, nuts, thick nut butters, popcorn, marshmallows, hard candy, hot dogs, very crusty bread, or any food in a round or coin-like shape.

Talking Texture with Feeding Expert and Pediatric Speech Therapist Jacqueline P. Henry, MA, SLP, CCC

Food comes in many different textures. You have probably heard the most about food textures in relation to baby food stages, usually beginning with smooth purées then transitioning to a chunkier purée. Many use baby cereal at this point. Next, meltable solids like puffs or soft crackers are introduced. Purées are often presented via a spoon with an adult setting pace and size of bites. Meltable solids allow for self-feeding. The last stage of most baby foods, which often contain chunks in a variety of textures, are where many kiddos begin to show difficulty managing and/or tolerating new textures. This can lead to meal-related stress for kids and anxiety for the parents, thus ending up in need of feeding therapy. Of course, many children do fine from beginning to end of the popular progression promoted so heavily in our society, but for some, it's the perfect storm.

After reviewing this progression of texture introduction with parents, I switch it up and dive into self-feeding as a more efficient alternative. Keep in mind, I work with children who have delayed or disordered eating and need intervention. I used BLW with my daughter and the results were so positive that I tossed the BLW components into my therapy toolbox. The benefits, in my opinion, are twofold. First, self-feeding builds confidence and promotes fine motor skills to get the food from plate to mouth. Second, exposure to food shapes and textures in a setting where the kiddo has control promotes a higher frequency of attempts and enjoyment. Imagine, as an adult, you had to attempt to do something you have never done before. There are two scenarios. In the first, you are in control of your learning and attempts to complete the task. In the second, someone is standing over you directing your every move, possibly even grabbing your hands and giving (unsolicited) hand-over-hand assistance. My blood pressure is inching upward just imagining it! In the second situation, I doubt you would learn the skill, but instead attach a stress reaction to the memory. As a child mouths toys, they are preparing their mouth for a wide range of food shapes and textures. In BLW, food is used in the same way. We aren't expecting a six-month-old to gain adequate nutrition from self-feeding, but as a way to sharpen food management skills. When mouthing food, the tongue darts around, chasing the food. Just like when you have something stuck in your teeth. Your tongue just can't stay away! Eventually, through self-feeding practice, the child will develop the side-to-side tongue movement needed to manage a piece of food while chewing. Really, it all comes down to giving you baby control and experience. Happy eating!

Priority Nutrients

One of the main concerns about starting solids or complementary foods is getting certain nutrients that *may* be at lower levels now in baby's body. At the time of our first edition, no research had been done to determine if babies following a baby-led weaning approach have any greater risk of iron deficiency than traditionally fed infants.[3] Now, emerging evidence states there is no iron deficiency seen in infants following a modified BLW approach—meaning the parents are instructed to provide high-iron food at each meal. Regardless of the feeding approach, iron is a top-priority nutrient when starting solid foods. Before you pop open a box of iron-fortified infant cereal, let's start with the 411 on iron. Iron carries oxygen throughout our bodies. If you consider what's happening the first year of a baby's life, particularly in brain development, you recognize the importance of oxygen getting to the brain.

In short, if a body does not have enough iron, oxygen struggles to move around the body, which is of particular importance to brain development and baby's immune system. Iron deficiency can cause anemia, which can lead to fatigue, growth, and learning issues.[4] We all need iron, but our babies, in a stage of crucial growth and development, absolutely need iron. Identifying iron deficiency anemia in infants can be challenging. It's best to beef up their iron intake from the start, literally. Long before fortified baby foods, most babies thrived on food sources of iron from the table.

Once upon a time, meats were considered hard for babies to digest and many thought an early introduction of meat may put them at risk for allergies and possibly even kidney distress. We realize now that this was not and is not the case. Meats are our first foods.

Leslie still remembers when Dr. Julie told her that the newest recommendation was to start with meats and iron-rich foods. She was so happy to hear her doctor say those words (because that was her plan anyway). We now know that iron-rich foods should be introduced to babies early on when they're developmentally ready and starting solids. While starting the process, baby still depends on milk feedings as a primary energy source. Both formula and breast milk provide some iron. Fortified infant formula has (what appears to be) ample iron at 10 to 13 milligrams (mg) per liter, yet the bioavailability, or how much the body can actually break down and use, of the iron is only around 4 percent.[5] Breast milk is thought to be very low in iron yet it has a very high bioavailability of approximately 50 percent.[6] So generally speaking, breast milk and formula may deliver about the same amount of iron based on bioavailability. Now, in the second part of infancy, baby just needs more iron.

The Recommended Daily Allowance (RDA) of iron for an infant seven to twelve months old is approximately 11 mg (only 0.7 mg absorbed) per day due to rapid growth within the first year of life. Now, if you want to use infant cereal, you can, but there are ample ways your baby can get iron sources without it. Although infant cereals have a high amount of iron per serving (18 mg) the actual bioavailability is roughly 3 percent, whereas the bioavailability of animal sources of iron is around 15.5 percent.[7] These sources of iron, coupled with a food high in vitamin C, or ascorbic acid, to increase the absorption of iron in baby's body can help baby get the iron he needs.

Particular nutrients like iron are key during this time of growth and development. Focus on foods that provide those nutrients because, after all, it's food we put on the plate, not a specific nutrient.

It's possible you're still wondering—must baby get iron only from fortified cereals? Simple, unfortified foods have been around a lot longer with greater bioavailability, so our opinion is no. We're not saying you can't use it; it can be a convenient way to get iron. We're just saying you shouldn't feel like it's a requirement that you use fortified cereals. Fortified cereals also only provide about ten calories per tablespoon, so that's not a lot of energy for baby. Neither of us used infant cereals, and our little ones' iron levels were just fine. We feel that if you're consistently offering iron-rich food sources, you're on the right path. Here are a few examples of high-bioavailable food sources. Most animal sources of iron have higher bioavailability, yet many plant sources offer iron benefits, as well.

Heme Iron Sources (Animal Sources)		
Food	*Baby-Sized Portion*	*Iron Content*
Egg, hard-boiled	½ large	0.3 milligrams
Beef, ground (85% lean)	1 ounce	0.83 milligrams
Beefsteak, top sirloin	1 ounce	0.97 milligrams
Beef liver, panfried	1 ounce	1.7 milligrams
Chicken liver, braised	1 ounce	3.3 milligrams
Nonheme Iron Sources (Plant-Based)		
Food	*Baby-Sized Portion*	*Iron Content*
Black beans	1 tablespoon	0.28 milligrams
Lentils	1 tablespoon	0.4 milligrams
MaltOMeal, made with water	1 tablespoon	1.1 milligrams
Chocolate, dark, 70-85%	0.5 ounce	1.69 milligrams

US Department of Agriculture, Agricultural Research Service. USDA National Nutrient Database for Standard Reference, Release 26 external link disclaimer. Nutrient Data Laboratory Home Page, 2013. (https://ndb.nal.usda.gov// Accessed on 09/13/2016)

Foods to Start With

We don't want you to get all caught up on the numbers. That's a recipe that can really get us stressed out—parents don't need any more of that. Instead, let's focus on getting in iron-rich foods at most meals and, when you can, pair them with foods that are a source of vitamin C, which is known to increase the absorption of the iron. When starting little ones on solids, stick with individual foods on the plate so we can monitor their progress. We'll move on to the family's favorite mixed meals at around seven to eight months of age. For now, these are foods we recommend starting with, and then we'll build from there. The BLISS Protocol suggests to build a meal in this fashion. Pick an iron-rich food, add a high-energy food, and also a fruit and/or vegetable side.[8] We feel that this template makes it much easier to build baby's plate to get the necessary starter foods.

Sample Vitamin C Sources

Broccoli	Pineapple
Cauliflower	Raspberries
Kiwi	Red bell pepper
Mango	Strawberries
Orange	Tomatoes
Papaya	

We've got those iron-rich foods down now, so let's talk about high-energy foods and fruits and veggies. High-energy foods are just that—foods that are calorically dense. Baby is growing at a tremendous rate, and when offering first foods, we want them to get as much energy and nutrition as they can in every little bite. We used high-energy foods like avocados, meats, regular (not low-fat) Greek yogurt, cheese, butter/oil for seasoning, runny nut butters, and eggs. These high-energy foods typically have higher amounts of fat, which are crucial for brain development, growth, and self-regulation. You'll also note that some of the foods overlap categories. Regular Greek yogurt is great for protein and provides high levels of energy. Avocado is a tasty, satisfying fruit, but we put it in the high-energy category because of the energy it provides as an excellent fat source. Just pick a spot for it on the plate and fill in the rest.

Next up on baby's plate is the fruit and/or vegetable side. As we mentioned, those higher in vitamin C are a good choice when serving up the iron-rich foods, but you don't have to do that at every meal. Baby can get lots of variety and introductions to food by offering a wide selection of fruits and veggies prepared in different ways. We've created this list for you so that, early on in the feeding process, all you have to do is pick one from each column to build your meal. This isn't a complete list. You'll add to this list with your own family foods, but we hope this will set you up for a great start. As you and baby gain more confidence with feeding, it'll become second nature.

Pick a Food from Each Column and Build Baby's Meal		
*Iron-rich food **Vitamin C source		
Protein Foods	**High-Energy Foods**	**Fruit/Vegetable Sides**
*Beef, sirloin, flank, flatiron, roast, finger-sliced	Avocado, ripe, sliced	Carrots, shredded or thin sticks, soft steamed
*Beef, ground, soft cooked or rolled into fingerlike sticks then cooked	Soft/runny nut butters (natural peanut or almond)	Banana, very ripe, cut in half

Pick a Food from Each Column and Build Baby's Meal *Iron-rich food **Vitamin C source		
Protein Foods	**High-Energy Foods**	**Fruit/Vegetable Sides**
*Eggs, scrambled or hard-boiled, cut into slices	Whole-fat, plain Greek yogurt	Pears, ripe and soft, thinly sliced
*Chicken, soft, white or dark meat, finger-sliced or ground	Extra-virgin olive oil	**Sweet potatoes, steamed or baked without skin
Fatty fish (salmon or trout fillets, skinless), small chunks	Chia seeds (or chia pudding)	Green beans, soft, boiled or steamed
*Tuna, canned chunk light, small chunks	Chocolate, dark 65% plus, broken into grippable pieces	*Lentils, cooked in chicken stock and canned tomatoes
*Pork, chops, tender-loin, or roast, tender and finger-sliced	Soft buttered toast, finger-sliced, or soft crackers, like grahams	*Beans, extra soft/smashable black, kidney, or pinto beans
*Turkey, soft, white or dark meat, finger-sliced	Olives, chopped	**Strawberries, sliced, soft fresh or frozen and defrosted (great texture at this stage)
*Turkey, ground, soft cooked or rolled into fingerlike sticks then cooked	Coconut milk (good for cooking with, not drinking as babies drink breast milk or formula)	**Raspberries, halved
*Game meat (venison, duck, rabbit, or elk)	Cheese, shredded or grated	**Tomatoes, thinly sliced
*Lamb, sliced or ground, soft cooked or rolled into fingerlike sticks then cooked	Whole-fat cottage cheese or ricotta cheese	**Kiwi, very ripe and core removed, sliced
*Beans (lentils or extra soft/smashable black, kidney, or pinto beans)		**Broccoli, raw or soft-steamed, stem with flower top for ease of holding

>>

Pick a Food from Each Column and Build Baby's Meal		
*Iron-rich food **Vitamin C source		
Protein Foods	**High-Energy Foods**	**Fruit/Vegetable Sides**
		**Orange, de-segmented without any inner skins at first

This *fill in the plate* method of building baby's meal makes it much easier to put a meal on the table. Pick one from the protein-rich foods, the high-energy foods, and fruit/vegetable side and just *fill in the plate*. Don't forget, we have our first foods recipes for you to try in chapter 14.

Here are some quick meal ideas that pair high-iron foods with high–vitamin C foods:

½ Boiled Egg
3 Raspberries
2 Soft Steamed
    Green Beans

2 Tbsp. Lentils
2 Frozen Strawberries
1 Raw Broccoli Stalk
    and Floret

1 oz. Sirloin Steak
1 Kiwi Wedge
1 Sweet Potato Finger

> If the food is slippery, try rolling it in almond meal (finely ground almond flour) or ground oatmeal so baby can get a good grip.

Miss A was not interested in playing with her food. Nope, this girl dove right in and insisted on chewing to swallow. Wendy Jo kicked off her daughter's eating adventures with boiled sweet potato wedges, a juicy wedge of steak, and avocado slices. Let's just say steak was the winner, not only for Miss A, but for Mama's confidence, too. Miss A sucked out every drop of juice from that steak finger and even sucked on a second piece. With meals, Wendy Jo had to ensure that the foods were a safe texture, because Miss A was going to find a way to swallow her food. After a couple weeks of meals, and a couple meal meltdowns had occurred in which Miss A wasn't getting in the food fast enough and was turning hangry (our favorite term for being hungry and angry), Wendy Jo realized she needed to breastfeed Miss A before her meals. This way, Miss A wasn't overly hungry and had more patience for learning to deal with the food. And then the learning process begins. We can look back and see clearly that Miss A was *Born to Eat.*

> Cooking influences the amount of iron lost in juices; therefore, it's hard to estimate the amount of iron lost. Research suggests that juices from the meat provide a source of iron.[9] Our little eaters can get the nutrient-rich benefit.

This may not be everyone's experience. Many babies may just play with their foods—smash it, roll it, toss it, or gnaw on it before they ever show interest in actually eating or swallowing the foods. There can be a variety of reasons this happens. The important thing to know is that all babies are different, and they will advance when they are ready. Avoid assuming a baby dislikes a food because they don't eat it; instead, recognize this is part of their learning process. Keep trying foods without expectations. Likes and dislikes come much later in a child's development. At this stage, all foods are fair game (unless there's a known allergy).

> Offer milk feedings prior to meals at the beginning. This way, baby isn't too hungry to skill build and doesn't move too fast with new foods and textures.

The Role of the Spoon

At first, if all baby does is gnaw on the spoon throughout the meal, that's okay! This is the time for learning. Nourishment comes soon. Little ones can use a helping hand; you can show them how to guide the spoon effectively to their mouths before food is even on it. The spoon can be used as a chewing toy, a tool for learning, and a mode of feeding. Parents can mimic how a spoon is used during playtime and mealtime, then reinforce spoon use by placing a loaded spoon on the high chair tray when it's time to start feeding. Helping little ones who are learning to self-feed by putting foods like yogurt, applesauce, ground meats, and other mashed foods on the spoon is an excellent way to get a beginner eater comfortable with spoons. Once your little one begins to toddle around, avoid letting them walk with a spoon in their mouth, as tripping and falling are frequent with new walkers.

Mealtimes may be better earlier for some or later for others. Choose what time of day your baby can have the most success. You may not be putting three meals on the table per day at first, so don't worry. Let your baby (and your intuition) guide you.

Caution Foods

There are foods that we suggest avoiding at least initially, like we mentioned earlier in our pre-feeding beginner safety checklist. These are foods that a baby's gums can break off in large chunks, but cannot chew before they swallow (e.g., raw apple, raw carrot,

Did You Know?

While your little one is beginning to explore foods, tastes, and textures, he's learning, as well. Let's break down some of the developmental skills baby is homing in on while eating. We'll start with the palmar and pincer (not pincher). A baby is born with the innate ability to grasp objects. By three months, he'll begin to work on this skill and will make significant progress as each month passes. Around four to seven months old, a baby will pick up larger foods, like carrots and broccoli, with an immature palmar grasp and draw them to her mouth.

She will likely be able to grasp smaller foods such as peas and blueberries by raking it toward her with her hand and squeezing it into her fist. Don't expect a precise grasp just yet. At around eight to twelve months, baby will start picking up those blueberries with a more refined pincer grasp using her thumb and forefinger.

raw celery, round foods, crumb-like foods). In chapter 14, we have an extensive list of foods that can pose choking risks and how to best modify or avoid these foods. Bigger pieces of food that break off into their mouth can pose a risk until a baby is ready to chew and swallow or chew and spit. Gagging is normal and part of the learning process. Once they learn how to handle a gag, babies then continue to learn which foods are easier for them to chew (or not chew) and will often spit out foods that they are not ready to swallow. This takes time to identify and can be different from infant to infant, so take your time and watch for those cues. We felt confident with these starter foods right away.

BORN TO EAT STARTER FOODS

1. Avocado, ¼ to ⅛ of an avocado sliced lengthwise.
2. Steamed carrots or sweet potatoes, 1-inch slices steamed to a very soft texture or mashed.
3. Beef, medium to medium-well steak slices, about baby's fist and a half in length.
4. Whole-fat Greek yogurt plain or with ½ teaspoon of nut butter swirled into 1 to 2 tablespoons of yogurt. This gets messy, but it's a great way to introduce nuts safely and a source of probiotics for baby. We'll touch more on probiotics in chapter 9.
5. Eggs, boiled or scrambled. Served boiled eggs thinly sliced, just the yolk, or mashed like egg salad.
6. Soft fruits like pears and kiwi sliced into strips.
7. High-allergen foods like milk, egg, peanut, tree nuts, soy, wheat, fish and shellfish. *Remember to discuss this progression with baby's pediatrician if you feel there's an allergy risk. Nut butters need to be added to yogurt or a thin layer on a soft piece of toast.* Peanut puffs are an excellent and safe way to introduce peanuts, similar to the product Bamba.
8. Steamed broccoli, stalk and floret, so baby can hold on to the stalk. We served steamed florets and removed the stalk from the table once the *tree* portion was gone. Go with your comfort level and what your baby's gnawing skills are at the start.

Wait until One Year for These Foods

Drinking Cow's Milk: Because baby should be consuming breast milk or infant formula. Other dairy forms are fine.

Honey: Due to risk of the toxin *Clostridium botulinum*, which can be very serious for an infant's gastrointestinal system.

Lunch Meats and Fresh Cheeses like goat and feta: Due to the possible growth of *Listeria monocytogenes* leading to listeriosis. Listeria can grow in refrigerator-like temperatures.

Just One Food at a Time? Not Necessarily.

There are families out there with infants who are at higher risk for food allergies. With this in mind, some recommendations for introducing foods included starting with one food per three to seven days and then trying a new food in the following days. We have friends and professional colleagues in this boat, and they have chosen to give it a little more time between introductions. That is perfectly fine! Chat with your pediatrician if you're concerned about a food allergy and make that choice together.

> Emerging research suggests that giving high-allergen foods as soon as a child is developmentally appropriate to consume solids may reduce the risk of the development of some food allergies.[10] In fact, the National Institutes of Allergy and Infectious Disease established new clinical guidelines for early introduction of allergens, particularly peanut and egg, at four to six months of age.[11] The American Academy of Pediatrics and the 2020 Dietary Guidelines for Americans have also endorsed these recommendations.[12]

If you don't have a family history of food allergies, there's no evidence to date that suggests a "one food at a time" approach prevents the development of an allergy. We introduced our little ones to what we ate from day one. We didn't do the one food per three to seven days progression, but some do—you're the parent, you choose what's right for you and your baby. We felt that introducing food variety in the same amount of our own family variety was beneficial. Research suggests introducing as many flavors and textures to babies as often as possible may increase the overall acceptance of foods later on in life.[13] For example, folks in India make curry dishes. You won't find a curried chicken on a kids' menu in the United States, yet babies in India eat curry all the time. It's all about exposure and family culture. It's up to you.

What does an allergic reaction look like?

When starting solids, it's a good idea to know how a food allergy reaction may appear. If you or your child have a family history of food allergies, speak to your pediatrician prior to starting solids to determine your child's level of risk.

The following symptoms could be signs of an allergy:

- Shortness of breath
- Wheezing, repetitive cough
- Pale or bluish skin
- Weak pulse
- Hives
- Swelling of the tongue or lips
- Vomiting and diarrhea
- Sudden fatigue
- Loss of consciousness

If you suspect any of these symptoms, call 911 or go to your nearest emergency room. For more information on food allergies, visit https://www.foodallergy.org.

Is Baby Eating Enough?

At this stage in the game, breast milk or formula are providing most of baby's nutrition. Don't let it worry you if they aren't eating much of the solid food you've offered at first. The truth of the matter is, your baby has their entire life ahead of them to eat. Take this slow. If you need to start with just one meal per day, that's fine.

You choose what you chew, as well as which foods your baby chews, but they choose how much. Remember the Division of Responsibility? This begins at first bite. Although the temptation to say *one more bite* may linger on your tongue and in your mind, let's not get in the habit of pressuring with those words. If you find your baby is getting frustrated with every bite, try feeding your baby with breast milk or formula before the meal. Remember—at first, we don't want baby to come to the plate super hungry. Her skills aren't ready to deliver the full nourishment of a meal. The only time Wendy Jo found herself coaching in food has been when Miss A was sick. Wendy Jo realized that she needed a reminder to *chew, chew, chew*. This helped her realize that the lack of appetite was related to Miss A being ill. During this time, she nursed a lot more and hardly ate at mealtimes. If this happens, don't panic. When your little one feels better, you can resume more solid food feedings.

What Is Coaching?

When we use the term *coaching*, we simply mean modeling an action while using supportive words like *chew, chew, chew*, or, as we move forward, the phrase *spit it out*. We use these only for reasons of safety and that's it. We do not recommend comments like *just a little more*, *keep eating*, or *that's enough*. This can feel like pressure to eat or stop eating and we want baby to lead the way.

Early on, little ones tend to check in more with the pediatrician. At first monthly, and once they hit about six months of age, about every two to three months. If your little one is filling diapers and maintaining their growth curve, it's most likely they're getting enough. We both had great experiences with our pediatrician's offices and knew that if we needed a quick check-in visit for reassurance, that wouldn't be a problem.

Chapter 5 References

1. "Infant Food and Feeding," American Academy of Pediatrics, accessed August 19, 2016, https://www.aap.org/en-us/advocacy-and-policy/aap-health-initiatives/HALF -Implementation-Guide/Age-Specific-Content/pages/infant-food-and-feeding.aspx.

2. Sonya L. Cameron, Anne-Louise M. Heath, and Rachael W. Taylor. "How Feasible Is Baby-Led Weaning as an Approach to Infant Feeding? A Review of the Evidence," *Nutrients* 4(11) (2012): 1575–1609, DOI:10.3390/nu4111575.

3. Lisa Daniels, Rachael W. Taylor, Sheila M. Williams, Rosalind S. Gibson, Elizabeth A. Fleming, Benjamin J. Wheeler, Barry J. Taylor, Jillian J. Haszard, and Anne-Louise M. Heath. "Impact of a Modified Version of Baby-Led Weaning on Iron Intact and Status: A Randomized Controlled Trial." *British Medical Journal Open* 8 (6) (2018), DOI: 10.1136/BMJOpen-2017-019036.

4. Robert D. Baker, Frank R. Greer, and the Committee on Nutrition, "From the American Academy of Pediatrics Clinical Report, Diagnosis and Prevention of Iron Deficiency and Iron-Deficiency Anemia in Infants and Young Children

(0–3 Years of Age)," *Pediatrics* 126 (5) (November 2010), accessed October 4, 2016, http://pediatrics.aappublications.org/content/126/5/1040.

5. Lena Davidsson, Peter Kastenmayer, Hanna Szajewska, Richard F. Hurrell, and Denis Barclay. "Iron bioavailability in infants from an infant cereal fortified with ferric pyrophosphate or ferrous fumarate," *American Journal of Clinical Nutrition* 71(6) (June 2000):1597–602, accessed October 4, 2016, http://ajcn.nutrition.org/content/71/6/1597.long.

6. U. M. Saarinen, M. A. Siimes, and P. R. Dallman. "Iron absorption in infants: high bioavailability of breast milk iron as indicated by the extrinsic tag method of iron absorption and by the concentration of serum ferritin," *Journal of Pediatrics* 91(1) (July 1977): 36–9, PR. http://www.ncbi.nlm.nih.gov/pubmed/577504.

7. Sonya L. Cameron, Anne-Louise M. Heath, and Rachael W. Taylor. "How Feasible Is Baby-Led Weaning as an Approach to Infant Feeding? A Review of the Evidence," *Nutrients* 4(11) (2012): 1575–1609, DOI:10.3390/nu4111575.

8. Lisa Daniels, Anne-Louise M. Heath, Sheila M. Williams, Sonya L. Cameron, Elizabeth A. Fleming, Barry J. Taylor, Ben J. Wheeler, Rosalind S. Gibson, and Rachael W. Taylor. "Baby-Led Introduction to SolidS (BLISS) study: a randomised controlled trial of a baby-led approach to complementary feeding," *BMC Pediatrics* 15 (2015): 179, DOI:10.1186/s12887-015-0491-8.

9. Roger Purchas, David Simcock, Trevor Knight, and Brian Wilkinson. "Variation in the form of iron in beef and lamb meat and losses of iron during cooking and storage," *International Journal of Food Science & Technology* 38 (2003): 827–837, DOI:10.1046/j.1365-2621.2003.00732.x.

10. Despo Ierodiakonou, Vanessa Garcia-Larsen, Andrew Logan, Annabel Groome, Sergio Cunha, Jennifer Chivinge, Zoe Robinson, Natalie Geoghegan, Katharine Jarrold, Tim Reeves, Nara Tagiyeva-Milne, Ulugbek Nurmatov, MD, Marialena Trivella, Jo Leonardi-Bee, and Robert J. Boyle, MD. "Timing of Allergenic Food Introduction to the Infant Diet and Risk of Allergic or Autoimmune Disease: A Systematic Review and Meta-analysis," *Journal of the American Medical Association* 316(11) (2016): 1181–1192, DOI:10.1001/jama.2016.12623.

11. National Institute of Allergy and Infectious Diseases-Sponsored Expert Panel. 2017 Addendum guidelines for the prevention of peanut allergy in the United States.

12. Dietary Guidelines Advisory Committee. Scientific Report of the 2020 Dietary Guidelines Advisory Committee: Advisory Report to the Secretary of Agriculture and the Secretary of Health and Human Services. 2020.

13. Forestell, C. A. "Flavor Perception and Preference Development in Human Infants" *Annals Nutrition Metabolism* 17 (2017): 70(suppl 3):17-25, https://doi.org/10.1159/000478759.

CHAPTER 6

EXPLORATION
(7 TO 8 MONTHS–THE BEGINNER)

Leslie's daughter, CC, loved being including in the family meal. She'd been so excited to try many first foods when she was just over six months old. Now CC was just over seven months and seemed to have a handle on picking up food, and actually eating it! She moved from smashing food with her palm and raking it toward her mouth to a more refined method. She was able to pick up a bean or berry now just with her thumb and forefinger. Leslie and her husband were excited to see her explore so many textures and try so many foods. Now, it was time to step it up a notch for little CC. She liked tomatoes, she loved beef, she could eat loads of beans—it was time to let CC experience mixed-ingredient meals, like her family's favorite chili. It's still her favorite food to date, even when it's 100 degrees out.

Is Baby Ready?

Baby Ann was grabbing for the foods on Mom's plate after she ate her ground beef crumbles, sliced tomatoes, and avocado. She picked up the smaller pieces of her sliced tomato with the tips of her fingers, a much more precise movement than when she started with solids a few weeks before. Now she was sitting with her parents trying to eat at breakfast and dinner.

- ✔ Ready, Baby Ann is showing signs of the pincer grasp and is ready to move forward.
- ❑ Not Ready

Baby Joe was happy to sit at the dinner table with Mom and Dad for all of his meals. He now consumed most of his meals and demanded to nurse less throughout the day.

- ✔ Ready, Baby Joe is progressing and ready to join in more meals.
- ❑ Not Ready

Baby Evan was really having a lot of fun with his food. He found it interesting to watch most of the food on his plate hit the floor. When he tried to use the side of his hand to rake food toward his mouth, he'd end up smashing more than he got in his mouth. He seemed content just playing with his spoon versus using it to eat food.

- ❑ Ready
- ✔ Not Ready, Baby Evan is still enjoying play with food and this is okay. Continue looking for signs of readiness to move forward with meals.

Is Your Little One Ready to Move On?

Hopefully by now you're feeling like this self-feeding stuff is really great! And it's messy but not that bad. As you're supporting your little one, you've likely noticed some changes in skills and how he's actually eating. It's time to check in and see how your baby is progressing. Is he eating more at each meal? How many meals per day does he enjoy with the family? Is his pincer grasp developing? And what goes in, must come out. Those diapers are likely changing, too. Many babies are just starting to take in enough food to alter their poo color. This is an excellent (and stinky) way to tell how much baby is eating. If baby's poo is still yellow, then it's likely he's still learning and playing with food versus eating most of it. The yellowish color suggests that the diet is still predominantly milk-based. The color turning more toward brown is a good indicator that baby is beginning to eat and digest more solid food. And it's likely that baby is graduating from a pre-eating beginner to a beginner eater.

Let's take a moment to see how your little one is progressing with feeding skills, texture tolerance, and food intake. Use this checklist to determine if baby is ready to move from pre-feeding beginner to a beginner.

- ☐ Eating more, 2 to 3 meals per day
- ☐ Grasping items with more palm and finger control
- ☐ Able to accept and tolerate a variety of textures (smooth, chewy, soft, lumpy, liquid-y)
- ☐ Getting spoon effectively in mouth
- ☐ Able to eat most of meal (3 to 6 tablespoons per meal)
- ☐ Ready for the introduction of a straw and open cup (filled with breast milk or formula at this stage). Practicing with both an open cup and straw cup are advantageous for the development of infant skills
- ☐ Banging, dropping, throwing, and smashing are fascinating baby at this stage
- ☐ Reaching out for more food or eating second helpings of food

If baby doesn't quite have all of these down, that's fine. Give it another week or so and reevaluate. Remember the timeline is one of readiness and skill development, not specific age. Once he's eating more and getting food to his mouth more effectively, we can continue with the *fill the plate* method and begin to add a larger variety of individual and mixed foods. But safety first! Let's review safety for the beginner.

Beginner Self-Feeder Safety Checklist

1. Babies are getting more mobile at this stage, so don't forget to strap them in at the table.
2. **Never** leave a baby unattended while eating. Although you may be gaining more confidence in their feeding capabilities, they can still get tired, relaxed, or overly excited and could take in too much at one time. Babies need to be watched and coached appropriately any time food is present.
3. Test the temperature and texture of the food by mashing between your fingers gently or pressing between your lips to make sure the food can be mashed with baby's gums. If not, it's not the right texture. Consider cooking the food longer or picking a different food.
4. Still offer foods that have been cut or are in the form of a finger so baby can pick them up. This should be about one and half times as long as baby's fist.
5. Don't offer foods that easily break off into small pieces or crumbs that could potentially block baby's airway, as they can pose a choking risk. Foods we recommend avoiding at this stage due to increased risk of choking include raw apples, whole grapes, whole cherry tomatoes, nuts, thick nut butters, popcorn, marshmallows, hard candy, hot dogs, very hard crusty bread, or any food in a round or coin-like shape.
6. If baby manages to break off small pieces of a harder food, remove from the table. Do not remove food from baby's mouth. Coach baby to spit out any foods that are unsafe. Then remove food from the table.
7. If your baby has teeth at this stage, it may be best to avoid raw foods that can break off easily (such as carrots, celery, apple, and broccoli). Their teeth may allow them to bite off more than they can chew, literally. These can be served cooked, and raw can be reintroduced when your baby shows signs of being skilled in chewing or spitting out foods they cannot swallow safely.

Priority Nutrients

With one month into the adventures of eating, there's a good chance your little one is still not eating all that much. Babies vary in intake, so don't fret if breast milk or infant formulas are still their main source of nutrition as they transition to solid foods through the end of their first year. As previously mentioned, iron is an important nutrient to focus on, and that continues throughout the first year (and throughout childhood). Feel free to visit chapter 5 from time to time if you need an iron-rich foods refresher. As we move on with the beginner eater, we'll focus on other important nutrients and foods that are excellent additions at the family dinner table and for baby's growth and development. We'll continue to focus on protein- and iron-rich foods on the plate and add foods that are sources of omega-3 fatty acids, vitamin D, zinc, and probiotics.

Omega-3 Fatty Acids

It's likely you're familiar with omega-3 fatty acids like docosahexaenoic acid, which is usually referred to as DHA. They're commonly found in prenatal vitamins and added to many products for growing infants and children. The thing to remember about omega-3 fats is that they are *essential* fatty acids. This means that your body cannot make them and they must be ingested through the diet. Omega-3 fatty acids, particularly DHA, are primary fats found in the brain and are essential for central nervous system and retinal development. There are actually three types of omega-3 fatty acids: ALA (alpha-linolenic acid), DHA (docosahexaenoic acid), and EPA (eicosapentaenoic acid). We're focusing primarily on DHA and its crucial role in the body of a developing infant and child. Researchers and food manufacturers alike have realized the importance of these fats across the life span. We are now even seeing omega-3 fats as an added component to foods that do not have them naturally. This is called a functional food, and we feel that it's a great and useful advance in food technology and manufacturing. It's a particularly helpful way to get in some nutrients that might not be accessible or readily available for some families or regions.

We suggest incorporating at least one food source of omega-3 fatty acids daily (and not just for baby).

Sources of Omega-3 Fatty Acids

*Anchovies	*Omega-3-enriched eggs
*Canned chunk light tuna	*Salmon
Chia seeds	*Sardines
*Crab	*Shrimp
Edamame	*Trout
Flaxseed oil	Walnuts
*Herring	

*Sources of DHA

Vitamin D

In recent years, vitamin D, also known as the sunshine vitamin, has gotten plenty of press. It's related to numerous processes in the body like bone health, immunity, and beyond. Many Americans have insufficient, if not deficient, levels. While the best source or way to convert vitamin D in the skin to its active and useful form is exposure to sunlight, too much time in the sun can be damaging to the skin. The *Born to Eat* team loves getting our vitamin D from the sunshine. However, we do know that a little can go a long way to provide vitamin D and can quickly turn into too much sun. Many children's and medical organizations recommend sunscreen for most all sun exposure. This is great for keeping skin safe, but not so good for vitamin D levels.

Low vitamin D is becoming an issue across the life span, yet this is of primary concern for breastfed infants and partially breastfed infants, since breast milk has low levels of vitamin D. Currently, the AAP recommends that all infants and children have a minimum intake of 400 IU (International Units) of vitamin D per day. This could be achieved by supplementation of vitamin D for babies who are breastfed or through fortified formula during infancy. It's very unlikely that an infant or child would reach the minimum intake level with food alone. There's a reason they call it the sunshine vitamin and not the fortified food vitamin.

While there are a few food sources that could provide 400 IU of vitamin D, an infant wouldn't consume the serving amount to get the needed vitamin amount. And, some sources, like swordfish, aren't recommended for infants due to high mercury levels. Sockeye salmon provides those great omega fats along with over 400 IU vitamin D per 3 ounces. Baby isn't likely to eat 3 ounces, but it's a solid start and a nutrient-dense food selection for baby's plate.

Sun exposure, in addition to supplementation, remains the best way to get this crucial vitamin. Because of this, recommendations are changing around the world and may include more sun exposure. Be sure to check with your pediatrician for the newest information on vitamin D.

Zinc

With foods like beef, poultry, dairy, eggs, nuts, beans, and shellfish landing on baby's plate, he'll be getting sources of zinc, as well. Zinc is an important mineral that aids in immune function and growth and development. It's hard to protect a baby from colds and illness, but we can support his immune system by making sure we're getting food sources of zinc on his plate. The good thing is that many food sources of zinc are also sources of iron, so you don't have to carry around a big list of foods and nutrients.

Probiotics

Along with omega-3s and vitamin D, probiotics are also popular in the media and with food marketers. There's also a focus on probiotics in emerging research. From helping a colicky baby and treatment of eczema to prevention of allergies, probiotics have gained ample attention for their role in infant nutrition.[1,2] Probiotics are the healthy gut microbes, or bacteria, that aid in digestion and have numerous protective attributes within the human body. Probiotics within the intestines are so important that the gut is often called the second brain, meaning our neurological and physical health are directly connected to and benefited by the health of our gut. Research has also suggested that infants who are introduced to family foods earlier have been found to have higher counts of gut bacteria.[3] Although probiotics are shown to be beneficial, the research is still unclear about which bacteria are most beneficial for particular ailments. The *Born to Eat* team feels it's best to get in a variety of bacteria from foods. Probiotics are found in fermented foods such as sauerkraut (German cabbage salad), cheese, yogurts, kefir (similar to a yogurt drink, but more probiotics), kimchi (Korean cabbage salad), sourdough breads, and miso (fermented soy paste). Mothers who breastfeed can pass probiotics on to their infants through breast milk, as well as prebiotics, which are the foods that feed probiotics.

Probiotics are beneficial for the entire family, not just your *Born to Eat* baby. If eating fermented foods is a challenge within your home, consider opting for a supplement. If you decide to use a probiotic supplement, select one found in the refrigerator section of your health food store that has at least 10 billion bacteria per serving and contains at least four bacterial strains. Talk to your family physician or registered dietitian for help selecting a particular brand or strains. If your baby needs to be on antibiotics for any reason, it's not a bad idea to speak to your physician about using a probiotic supplement following the course of the medicine. Antibiotics kill not only bad bacteria, but also the good. It's imperative to restore the healthy gut microflora once your infant has had their final dose of antibiotics. In addition to lots of Greek yogurt, CC likes her chewable daily probiotic and asks for her *pro-body-otic* every morning.

Adding More Foods, Textures, and Meals

Now you know even more about priority nutrients. These nutrients aren't just important for infants, but they're smart nutrients for the whole family. We've given you lists of foods with varying nutritional properties, and it's important to remember that we don't just eat nutrients, we eat food. With the suggestions we've provided about the nutrients, we can plan some tasty family meals. These foods can be added to family meals or incorporated into your family's favorite recipes. This isn't just the time to feed baby well; it's an opportunity to improve nutrition, variety, and food enjoyment for the whole family.

Early on in the feeding process, Leslie remembers being told to avoid spicy foods and flavors with her little one. While she wasn't going to feed CC a habanero pepper straight from the garden, she added jalapeños to her pot of chili and enchilada bake just like always. Leslie didn't (and still doesn't) believe that having a baby meant the whole family had to eat boring, bland food. Just like with every child (and adult), it was important for CC to experience a variety of flavors and decide for herself whether a food was too spicy or just right. Like we mentioned, that same chili is still CC's favorite food, jalapeños, chili powder, and all. On the flip side, it's totally fine to offer a not-so-spicy option, as well. Some parents (and babies) may have issues with reflux and spice may not be the best addition. Not everyone prefers a spicy kick and that's okay!

We feel that variety is actually the true spice of life and how much variety you introduce to your little one is up to you. Just like what you chew is up to you, how you season and spice is up to you, as well. If you can tell your little one is getting a handle on this eating stuff, the family's favorite mixed foods are fair game. Whether you're having lasagna, tacos, burgers, or going out for Thai food, your little one may be ready to be adventurous in his eating, too. Exposure to new foods is key to a more advanced and accepting palate in the years to come. You can break down your dinner for baby in a baby-friendly fashion. Like CC's chili, at first Leslie served it separated on the plate into beans, beef, tomatoes, and shredded cheese.

Don't worry if baby seems turned off by some of the foods offered; they are still exploring and trying to mentally process their experiences. It's a common misinterpretation that while feeding babies, their facial responses are indicative of them liking or disliking a food. At this stage, it's still about discovery, and they're figuring out what a food tastes like, feels like, smells like, crunches, squashes, and smears like—they are not yet deciding whether or not they like or dislike foods. When at all possible, it's best to avoid a reaction of negativity. We still have to watch our facial expressions at times. We all know the concerned scowl look that accompanies the leading question, *Oh, you don't like it?* We have to coach ourselves as parents and others involved in the family meal to avoid phrases like, *Oh, he doesn't like it* or *He hates it.*

This is the time to stay positive and curious with our own reactions while eating and with baby's experience. If you'd like, you can even dial up the reaction of how much you enjoy each bite saying *Yummy, this is so good!* For those of us who truly have negative preference for say, broccoli, this is possibly the time to try it again, or at the very least don't say anything negative about it when it's on our plates. It's important that baby see similar foods on our plates. We're modeling variety, adventure, and trust with our food. If caregivers don't put broccoli on their plate and show baby how to eat and enjoy it, why would baby want to try it? Our babies are watching and learning. Babies and children alike learn by what foods are provided for them to eat and explore. Parents and caregivers then model how it's eaten and enjoyed.

As we're exploring more foods, it may be tempting to offer baby a bite, but remember it's best that they self-feed and self-regulate. If baby reaches for food on another's plate, place a safe piece of that food or offering on their plate, and let them explore. If the family meal happens to be something extremely spicy, remember that babies can be more sensitive to it, so watch them closely for any flushing or an immediate need for breast milk, formula, or water after a spicy bite. Some babies like spicy food, so it's okay to introduce them to these foods as we mentioned with CC's chili. Just stay alert; you will surely find out whether your little one can take the heat. Keep a non-spicy alterative on the back burner just in case.

Did You Know?

Exposure to new foods is key to a more advanced and accepting palate in the years to come. It can take ten, twenty, or *even more* introductions of a food before it's accepted. That goes for both the little ones and big ones in the family. We all have different temperaments that can impact our eating and acceptance of foods. Sometimes it's easy, and sometimes it's not. Just don't give up!

Our Favorite Beginner Mixed-Food Meals

It's time to introduce some of your favorite family meals. Those meals don't have to be your holiday best recipes; they can just be simple and tasty. Some of our favorite beginner entrées were chicken pot pie, avocado chicken salad, chili, spaghetti and meatballs, chicken curry, shredded pork roast, and a simple pot roast. There are so many options. We're sharing our favorite family dinner recipes with you in chapter 17. Before you know it, you'll add your own favorites to the list!

Is Baby Getting Enough?

At this stage, babies should be sitting down with the family, or caregivers, two to three meals per day. Whether baby eats is up to them. The Division of Responsibility for this age suggests the parent or caregiver is responsible for *what* food will be offered while baby decides on *how much* to eat.[4] While you're enjoying your own meal, you're demonstrating how to chew and savor each bite of new food. Now that you've expanded baby's variety, you may notice that he's excited to see new foods or maybe even unsure at the sight of new mixed meal. But that's okay. Continue to consistently offer the new foods.

Since baby is in charge of how much to eat without feeding help or coaching him to eat more, we as parents can begin to worry if he's getting enough. If baby is still taking milk feedings and starting to actually eat some of his offered foods during mealtimes or snack times, it's very likely that baby's growth, measured by length and weight at the pediatrician's office, is right on track for *his* individual body. Babies follow their own growth curves; some stay at the same percentile curve throughout infancy while others may have bumps higher or lower visit to visit. If your child has a large bump up or down on the curve, this can be concerning, but is often normal within the first six months (and even up to age two). Sometimes it can be a fluke, a bout of sickness, or even a measurement error. Regardless, it's a good idea to follow up and repeat the measures so you and your pediatrician can determine the next steps. Purposeful weight loss is never a goal.

Should You Worry about the Weight?

Growth around a stable percentile is reassuring, but it is not uncommon for babies' weight to shift up or down on the growth chart within the first six months and even up to two years of age.[5,6] Family doctor and childhood feeding specialist Dr. Katja Rowell says, "While weight loss and sudden changes are always worrisome, if baby is doing well overall, weight percentiles moving up or down isn't always concerning, but warrants a thorough history and exam." This is an important tidbit for us as parents because as soon as a doctor puts a stigmatizing label like *underweight*, *overw*ight*, or *ob*se* on our kids, we're going to worry and be tempted to take our feeding strategy in a different   >>

direction—our doctors might even ask us to. This can lead to food pushing if our little one is labeled underweight or restricting if labeled overw*ight, which is likely to backfire (more on this in chapter 8).

Where your child is weight-wise may be exactly where they need to be no matter the label. *Underweight* and *ob*se* labels sound scary, but if baby is bigger or smaller than average and growing in a steady way, that is likely to be healthy.[7] We've seen many clients where a misguided worry about weight led to feeding problems and can make weight concerns worse. We are *Born to Eat*, and with that comes times of learning, growth, and weight fluctuations.

Development Through Food Exploration

These are exciting times. Hopefully, you and baby are getting the swing of self-feeding and feeling more confident about the baby-led weaning approach. As parents, we're learning our role in the feeding process while baby is learning his role. Most likely, he's also learning and developing loads of skills right before your eyes.

The pincer grasp, which may start around six or seven months, is usually more efficient around nine to twelve months. During this stage, you can watch how baby is progressing from a clumsy grasp to a more fine movement. As finger dexterity improves, baby will be able to feed himself more efficiently. This allows baby to pick up foods with his thumb and forefinger just like CC was starting to do with her beans. Baby's fine motor skills will quickly become stronger and he may also want to use a utensil more often, though more likely he will hold utensil with one hand and feed with the other. Around this same time, baby also develops a love for throwing. Be prepared for flying objects! Cause and effect are fun at this age, so when your baby tests how quickly that sweet potato wedge can drop to the floor, don't fret—it's normal, it's expected, and truly is a part of the learning process. Just have another slice at the ready, because he'll quickly realize he can't get that one back to eat.

American Sign Language and Feeding

If you're interested in using American Sign Language with your baby, which we both did, this is an excellent time to introduce these helpful food-related signs. We found these signs very helpful in understanding baby's cues and supporting responsive eating before baby talks.

<u>All finished or all done:</u> holding both hands up and waving them. When your baby is starting to throw more things off the table then put to their mouth, then it's a great time to ask if they're all finished. Be sure to give them some time to process the question before taking their food away.

<u>More:</u> bring fingers to your thumbs on both hands then tap thumbs while keeping your hands in this position.

<u>Milk:</u> squeeze your hands like you are milking an udder on a cow.

<u>Water:</u> make a W with your fingers and bring it to your lips. This isn't exclusive to water you drink, so you can talk about water as it relates to a pool, rain, a puddle, or in the bath.

<u>Food or eat:</u> pinch fingers to thumb and bring up to your mouth. "It's time to eat," is a great way to indicate mealtime and using this sign.

>>

The more consistently you use these signs, the quicker your baby will grasp them and use the signs to ease communication barriers. Your baby may not master the sign until they have excellent finger dexterity, so look for any evidence that they are trying to use the sign and praise them with utter excitement to encourage them to continue trying and using sign language. For example, Miss A still signed the word *water* by bringing only one finger up to her mouth at sixteen months old, but it was also her first sign at seven months old. She would also use the sign for water any time she wanted to sip what Mom and Dad were drinking.

Drinking from a Cup

You may have already started playing with an open cup, and that's great. If not, no worries. Now is the time to give baby an open cup. As we mentioned in chapter 5, we love the EZPZ tiny cup. You can start by adding formula, breast milk, or water to the cup. We suggest no more than 1 to 2 tablespoons in the cup, once or twice a day. Right now baby is simply learning technique and adding a little hydration.

CHAPTER 6 REFERENCES

1. Jisheng Gao, Hongwei Wu, and Jinfeng Liu. "Importance of gut microbiota in health and diseases of new born infants (Review)," *Experimental and Therapeutic Medicine* 12(1): (July 2016): 28–32, published online April 11, 2016, DOI: 10.3892/etm.2016.3253 PMCID: PMC4906629.

2. Erin C. Davis, Andrew M. Dinsmoor, Mei Wang, and Sharon M. Donovan. "Microbiome Composition in Pediatric Populations from Birth to Adolescence: Impact of Diet and Prebiotic and Probiotic Interventions" *Digestive Diseases and Sciences* 65 (2020): 706–722, DOI: 10.1007/s10620-020-06092-x.

3. Martin Frederik Laursen, Louise B. B. Andersen, Kim F. Michaelsen, Christian Mølgaard, Ellen Trolle, Martin Iain Bahl, and Tine Rask Licht. "Host-Microbe Biology Infant Gut Microbiota Development Is Driven by Transition to Family Foods Independent of Maternal Obesity," *mSphere* 1(1) (January–February 2016): e00069-15. Published online 2016 Feb 10. DOI: 10.1128/mSphere.00069-15 PMCID: PMC4863607http://www.ncbi.nlm.nih.gov/pmc/articles/PMC4863607/.

4. "Ellyn Satter's Division of Responsibility in Feeding," Ellyn Satter Institute, accessed September 20, 2016, http://ellynsatterinstitute.org/dor/divisionofresponsibilityin feeding.php.

5. Arthur Jaffe, "Failure to Thrive: Current Clinical Concepts," *Pediatrics in Review*, 32(3), (March 2011): 100–107. DOI: 10.1542/pir.32-3-100.

6. Zuguo Mei, Laurence Grummer-Strawn, Diane Thompson, William Dietz, "Shifts in Percentiles of Growth During Early Childhood: Analysis of Longitudinal Data From the California Child Health and Development Study," *Pediatrics*, 113 (6), (June 2004): e617–e627, accessed October 12, 2016.

7. James Ledler, Lewis Rose, "Assessment of Abnormal Growth Curves," *American Family Physician*, 58(1), (July 1998): 153–158, accessed October 12, 2016.

CHAPTER 7

THIS STUFF IS TASTY
(9 TO 12 MONTHS–THE NOVICE)

> "Adopt the pace of nature: her secret is patience."
> —Ralph Waldo Emerson

Leslie took CC to the office a couple times a week. CC loved looking around at all the nutritionist stuff while Leslie did administrative tasks or met with other dietitians in the office. CC was about ten months old and eating like a champ. Leslie carried snacks like peeled clementines with her because CC loved them. One day, while Leslie was having a discussion with a coworker, she could tell CC was hungry so she gave her a piece of the clementine. A few seconds later, Leslie noticed that she was too quiet and looked over to see CC's scared, red face, and watering eyes. Leslie quickly grabbed CC out of her car seat and set her upright. CC was able to control the clementine and swallow it with no problem once she was sitting upright. They'd both gotten a bit too comfortable since she had been self-feeding so well, and Leslie didn't think a thing about giving CC a snack while reclined in her car seat. This was a very scary (and embarrassing) lesson in feeding safety, and Leslie never did that again! It could happen to any one of us, even a nutrition pro.

At this stage, it's tempting to be more relaxed with food just because you've seen them gain skills, make great strides, and begin to eat like a toddler. But the truth is they're still babies and they get tired, get overly excited, or can be too relaxed. It's always important to stay tuned in while your little one eats. We feel it's important to remind caregivers and ourselves that attention toward monitoring little ones is still a priority while they continue on their eating journeys.

Milestones

From crawling to walking to teething, your little one is likely reaching huge milestones in the final three months of her first year. She's really starting to master her pincer grasp and is able to pick up the tiny blueberry or a pitted cherry and plop it in her mouth. She's probably getting confident in her own skills at this point and may be excited to use utensils, too. This is all part of the natural progression of raising babies who are *Born to Eat*. What you offer also helps her master skills to become a much neater eater, but she's not quite there yet.

In addition to finger dexterity, you will notice your little one might be a bit more active at this age, as she's learning to stand or possibly walk or still mastering her crawl. Because of this need to move, you may find keeping her in her high chair to be a bit more challenging. It's tempting to put their food on the ground and let them graze, but as convenient as it may seem, babies are more apt to choke unless seated properly while eating. If your little one wants to move, let her down and then ask again if she's ready to eat in five or ten minutes (this is the perfect time to sign *food* or *more*). If not, you can put the food away and try again later. A baby's attention span is short, but she'll likely let you know when she's hungry again, or her fussing will be your first clue.

To help at mealtimes, try engaging your little one around food by introducing food to her or try playing a game of peekaboo with foods on her plate to get her interested in sitting at the table. This helps with creating habits, and by having your little one eat with you at meals, she's growing more accustomed to this behavior and will be more apt to sit longer and longer at a meal with each passing month.

Trust your intuition and assessment of your little one's progression. Find a pediatrician you trust and they'll have no problem with you being a proactive parent versus a reactive one. Keep track of areas of concern to share with your pediatrician and have things written out prior to your appointment. This can keep you both on track so you don't feel rushed or pass over a concern.

Chomp Chomp

Teething is likely in full swing by now. Even if teeth haven't popped yet, your little one is probably gumming everything in sight and drooling like a river. She may want to put everything in her mouth to help find relief for her aching gums or just enjoy the sensation of something new. Food items and nonfood items are a challenge to decipher for a teething baby or toddler on the move. Wendy Jo's pediatrician, Dr. Dave, shared a great tip with her.

> Dr. Dave says it's best to go around the house with an empty toilet paper roll and remove anything off the floor that could possibly fit through the hole, as anything smaller than that hole can fit nicely down your little one's throat. Thanks, Dr. Dave!

Babies get teeth at varying times; some may have six by now and some may not even have one. If you stick your finger in their mouth, they'll be sure to show you how well they can gum. *OUCH!* Great teething foods include frozen and slightly thawed bananas, cold cucumber sticks, or a cold slice of steak. Just like at every other stage, each baby is different. Wendy Jo's little one had a taste for sand, leaves, rocks, and basically anything she get her hands on while CC wasn't much of a chewer of things other than food.

Now that we've covered some milestones, let's see whether a baby is ready to move ahead with her eating. If all of a sudden you notice your little one is not wanting to eat as much or crying out when eating, don't assume they're becoming picky eaters. It's not uncommon for a baby to turn down food while teething, as it may hurt their gums until the tooth breaks through the gumline. If they're nursing or have a greater desire for formula instead of food, chalk it up to teething. During this time, keep offering foods, more breast milk or formula feedings, and in time, they'll return to their normal eating patterns.

> Wendy Jo's daughter had three days where she would only choose to eat softer foods offered on her plate, like berries and yogurt, then *pop*! There was her first tooth.

With the addition of new teeth, your little one may be ready for some new textures. Up to this point, vegetables and fruit were very soft. It may be time to try a crunchier green bean, a wedge of cantaloupe, or steamed broccoli. If she's ready, she will take little nibbles, chew up each piece, and continue on with her meal. If she's not ready for this texture, she may gag or spit out the food and leave it on her plate. Keep offering a new texture every couple days so she can continue to work on the skill and let you know when she's ready to advance. All skills take practice, and no one is an expert at first bite. Your little one is entering into the novice stage of eating.

Is Baby Ready?

Baby Dayne was nine months old. He'd been fidgety and fussy sitting through mealtimes and crying when he took a bite of food. He had a couple new teeth erupting.

- ❑ Ready
- ✔ Not Ready, new teeth can make it a challenge to try out new foods. Give Baby Dayne a couple more weeks or until the pain of new teeth fade.

Baby Simone was ten months old, and blueberries were her new favorite food. She loved picking up one blueberry half at a time and could easily eat ½ cup or more at breakfast.

- ✔ Ready, looks like Baby Simone has the pincer grasp now.
- ❑ Not Ready

Baby Maya was nine months old. She was served a steamed green bean just like her parents like them, al dente. At first bite, she chewed, made a gagging noise, and spit out the green bean. She went for her raspberry instead and left the green bean on her plate.

- ❑ Ready
- ✔ Not Ready, advancing Baby Maya to an al dente texture may be a bit early. Steam her green beans a bit longer and try again in a couple weeks. Bravo to Baby Maya for recognizing this and spitting out her green bean.

Now that you have a better idea where your novice eater is in regards to progression of eating, let's review our safety checklist for this skill level. You will note that some things have changed as your little one grows and has more skills.

Novice Safety Checklist

1. Secure baby upright in a high chair or feeding seat. Baby should never be reclined, eating in a car seat (thank you, Leslie, for that reminder), or eating in someone's lap. This allows the parent or caregiver to evaluate how baby is doing at all times.

2. **Never** leave baby alone when eating. It's more tempting to turn your back while she's eating at this age or feed her on the floor, but risks are still present, and it's best to tune in to each bite.

3. Let baby put food in her mouth. She needs to be in control of how fast the food enters her mouth or how much she eats at all times. As tempting as it is, especially if baby slows eating a bit with teething, you don't have to help. As baby progresses with eating a variety of foods, she may still need some coaching to chew or spit out foods.

4. If the food has been cooked, continue to test the temperature of the food to ensure it has cooled enough for baby to test. Even something perceived as warm by the caregiver may be felt as hot by a baby. She may be able to handle warmer items and be taught to blow on her food to cool down a hot bite.

5. She may now be ready for vegetables that are a bit more al dente over very soft vegetables. Let her test the new texture and advance as you see fit.

6. Foods can now be offered in smaller pieces, about the size of a pinky nail or in wedges, depending on the food.

7. Don't offer foods that easily break off into small pieces or crumbs that could potentially block the airway of baby, as they can pose a choking risk. Foods we recommend still avoiding at *this stage* due to increased risk of choking include raw apples, whole grapes, whole cherry tomatoes, other raw fruits or vegetables with tough skins, nuts, thick nut butters, popcorn, marshmallows, hard candy, hot dogs, very crusty bread, or any food in a round or coin-like shape.

What Goes In Must Come Out

We're dietitians and have no problem talking about your little one's food exit strategy. Let's talk poo—appropriate potty talk, of course. With the advances in your little one's eating, you'll notice changes in her diaper. As gross as it can be, a diaper has a story to tell. A baby who still is taking in more formula or breast milk has a more yellow hue to the poop; whereas a baby who is eating more has very identifiable food in the

poo (*poo* sounds a lot better than *fecal matter* or *stools*). The color will become darker brown and will start to take on a more solid form. You may not have the same perception and wish to discard that stinky diaper as quick as can be—we get it—but the diaper speaks volumes about food intake. Randomly pick a day and check out the contents. This will help you know whether your little one is eating more food over just playing with the plate or tossing it overboard to feed her favorite pooch. It will also give you an indication of how well she's chewing up the food before swallowing. Does a blueberry half make its way out? Perhaps cut them in half, if so. Or, are you finding beans make their way out just as they went in? Again, a good time to cut the bean in half.

As gross as it is, poo can provide some value in letting the parent know just how well a little one is eating. Again, as icky as this may sound, your pediatrician may ask you questions about this, and you'll know exactly why.

Now that you know the basic ins and outs of poo, it's time to discuss the nutrients your little one needs at this time to continue to thrive. Remember, the *Born to Eat* team doesn't advocate eating nutrients. We, as humans, eat food versus single nutrients. Ramp up the offerings of family foods to ensure the baby is getting adequate nutrition.

Grow Baby, Grow

As you have probably noticed, your baby has been rapidly changing sizes in baby clothes and their little head keeps growing. With all that growing, two additional key nutrients to focus on over the next couple months are zinc and selenium. We've touched on zinc before, but we're digging a little deeper now.

These two nutrients are antioxidant powerhouses, meaning they inhibit oxidation at the cellular level. Antioxidants are important in fighting cell damage by free radicals. Antioxidants, such as zinc and selenium, are important dietary additions for your growing infant. As your baby continues to grow, so will their appetite, making it easier to get in a greater variety of nutrients.

ZINC

Wendy Jo's college professor loved to say, "I Zinc Therefore I am." A little play on words, but definitely shows the importance of this antioxidant. Zinc plays an important role in metabolism and digestion and is often linked to skin issues, such as eczema. The good news is, if you've stuck to our suggestions of first foods, your baby is likely getting enough, because beef is a star player in delivering zinc—just 1 ounce delivers exactly what your baby needs. Other solid zinc providers include beans, almond butter (she's not quite ready for whole or chopped nuts), yogurt, ricotta cheese, and peas. Red meat takes center stage for zinc, but the rest are great sources, too.

If you're concerned about taking in too much zinc, don't be. When you stick with foods in their whole food form, it's hard to chew too much zinc-rich food. People, regardless of age, are more at risk of overdoing nutrients when they add in many fortified foods or supplements. We recommend sticking with food sources unless your doctor suggests otherwise.

SELENIUM

Selenium is a key antioxidant involved with vitamin C, thyroid health, and the body's response to stress. When a body comes under stress, the need for selenium increases because selenium is part of the glutathione peroxidases enzyme mechanism (what?!). In short, it's a big deal when our body is dealing with severe stress. Breast milk has selenium, so if you have continued breastfeeding, your little one is still taking in selenium. Selenium wasn't always a mandatory ingredient in infant formula. According to the Food and Drug Administration's official website, selenium was added to the mandated list of nutrients in infant formulas in June 2015. Selenium is a big deal, but a small amount goes a long way.

Just like an adult, the recommendation for including seafood in an infant and child's diet is about two to three times per week. If you keep this in mind, your baby is most likely getting in adequate amounts of selenium. Seafood is one of the top sources of selenium: it can be found in tuna, shrimp, and salmon. If you're not able to eat seafood or enjoy it as frequently as suggested, selenium can also be found in mushrooms, asparagus, eggs, turkey, chicken, and sunflower seeds.

How Much Is Enough? Or Too Much?

One of the most frequent questions the *Born to Eat* team gets is in regard to quantity of food. How much is enough food for a baby? The truth is the range in amounts will vary, and a nine-month-old may or may not eat as much as a twelve-month-old, and Johnny next door may eat less than Sue down the street but more than Robbie from daycare. The goal is that by the time baby hits their first birthday, they can sustain themselves with foods, transition to whole cow's milk from a cup, and no longer need breast milk or formula. We will cover more on that in the next chapter. Rest assured, your little one is working on eating more, developing precise self-feeding skills, and learning from you every time you sit down to a enjoy a meal together.

Dishing It Up

By now, you're seeing that your baby truly can enjoy eating what you eat without making special meals or only serving up kid-friendly foods. At this stage, baby can likely transition from isolated foods like spaghetti with meatballs on the side to normally plated mixed meals like spaghetti with meatballs on top. Remember, it's

Spaghetti and Meatballs
Finger of Bread
4 Green Beans

best to put less on a plate so your little one doesn't get overwhelmed. But don't forget to offer seconds and even thirds if your little one indicates they want more (reaching for more, signing more, opening mouth, sucking on fist). We don't want to overwhelm baby, and we sure don't want to restrict them either (this can lead to food preoccupation later on). If baby is leading the way, she will likely eat to meet her needs. Sometimes she'll eat a lot and other times a little. Baby will also let you know when she's full by losing interest in the meal, appearing distracted, pulling off bib, or trying to get out of the high chair. These actions let you know baby is done with mealtime.

Here is a sample three-day menu for your nine- to twelve-month-old. Note the range in amounts that you can start with and offer more as needed. These amounts are not serving sizes; they're merely suggestions for getting started. Go with your gut and recent experiences of what your baby has eaten.

Meal	Sample Day 1	Sample Day 2	Sample Day 3
Breakfast	❑ ½–1 boiled egg ❑ 2 tablespoons–¼ cup plain, whole-fat, Greek yogurt ❑ 2 tablespoons–¼ cup blueberries	❑ 1 slice (cut into thin strips) thinly smeared almond butter toast ❑ 1 mini-muffin frittata (pg 182) ❑ 5–10 raspberries	❑ 2 tablespoons–¼ cup Beefy Breakfast Sausage (page 197) ❑ 2 tablespoons sweet potato hash brown ❑ 2–4 strawberries
Snack	❑ 2 tablespoons hummus ❑ 2 pretzels	❑ ¼ cup whole-grain O cereal ❑ 2 tablespoons–¼ cup plain, whole-fat, Greek yogurt	❑ 2 tablespoons applesauce ❑ ¼ cup grated cheese
Lunch	❑ 2 tablespoons–¼ cup Chunk Light Tuna Salad (page 205) ❑ ⅛–¼ avocado slices or mashed and spread on bread or crackers ❑ 2 whole-grain crackers or ½ slice whole-grain bread ❑ 2 tablespoons canned (in juice or water) mandarin oranges	❑ ¼ cup lentil soup ❑ ¼ grilled cheese sandwich (cut into ½-inch bites) ❑ ¼–½ kiwi fruit	❑ 2 tablespoons–¼ cup cottage or ricotta cheese ❑ 2–4 zucchini finger fritters ❑ 2–3 cherry tomato halves with olive oil and lemon juice ❑ 4–6 blackberries

Meal	Sample Day 1	Sample Day 2	Sample Day 3
Snack	❑ 2 tablespoons cottage cheese or ricotta cheese ❑ ¼ very ripe pear or 1 very small pear that baby can hold to eat	❑ ¼–½ boiled egg or egg salad ❑ 1–2 whole-grain crackers	❑ 1 (2-inch) cucumber spear ❑ 2–4 quartered olives, without seed ❑ 2–4 tablespoons whole fat, plain Greek yogurt
Dinner	❑ ¼–½ cup spaghetti with meat sauce	❑ ½–1 whole grilled salmon patties ❑ 2–4 steamed green beans ❑ ¼ cup oven-roasted potato wedges	❑ ¼–½ cup Single-Crust Chicken Pot Pie (page 237) ❑ 1 square dark chocolate

In real life, it looks a little different for every family. CC ate a good serving of fruit and eggs most mornings shortly after waking while Miss A had breakfast broken up into two snack-like meals. Times are not carved in stone nor are the number of meals offered. What is certain is that your little one has a smaller stomach and does need to eat more frequently than an adult. From nine to twelve months of age, your little one will be moving toward eating roughly three meals and two to three snacks per day. Don't feel as though you ever have to follow this like it's a diet or scripted meal plan. It's not! The idea of this meal plan menu example is to show variety and that your baby can eat what you eat.

You Choose What, They Choose How Much

Just like the beginner eater, Ellyn Satter's Division of Responsibility holds true for this age, as well. The Division of Responsibility suggests the parent or caregiver is responsible for *what* food will be offered while baby decides on *how much* to eat. Our perception of what is enough may not match what baby really wants or needs. If you feel they're not eating enough, offer meals more frequently throughout the day, offer high-fat, nutrient-dense foods, and skip beverages until after mealtimes (liquids can be too filling and cause lower intake of solid foods at meals). At this point, you can avoid nursing or giving infant formula to your baby until after they've finished their meal.

Time Flies

Congrats! You're off to a great start, and your baby has an excellent foundation for eating. Next up is baby's first birthday, and with that comes a toddler with an independent mind and palate. The *Born to Eat* team has you covered, and chapters 8 and 9 tackle the more selective palate and creative ways to keep your toddler on the self-feeding path.

Journal Notes

ONE YEAR! YAY! RECORD SOME OF YOUR FAVORITE MOMENTS HERE.

_____

_____

_____

_____

_____

_____

_____

_____

_____

CHAPTER 8

I'M ON THE MOVE
(12 TO 24 MONTHS—THE PRE-ADVANCED EATER)

> "Silence is golden—unless you have a toddler. In that case, silence is very, very suspicious."
>
> —Anonymous

The cake smash. It's the one-year-old's rite of passage into the food world. Hopefully by the time your little one smears icing across his hair and anyone nearby, he has experienced much of what the family table has to offer. And in every possible texture. This can be such a fun time for food adventuring and dining as a family. Not only is he eating a variety of foods and textures, but he's likely hungry for more since he can walk and explore on his own. He may also decide he'd rather explore than eat. Your baby has graduated to a toddler, and his rate of growth development has slowed down, so if you do notice a drop in intake, don't let it get you overly concerned; on the other hand, if his newfound ability to walk has turned into a run, then his eating may be off and running, too.

It's possible you're feeling like you have this feeding thing down! We sure did. Year One can lead to many food adventures for you and the little one, like ordering from a real menu. Before he orders that chicken Parmesan, let's take a moment to see how this new toddler is progressing with feeding skills, texture tolerance, and food intake. Use this checklist to determine if your toddler is ready to move from a novice eater to the pre-advanced eater. By now, your little one is likely:

- Eating approximately three meals and two or three snacks per day
- Grasping items with a fine pincer grasp
- Handling almost all textures
- Biting and chewing most foods
- Holding and using a spoon more effectively
- Using a straw cup and open cup with more confidence during mealtimes
- Using more control getting food into his mouth and spilling less
- Asking for more food as needed

Remember, each toddler is developing at his own pace. These are general markers of progressing in feeding and eating skills. Now that he's more mobile and having tons of fun around the house, we have to keep in mind new or changing areas of concern. Let's review safety now that your little one has graduated to a toddler or pre-advanced eater.

The Pre-Advanced Eater Safety Checklist

1. Toddler eats at the table in high chair, not walking around or while playing.
2. Turn off distractions, such as television or a toy, so he can focus on his food. Distractions can lead to accidents while eating, in addition to creating a habit of mindless eating.
3. **Never** leave him unattended while eating. Although his feeding skills have improved dramatically, it's a good idea to stay close while eating. Depending on how many teeth he has and his chewing competency, choking can still be a risk.
4. Continue to test the temperature of cooked and mixed meals to make sure they're not too hot for him to handle. Just like testing with texture, you can teach him to test by taking a bite or placing it to his lip.
5. Foods can be offered in smaller pieces now that your little one is chewing more efficiently. For example, instead of fingers of steak, you can cut into smaller bites. Although children don't get their grinding molars until about two to three years old, they can gum, gnaw, and chew meats quite well, especially with preparations that keep it moist and tender.
6. Foods that were once avoided whole can be included depending on your little one's chewing development. If needed, you can still cut round foods like grapes

(in halves from stem end to point, not around the middle), cherry tomatoes, hot dogs, etc. in half.

7. There still may be foods that are hard for your toddler to manipulate with his gums, teeth, or chewing skills. Modify the texture as needed—like pulling the strings from an orange section or chopping nuts.

Is Little One Ready to Move On?

Let's look and see if your little one is ready to move into pre-advanced eating.

Little Debbie used to struggle with her spoon while eating her oatmeal at breakfast and enjoyed using her hands instead. Occasionally she would try the spoon throughout the meal.

- ❑   Ready
- ✔   Not Ready, Little Debbie needs more time working with her spoon skills.

Little Johnny is doing great using his open cup and spoon during most meals. He's now able to eat thin liquids, like soup with his spoon with minimum spillage.

- ✔   Ready, Little Johnny seems to be eating well with his spoon.
- ❑   Not Ready

Little Maxie is using her baby signs to ask for more food at mealtimes. She seems to be honoring her own hunger cues in a growing body.

- ✔   Ready, Little Maxie is eating well and getting used to honoring her body's cues.
- ❑   Not Ready

Don't Freak Out

For the last year, you've likely watched your baby become a happy and interested eater. It isn't uncommon for this interest and appetite to decrease, though. This is normal since the growth velocity has slowed dramatically from those early months of life. When we've counseled parents of one- to two-year-olds, we often hear that they wished they had known that was normal. We love our kids and want them to be nourished. It's very tempting to stray from the Division of Responsibility when we feel desperate for them to eat or to get enough. We've been tempted to say "just one more bite" or "just finish your carrots," as well, but we have to trust that the same intuition that helped them feed themselves to this point will also help them stay nourished enough to sustain their growth and development by self-regulation. They will continue to learn and explore without the pressure from "just try it" or "but, you like it!" They are *Born to Eat*, and their bodies will respond accordingly.

Research suggests that a controlling parenting style, whether it's pushing a child to eat more or restricting their intake, leads to poor self-regulation.[1] It seems that controlling parental styles have the exact opposite outcome of what the parent is trying to control. If the diet is being restricted, it's very likely the child will eat more when given the chance and is linked to weight dysregulation. On the flip side, if the child is pressured to eat, those behaviors can result in difficulty eating, less enjoyment of food, and weight faltering. The bottom line is, no matter how strong the urge is to control our little one's intake can be, make every attempt to avoid it.

> This is a great time to check out the book *How to Raise an Intuitive Eater: Raising the Next Generation with Food and Body Confidence* by Sumner Brooks, MPH, RDN and Amee Severson, MPP-D, RDN. It's a wonderful resource for parents and caregivers.
>
> We also love the Easy Bites app founded by Natalia Stasenko, Registered Dietitian, and Responsive Feeding Specialist.
>
> If you're on Instagram, you may also like these accounts.
>
> - @kids.eat.in.color
> - @kid.food.explorers
> - @pediatric.dietitian
> - @EasyBites.App
> - @Nutrition.for.Littles
> - @NicolecruzRD
> - @CrystalKarges
> - @NutriChicos
> - @Oona_Hanson
> - @KatieBartelsRD_

Let's take a moment to review our role as a parent following the Division of Responsibility supporting a self-regulating eater. Parents remain in charge of *when* food is offered, *what* food is offered, and *where* it will be eaten or served. An additional role on our part is to *trust*. Trust that our *Born to Eat* child can do just that and follow their role. We're trusting that our little one will follow his role to decide *whether or if* he'll eat and *how much*. We've watched these beautiful skills develop in the families we've counseled along with our own kids. It's totally doable.

Breaking down the roles at a meal may look a bit like this scenario. Mom makes dinner at six o'clock (when) and puts roasted sweet potatoes, asparagus, strawberries, and barbeque chicken (what) on David's plate. Dad sets the table in the kitchen (where). David gets seated in his high chair and begins to eat his sweet potatoes, strawberries, and chicken (whether). He's unsure about the asparagus but explores. He left most of the asparagus and half of his sweet potatoes on his plate (how much) and pushed it away to signal that he was finished. Mom and Dad have

seen him eat everything on his dinner plate with the exact same menu. Although they're concerned about him getting enough, they trust he's self-regulating for his needs at that moment and don't encourage him to eat more. David and his parents are respecting their roles and trusting each other in their responsibilities.

Nutrition versus Nutrients

Now that your little one is a year old, it's recommended to add whole cow's milk as a beverage in place of infant formula. Some may still be breastfeeding on demand or putting breast milk in a cup, and that's cool, too. Do what works best for you and your little one. Just remember that beverages like milk can fill your little one's tummy quickly and decrease the amount of food eaten at a meal. Milk can be offered with a small snack or after the meal so more solid foods may be eaten.

To Drink or Not to Drink

Another frequent question that comes up around this time is about beverages. Fruit juices are a hot-button topic. The American Academy of Pediatrics recommends a maximum amount of 4 ounces of juice per day for toddlers 1 to 3 years of age. Like with food, we trust our toddlers to regulate their intake of juices based on what we provide according

>>

to the guidelines. If you choose to use juice at this age, be sure that the juice you choose is 100 percent fruit juice. We do believe some juices have a benefit and a possible place in a child's life. After all, many of us enjoy the occasional diversion from water. Of 100 percent juice options, our top picks serve a purpose and can complement an occasional meal or a snack. We've added small amounts of these juices to yogurt, water, cooked foods, oats, and popsicles to add flavor changes and functional benefits. The nutrients delivered in 1 to 2 ounces of these juices per day aren't easily attainable through whole foods:

- Concord grape juice: The benefits an adult can get from drinking wine can be found in the dark juices of Concord grapes. From research on brain function to heart health, Concord grapes have been earning a lot of positive press for their nutritional attributes.[2,3]
- Tart cherry juice: It may be too tart for your palate, but may be just right for your little one. Tart cherry juice may help with sleep, so perhaps reserve the 1- to 2-ounce serving for after dinner.[4]
- Cranberry juice: Another tart juice with promising research. Cranberry juice may help prevent recurrent urinary tract infections in adults and children alike.[5]
- Orange juice: Orange juice offers a great source of vitamin C and many fortified options provide Vitamin D, as well. This will complement your meal to help with the absorption of iron from other food sources.

This is a great time to continue working with an open cup and straw. We like silicone and stainless steel options. Here's another trick from Dr. Dave: place a straw in a cup of water and cover the straw opening with a finger. While holding your finger in place, give it to your infant and allow them to suck the beverage from the straw before releasing your finger. This can aid in teaching your little one how to suck up liquids from a straw.

We've mentioned before that we eat food, not nutrients. While our foods provide great nutrients, we don't sit down to a plate of vitamin C and omega-3 fatty acids. We're sitting down to grilled salmon and roasted red peppers. Now that your little one is a year old, his meals are likely looking a lot like yours except on a smaller scale. When we're thinking of nutrients and nutrition overall, we can focus on the same thing we'd want you to focus on for the whole family: balance. If you were sitting across from us in our respective counseling offices, we'd tell you to fill your plate with colorful fruits and vegetables, muscle-supporting proteins, satisfying fats, and energy-giving carbohydrates. And the way we teach it is visual, just like creating that first plate for baby. We use the Plate Method.

Don't worry too much about getting the balance just right. It's about balance over time, not every time. And, when we talk about balance, remember that you are in charge of what that means to you and your family—not us.

We've both experienced a meal where our little ones only eat the sweet potatoes or the brownie. As parents (and nutrition experts) we, of course, want our kids to eat well; however, the *how* a child eats, developing feeding and eating behaviors early on, may be even more important than *what* they eat in the beginning. In our nutrition counseling offices, we've seen the damage that the lack of body trust can cause over time.

These early years can be so important in feeding and eating behavior development.

> Development through discovery, without pressure, is the way to build trust—trust in the adults around them, trust in food, and trust in their own body.
> —Katja Rowell, MD, coauthor of *Helping Your Child with Extreme Picky Eating*

It's common during this time for your little one to have more preferences. He may only eat the eggs on his breakfast plate and not the toast. This is also okay. As parents, we continue to offer the foods even though we know that he may not eat it from one day to the next. Many parents worry at this stage that their children may be becoming picky eaters. There's typical picky eating, which is normal like described above, and then there's extreme picky eating. Sometimes a typical picky eating sixteen-month-old will start eating fewer and fewer foods or textures.

There are a variety of reasons for this, and as parents, we don't want to make a normal issue a problematic one. For example, say CC stopped eating broccoli (she did) for a while and we stopped offering it to her saying she's picky (we didn't). Then the same

> What we eat is important, but having a hyper focus on eating certain foods, or not eating certain foods, can backfire. When food is a big deal, it may always be a big deal.

thing happens with tomatoes, and we say "Oh, she's picky and won't eat those foods." It's possible we took a typical one-year-old eater and helped create a very picky one. Remember, when food's a big deal, it's a big deal.

Is It Typical Picky Eating or Extreme?

About half of all young children are considered "picky" at some point. Most picky eating behaviors are part of normal eating stages. All parents need more information and support to identify typical picky eating, how not to make matters worse, how to support a healthy relationship to food, when to seek professional help, and how to find the right help. We define *extreme picky eating* (EPE) as not eating enough quantity or variety to support healthy emotional, physical, or social development; or eating patterns that are a significant source of conflict or worry. Extreme picky eating is an umbrella term that covers labels including: *selective eating, food aversion, feeding disorder, ARFID* (avoidant restrictive food intake disorder), *problem feeder*, and *infantile anorexia* (older term).

Anything that makes getting food to the mouth, chewing, swallowing, and digesting difficult, painful, or uncomfortable increases the odds a child will struggle with more extreme picky eating. How a child is fed also plays a critical role. Here are some signs that parents may be dealing with more extreme picky eating, often linked with medical challenges, oral-motor or sensory difficulties, anxiety, autism spectrum, temperament, and feeding history. These are complex problems with many factors that must be considered and addressed.

- ❏ Not able to gum or chew with molars by 15 to 18 months
- ❏ Falling off growth curve, losing weight
- ❏ Struggled with breast or bottle feeding and/or transition to solids (versus the child who does well until 15 to 18 months when typical picky eating phase usually starts)
- ❏ Choking, vomiting regularly, aspirating
- ❏ Pain or distress with eating or digesting
- ❏ Pocketing or "cheeking" food (functional or behavioral)

>>

❑ Avoids entire food groups
❑ Stuck at a transition, e.g., can't get beyond spoon or purées
❑ Small number of "safe" or accepted foods, may be particular packaging or brand
❑ Child is anxious or upset out of proportion, beyond typical toddler tantrum
❑ Showed little interest in food/eating all along
❑ Never mouthed foods or objects (sensorimotor clues)
❑ Can't go to sleepovers or parties due to limited accepted food and/or anxiety
❑ Teased by peers, or extreme attention from adults (family, teachers) around child's eating
❑ History of forced or pressured feeding and reluctance to eat

From Dr. Katja Rowell, feeding expert and author, with coauthor Jenny McGlothlin SLP. *Helping Your Child with Extreme Picky Eating: A Step-by-Step Guide for Overcoming Selective Eating, Food Aversion, and Feeding Disorders.*

Chapter 8 References

1. Brown, A., and M. D. Lee. Early influences on child satiety-responsiveness: the role of weaning style. *Pediatric Obesity*, 10 (2015): 57–66. DOI:10.1111 /j.2047-6310.2013.00207.x

2. Daniel J. Lamport, Claire L. Lawton, Natasha Merat, Hamish Jamson, Kyriaki Myrissa, Denise Hofman, Helen K. Chadwick, Frits Quadt, JoLynne D. Wightman, and Louise Dye. "Concord grape juice, cognitive function, and driving performance: a 12-wk, placebo-controlled, randomized crossover trial in mothers of preteen children," *American Journal of Clinical Nutrition* 103(3) (March 2016): 775–83, date of Epublication February 10, 2016, DOI: 10.3945/ajcn.115.114553.

3. Lisa M. Vislocky and Maria Louise Fernandez. "Grapes and Grape Products: Their Role in Health." *Nutrition Today* 48 (1) (2013): 47–51, DOI: 10.1111/j.1753-4887.2010.00335.x

4. G. Howatson, P. G. Bell, J. Tallent, B. Middleton, M. P. McHugh, and J. Ellis. "Effect of tart cherry juice (Prunus cerasus) on melatonin levels and enhanced sleep quality," *European Journal of Nutrition* 51 (8) (December 2012): 909–16, ePublication October 30, 2011, DOI: 10.1007/s00394-011-0263-7.

5. Ran D. Goldman, "Cranberry juice for urinary tract infection in children," *Canadian Family Physician* 58(4) (April 2012): 398–401, accessed October 5, 2016, http://www.cfp.ca/content/58/4/398.full.

CHAPTER 9

I DON'T LIKE THAT . . . TODAY
(24 TO 36 MONTHS–THE ADVANCED EATER)

> "What a precious gift we can bestow upon our children, if we teach them that they are born with a profound wisdom about eating that they can trust all of their lives."
> —Elyse Resch, MS, RDN, CEDS-S coauthor of *Intuitive Eating*

Zoe was so excited to head to preschool. She'd seen all the big kids get backpacks and lunch boxes. It was her time to carry her own lunch box, and she couldn't wait to help fill it up. Every single day, she wanted a cheese quesadilla, and that was it! Her mom was getting frustrated and did everything she could to get her to try something different, but cheese quesadillas were her favorite. After two weeks of cheese quesadillas, her mom decided to get Zoe in the kitchen for a little exploration. They made different types of quesadillas, cheese and fruit kebabs, and cracker sandwiches. She and Zoe had a fun new list of lunch box foods. Mom also stopped asking her what she wanted for lunch each morning because she remembered that part of her role was to decide the *what*. She now had a new list of fun foods Zoe liked and packed accordingly.

Time to Fly

By now, your little one has moved into eating almost all foods or at least all textures foods can come in, with the exceptions of obvious choking hazards, like nuts, popcorn, and marshmallows. She can now use an open cup, sip from a straw, scoop with a spoon, and handle a fork. You may even brave the notion of helping your little one use a butter knife or child-safe knife with meals. Don't be shocked! Children all over the world learn how to use knives at an early age. As with everything, practice and a safe setting make for the best ways to learn. It's time. She has her wings, it's time to let her soar. Figuratively speaking, of course!

In addition to her soaring through her skills with utensils, she most likely has most of her teeth. Having a full set of choppers greatly improves her chewing capabilities and can give her more confidence when taking bites. But she may still try to bite off more than she can chew (don't we all?). Even while using her silverware and open cup and chomping down on her steak, there are still skills that need to be safely practiced and monitored. At this point, your little one may:

- Eat the same foods as the rest of the family
- Feed herself well with a spoon and fork
- Have definite food likes and dislikes
- Refuse certain foods or can become more picky
- Wipe her own mouth and hands with a napkin or cloth
- Start to serve herself at the table with minor spills
- Pour liquids into her cup from a small container

If these skills seem far from where your little one is right now, it's okay. Some little ones need a bit more encouragement and practice before they're ready to be an advanced eater. All children develop differently on their own timeline, and don't forget that time-based milestones are generalizations.

Is Little One Ready to Move On?

Let's look and see if your little one is ready to move into advanced eating.

Isla used an open cup and silverware when she enjoyed her mini hamburger, salad, and chocolate banana smoothie at dinner. She enjoyed showing off her skills of eating and drinking like her parents.

- ✔ Ready, Isla is eating and drinking well using her utensils and cup.
- ❑ Not Ready

Jack loved picking out his own snacks. When Mom said it was snack time, he was able to open the snack drawer and pick out some crackers. He asked his mom for cheese to complete his afternoon snack. He knew he needed to ask for help when necessary.

- ✔ Ready, Jack is asking for help and making choices based on the options Mom is providing.
- ❑ Not Ready

Audrey struggled eating her soup and got frustrated with her meal. She wanted to use her spoon, but the soup kept getting all over her shirt instead.

- ❑ Ready
- ✔ Not Ready, Audrey may still need some help with a bigger, little-kid-friendly spoon with lots of praise at each try.

The Advanced Eater Safety Checklist

Although your little one is growing by leaps and bounds and acting less like a toddler and more like a little girl ready to soar, there are still things we must continue to do to make the eating table a safe zone.

1. Toddler continues to eat at the table in high chair, booster seat supported with a footrest, or toddler chair and is not walking around or eating while playing.

2. Distractions continue to be removed. Continue to foster the habit of being mindful during mealtimes.

3. Continue to stay present with your little one while eating.

4. Continue to test the temperature of cooked and mixed meals to make sure they're not too hot for her to handle, and encourage her to test the food and blow on it if needed.

5. Continue to provide appropriately sized pieces of food and coach child while chewing or offer to cut smaller when you see her struggling.

6. Continue to advance previously avoided foods and cut round foods in half lengthwise.

7. Continue to modify the texture as needed based on your little one's comfort level.

Nutrients to Consider

Growth and development may slow after infancy, but your little one still has a need for many nutrients via her nutritional intake. Your little one may be experiencing a lot of changes within her second and third years. If you're a parent, you're probably excited to refer to her as a two- or three-year-old instead of counting all the months! If your little one has started a daycare or preschool, or she is experiencing longer times away from home, you may notice that her eating patterns vary when she's is away. This is often a time when toddlers can experience changes in food preferences, hydration issues, and even experience constipation.

At this age, busy is the name of the game. Stop to drink? Stop to potty? Or go in a strange potty? Those are all legitimate concerns and considerations of a two-and-half-year-old. That's right! We even have to engage in potty talk to get an understanding of what's going on with our little ones, especially if they're away during the day. While some may not consider potty talk part of nutrition, it can provide a lot of important information. We can ask questions like when did she poo at school, did she have one today, did it hurt? These questions can tell us if she's holding back and not going potty when needed or if she's not well-hydrated. There's a reason why dietitians have lots of potty talks, even with grown-ups. When we ask you *how's it going*, you're going to think twice about what we mean. When we're asking about kids, we're looking for information that tells us if your little one is getting enough food, fiber, and/or water from day to day.

In addition to fiber and water needs, there are some additional nutrients that children in the United States often lack, such as calcium and potassium. With a focused intake of fruits and vegetables, with fewer overly processed foods, nutrient deficiencies like these shouldn't be an issue.

FIBER

There's a good chance your little one is pottying just fine with all the whole foods she's eating, but just in case she experiences constipation, let's look at fiber needs for toddlers. According to the Academy of American Pediatrics, children two and older should take in 5 grams of dietary fiber plus their age.[1] So if she is two or three, she should eat about 7 to 8 grams per day and up to 17 to 18 grams per day. If you're providing plenty of fruits and veggies, it's likely she's getting enough. You do not need to plan to hit the high end of fiber every day or count up the grams (please don't). Too much fiber can also cause issues like bloating, gas, diarrhea, and with too little water, even constipation. This is true for us adults, too.

Parents often take note of fiber needs when their toddler is being potty trained. If your little one has an adequate amount of fiber in her diet, her poo will be better formed and will likely have an easier exit on the potty. Having a little one strain on the potty is not an enjoyable process. High-fiber foods include all berries, beans, broccoli, cabbage, peas, nuts, and potatoes with their skin. Before you open up a box of twiglike cereal or opt for a fiber supplement, try a daily dose of blackberries or raspberries. One cup of berries has a whopping 8 grams of fiber, and it's a super tasty fiber vehicle. We don't believe that you have to buy a bunch of fiber-spiked foods to get enough fiber. It can be done the old-fashioned way, with fruits and veggies.

WATER

When taking in enough fiber, it's equally important to stay hydrated. Fiber takes up fluid to help it form and exit our bodies. Toddlers and preschoolers are active little beings. With their high activity levels from running, jumping, swinging, sliding, and constant playing comes an increased need of fluids. According to the Institute of Medicine's *Dietary Reference Intakes for Electrolytes and Water,* the Adequate Intake (AI) for water for children aged one to three is 1.3 liters per day. That's about 44 fluid ounces, or roughly five and a half 8-ounce cups of water. Water is the beverage of choice for a toddler and preschooler. This is followed by milk (up to three 8-ounce cups per day) and, if desired, up to 4 ounces of 100 percent fruit juice per day. In addition to water, milk, and juice, some of your little one's fluid needs can be met with soups, yogurts, juicy fruits, and vegetables. Water can be obtained in a variety of ways, not just water consumption.

Toddlers often lack the ability to know they're thirsty or often forget to slow down to drink. If you find her urine is a dark yellow or is very strong smelling when she uses the potty then it's time to ramp up her fluids. Add fresh fruit to her water, make fruit ice cubes, add a splash of fruit juice, or make her some herbal tea like chamomile to help encourage her to drink water more frequently throughout the day. There are safe teas that are just for little ones these days. Who knew? Wendy Jo and Miss A have nighttime tea together. But don't forget that much like food, fluid needs can vary from child to child. Some need more and some need less. Some can even drink more than we do!

Calcium

The bone-building mineral, calcium, is a key nutrient for both babies and toddlers. Most think of bones when they refer to calcium, but it actually plays an important role in muscle contraction, nerve responses, enzymes, and hormone responses. Having a deficiency in calcium can equate to the body taking what it needs from bone. This can spell trouble for a toddler with growing and developing bones. Although milk has long received the fame as a source of calcium, other excellent sources can be included in the diet, as well. Almonds, yogurt, kefir, cheese, calcium-fortified orange juice, white beans, collard greens, and broccoli all provide some calcium. A child who drinks at least 2½ cups of milk per day is getting in enough calcium in a day. Breast milk has less than a third of the calcium that whole milk contains so, if breastmilk is still your toddler's drink of choice, look to add in yogurt, cheese, almonds, and greens throughout the day. But don't forget about that sunshine vitamin, vitamin D. Vitamin D is needed for calcium absorption. It's likely you're still supplementing with vitamin D since it's hard to get enough in food (this is true for little ones and their adults). Leslie gives CC a probiotic (which she calls her *pro-body-otic*) that also contains vitamin D each day.

Potassium

A diet rich in fruits and vegetables will cover a toddler's needs of potassium, but if you're concerned that your little one is not getting enough, there's nothing wrong with a multiple vitamin and mineral daily supplement. Potassium plays an important role in blood pressure regulation, muscle functions, and heart contractions. A toddler who is deficient in potassium can seem fatigued, much like with iron deficiency. Potassium is found in most fresh fruits and vegetables with excellent sources being roasted potatoes, dried apricots, bananas, raisins, sunflower seeds, lima beans, almonds, and acorn squash. If your little one eats a variety of foods, then this nutrient won't be a concern unless underlying conditions are present.

Farewell Clean Plate Club

The *Born to Eat* team doesn't promote the *clean plate club*. Leslie jokingly says it took her almost twenty years to unlearn the not-so-mindful habits of the clean plate club. There's more truth to that than joke.

The American Academy of Pediatrics reminds physicians and parents that children have an innate ability to self-regulate their food intake at this age. The AAP cautions parents that these three practices are associated with weight dysregulation in toddlers:

- feeding in response to emotional distress,
- using food as a reward, and
- excessive prompting or encouragement to eat.

It's tempting to prompt or encourage your child to eat more, take one more bite, or finish their plate. We get those urges, too! It's how many of us were raised, and we know our parents did the best they could with the information they had at the time. If you're ever in doubt, think back to Ellyn Satter's Division of Responsibility. As parents, we are responsible for *what* they are offered to eat, *when* they eat, and *where* they eat. Our little ones are in charge of *if* they eat and *how much* they eat.

Don't forget that just like how a meal can look different from family to family, bodies look different, as well. There is no such thing as a perfect body or weight. This is a great time to start conversations about how bodies are different and worthy no matter their shape or size.

Shake It Up

Before you say, "one more bite" or "come on, you can eat more" when you find your toddler falling into a food rut, let us reassure you, they are normal. Food jags, or when a child only wants a certain food or foods, normally only last a few weeks. Kids often get fixated on one food or another for a bit of time and then can quickly shift out of it or onto another food. Instead of focusing just on their food intake or encouraging them to have another bite, try shaking things up a bit. The joke about toddlers hating all the foods they loved yesterday can be oh so true.

If we don't make food a big deal, it likely won't end up being a big deal. When we engage in food fights or become a short-order cook, we could be inviting more struggles. There are things you can try that may help when you find your toddler refusing foods—even if it was a favorite yesterday. Changing up the texture, preparing the food with different spices, adding a sauce, putting it on a pizza, stuffing it into a quesadilla, adding into a soup, or topping it with cheese can be the small tweak needed to make a food more appealing to a free-thinking toddler.

Try shaking up the texture or look of these common foods:	
Eggs	Boiled, scrambled, cheesy, egg salad, deviled eggs, egg muffin, frittata, quiche, or omelet
Meats	Steak finger, ground, chopped, in sauce, burgers, meatballs, meat muffin cups, kebabs, chili, or stew
Beans	Refried, hummus or dip, soup, added to quesadillas, bean patties (falafel), or mixed with ground meat in sauce
Greens	Salad, sautéed with garlic, chopped in scrambled eggs, chopped into burgers or meatballs, added into sauces, or smoothies
Fruit	Sliced, fruit stacks or kebabs, mixed in yogurt, baked, or mixed in oats

We don't believe in hiding foods or being dishonest with your little one. Empower her to help you in the kitchen and work with the different textures and preparation methods of foods. Even if she chooses not to taste or eat what she makes, it helps that she played with the food and learned new skills in the kitchen. Remember, picky eating or the occasional food jag is normal at times. If you feel that you have an extreme picky eater on your hands, refer back to Dr. Rowell's suggestions in chapter 8.

Are You Really Going to Eat That?

These can be trying times as parents, we know! As dietitians, we often hear comments like, "You let your kid eat that?" How we'd like to respond is, "It's rude to comment on my food or my kid's food and it's really not your business," but we refrain . . . usually. Most of the time, we tend to say, "Food is food." Time and time again in our counseling offices, we get the question about having certain foods in the house. Parents ask us if they should just keep those certain foods out of the house altogether. Unless your child or family member has a food allergy, the answer is no and this is why.

Leslie uses this example over and over in her office. It's an example, but one she's witnessed in person many times. Two upset parents sit down in Leslie's office to discuss their family food choices but mainly those of little Johnny, who is now three years old. They give Leslie some background information about foods in their home and then they tell her what happened last week at a friend's party. Little Johnny isn't allowed to have chips or cookies at home. His parents feel like they're poor choices and have decided not to allow them in the home. They, his parents, are the nutritional gatekeepers of the home. However, little Johnny gets invited to a birthday party and chips and cookies are present. Little Johnny eats as much as he can until he feels sick from overeating. His parents have told him what a poor choice he made in eating those items and that it's "unhealthy." They were very upset with him and thought they could use some help navigating food selections. That's why they're sitting in Leslie's office without little Johnny.

Leslie and little Johnny's parents talk about their roles as food providers and little Johnny's role as an eater. They discuss how not all foods are nutritionally equal, but we want them to be emotionally neutral. All foods, regardless of their perceived nutritional quality, need to be offered to our children. If little Johnny felt like those foods were off-limits or taboo, or that he may not get them again for a long time, he may eat as much as possible. Scarcity can occur with food insecurity and food restriction.

Remember, when food is a big deal, it's a big deal! Leslie and Johnny's parents developed a plan to incorporate those foods into their weekly menus. Leslie suggested that they not mention anything about those foods now being on his plate or in his lunch box. She also recommended that they be part of a meal without some sort of special name and not something that comes afterward like *dessert*. This would allow little Johnny to self-regulate versus eating a meal just to get to his cookies and possibly overeat them. They, as the nutritional gatekeepers, learned that he could be trusted with those foods, and when they didn't make the food a big deal, it became less of a desirable, or special, food for him. At first, he ate them all and ate them first. But, over time, little Johnny would even leave part of the cookie on his plate at dinner. The cookie was no longer a big deal.

> To keep food emotionally neutral, we believe it's best to call food by its name. Using terms like dessert, treat, or sweet can undermine this approach. Let's call a cookie a cookie, a carrot a carrot, and a cake a cake. Because food is food.

We, as nutritional gatekeepers, have the very important job of providing a variety of foods, even those we'd rather our kids eat less often. As we've mentioned before, the *how* we eat at this stage in life may very well be as important as the *what*. The *what* comes in time. If they know they can trust their bodies, and that you do too, they're more likely to be adventurous with foods of

Mini Burger
Cherry Tomatoes
Cookie

all kinds later on. Supporting a child's autonomy encourages children to trust their instincts and parents trust their little one's instincts, as well. The more we learn to trust ourselves, the more we model for our children to trust themselves.

> As Born to Eat parents, we not only get to provide a variety of foods to our kids, but we have the pleasure and opportunity to teach them how to deal with all foods, regardless of their nutritional quality.

Variety and Exploration

Variety and exploration starts at home and continues during the childhood experience. One of the most common experiences, or challenges, can be when your little one starts daycare or preschool at this age. We've both experienced packing lunches and snacks for time away from home. These are a few of our favorite go-to options.

Morning Snack	Lunch	Afternoon Snack
Orange Cottage Cheese Muffin (page 192)	Ham & cheese quesadilla + strawberry & blueberry skewers (on straws) + cherry tomatoes	Almond butter–topped crackers + dried apricots
Pretzels	Parfait with Greek yogurt, granola, and berries	Cheese stick + cherry tomatoes
Banana + peanut butter	Nacho tortilla chips with beef & melted cheese + sliced avocado	Plain Greek yogurt + sliced fruit

Greek yogurt + frozen fruit smoothie	Avocado Chicken Salad (page 202) wrap + carrot sticks	Trail mix
Applesauce	Turkey apple sandwich squares + snap peas	Cookie + milk

If you're worried that daycare or preschool personnel may not support your child's ability to self-regulate and use the Division of Responsibility, try using a lunch box card, like the one from our friend, Dr. Katja Rowell, The Feeding Doctor. She suggests that if someone asks your child to eat certain foods, have your child hand over the card on page 114. Leslie uses this in CC's lunch box. Feel free to make copies of the card by visiting https://www.thefeedingdoctor.com/.

Chapter 9 Reference

1. Christine L. Williams, Marguerite Bollella, and Ernst L. Wynder. "A New Recommendation for Dietary Fiber in Childhood," *Pediatrics* 96 (5) (November 1995), accessed August 4, 2016, http://pediatrics.aappublications.org/content/96/5/985.

Lunch Box Card

Hello!

Please allow _____ to decide how much to eat, and in what order, from what I have packed. Even if it means all they eat for lunch is "dessert," or if they start with dessert.

I trust that _____ can rely on hunger and fullness signals to know how much to eat. If they need help opening containers, I thank you for that help. Otherwise, _____ should be good to go.

Please call my cell _____ if you have any questions.

Thank you for all you do for our children.

Hello!

Please allow _____ to decide how much to eat, and in what order, from what I have packed. Even if it means all they eat for lunch is "dessert," or if they start with dessert.

I trust that _____ can rely on hunger and fullness signals to know how much to eat. Otherwise, _____ should be good to go.

Please call my cell _____ if you have any questions.

Thank you for all you do for our children.

Hello!

Please allow _____ to decide how much to eat, and in what order, from what I have packed. Even if it means all they eat for lunch is "dessert," or if they start with dessert.

If _____ needs help opening containers, I thank you for that help. Otherwise, _____ should be good to go.

Please call my cell _____ if you have any questions.

Thank you for all you do for our children.

Hello!

Please allow _____ to decide how much to eat, and in what order, from what I have packed. Even if it means all they eat for lunch is "dessert," or if they start with dessert.

Please call my cell _____ if you have any questions.

Thank you for all you do for our children.

Used with permission by Katja Rowell, MD, from her 2012 book, *Love Me, Feed Me.* Updated 2022. https://www.thefeedingdoctor.com/

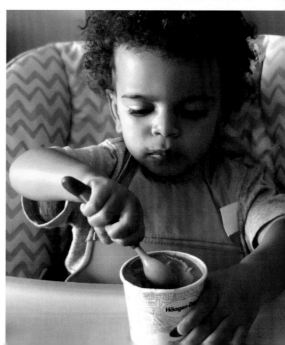

PART 3

THE *BORN TO EAT* FAMILY

Born to Eat isn't just a way of fostering a self-feeding or self-regulating child; it's a philosophy for the whole family. We believe that having a healthy relationship with food starts at home even if you didn't grow up that way. The *Born to Eat* approach starts with baby but must be fostered in the family environment by supporting body trust, celebrating body diversity, acknowledging differences in abilities, finding pleasure in eating, taking care of ourselves, and planning for meals as a family. We believe we are all *Born to Eat*, not just our kids. We'll show you how to embrace it in this part of the book.

> "When you support your body, eat based on hunger and appetite, and acknowledge pleasure, you are more likely to maintain a stable body weight and enjoy improved nutrition—and to pass those values and skills on to your children."
>
> —Katja Rowell, MD

CHAPTER 10

IT'S A FAMILY AFFAIR

> "We cannot solve our problems with the same thinking we used when we created them."
> —Albert Einstein

Kelly didn't trust herself with food. She was pretty sure her mom didn't either. When she was younger, her mom would hide food from her. At first, she didn't notice, but then it became a trend. She remembered being with her at the grocery store when they bought the chips and crackers together, but when she went to grab a snack, they weren't there. One day she found the chips. Not in a normal place to store food, but an obscure spot that could only be a hiding spot.

As an adult, she realized her mom could have been hiding the chips from her just so she could get some for herself. But she sure didn't hide the apples. When she was young, Kelly interpreted this as a sign that she wasn't to be trusted with food and, in turn, she couldn't trust her own body. Something must've been wrong with her. As Kelly became an adult, she struggled with self-regulation and body trust. She moved from one diet to another until she realized dieting wasn't the answer. Kelly began working with a an Intuitive Eating–aligned dietitian that supported her through the realization of how that experience had impacted her eating behaviors and body trust. She had carried so much shame about not being able to be trusted with food and had based many of her health and body choices on this experience.

Regardless of the initial intention of the hidden or restricted food, it had left a mark on her life. But she realized it didn't have to remain that way. Kelly was ready to truly take care of herself and that meant letting go of dieting, dieting tools, diet food, and those who didn't support her body confidence. She realized that trusting her body, practicing self-care, and combating the negative voice in her head would take some work. This may have impacted her life, but she wasn't going to let it do the same in her daughter's life. She knew that dieting, restricting, or demonizing food in any way at home could undermine self-regulation and body trust for everyone under her roof. *Body distrust and body hatred are learned.* Kelly was going to do what she could to make her home a safe zone.

> We grew up in a time when dieting was routinely recommended by health professionals and considered healthy. Even though many still recommend dieting as a means to health, we now know better. Our children don't have to have the same experiences with dieting and body distrust. We can break the cycle with the *Born to Eat* approach.

This is just one story of how our development around food and eating can impact our lives, and subsequently our kids' lives. They're not all like this one. Some may be, yet so many of us have wonderful family influences, but may have been negatively impacted by the predatory marketing of the dieting and weight-loss industry. And then there's the media, Photoshop, social media, and filters for everything!

Think back to the days when the only thing we needed filtered was coffee—no calories to count, no nutrition labels to scratch our heads over, and no apps to obsessively track the aforementioned numbers that may not make a difference in our health at all. We ate plain ol' food (most of which didn't have labels), we didn't even know about calories, and we made it as a population. It's very likely that in those times, the self-regulation with food that was developed and fostered in infancy and through childhood led to self-regulating adults. They didn't have all the numbers getting in the way of listening to their bodies.

> "With the research we have to date, it's not ethical to recommend any kind of dieting."
> —Evelyn Tribole, MS, RD, CEDS-S, and coauthor of *Intuitive Eating*

In our dieting-obsessed culture, few people make it to adulthood trusting their bodies. Today, there's a lot of background noise telling us to eat this, or eat that, now don't eat that, okay now you can have that but only if it's clean (whatever that means), organic, and

> *Born to Eat* kids need *Born to Eat* parents!

passed through a filter of solid gold (slight exaggeration). No wonder it's hard to feel like we're feeding ourselves well. But, there is hope. And thank goodness we are *what you chew is up to you* kind of people!

With our collective experiences, we've been counseling adults, families, and age-

> "It's impossible to feel in control around a food if you are never allowed to get enough of it."
>
> —Natalia Stasenko, RD

appropriate children for almost four decades. In that time, we've found that *it is possible* to regain self-regulation and body trust, and do so while living in a dieting culture. The clients we've had the privilege to work with have taught us so much. While they're all so very different in the lives they lead, they all have one thing in common: they felt too busy and overwhelmed to take steps toward health that weren't in the form of diets. In fact, we realized that they didn't even know there *was* something else.

We like to think "be reasonable and listen to your body" is a very sexy message, but it just hasn't made it to the mainstream. But, it is becoming more mainstream that a focus on weight isn't actually the path to health or wellness. In fact, weight-loss dieting moves us further away from it! Health is about how you define it. The Association for Size Diversity and Health (ASDAH) suggests that health cannot be characterized as simply the absence of physical or mental illness, limitation, or disease. ASDAH suggests that "health exists on a continuum that varies with time and circumstance for each individual." We couldn't agree more.

As we move forward, we think it's important to let you know we also believe in fostering a Health at Every Size® approach (or HAES®). The HAES® model rejects the conventional practice of using weight, or body mass index, as a proxy for health. There are five key principles of the Health at Every Size® Approach.

- Weight Inclusivity
- Respectful Care
- Health Enhancement
- Life-Enhancing Movement
- Eating for Well-Being

Yes! You can do all of these things without focusing on weight. What a liberating and compassionate way to promote health for every BODY.
For more information about HAES,® please visit https://asdah.org/.

How do we even start to listen to our bodies and trust them again if we've been swayed by dieting? It's possible, because we are, all of us young and old, *Born to Eat*. We have what it takes. It just takes time to turn up the volume on our self-regulation that the dieting world may have put on mute. Now, we realize that not everyone is caught up in the shaming dieting world, and that is fantastic! However, many are and it's affecting our health and happiness not just as individuals, but as families, too.

Like many of our clients, we feel too busy for self-care or self-observation at times. But without the self-observation of how our own feeding development and eating behaviors have impacted us, we don't even know where to start. This is the only way to find out what self-care may look like for us individually. Nothing changes for good without some nonjudgmental observation around our own beliefs and behaviors. This is a family affair, and there's no better time to create a whole family of self-regulating and body-trusting humans than when you're teaching your little one to do the same.

You, in addition to your little one, have to be a priority, and that isn't selfish. You read that right—self-care is *not* selfish. It's similar to the *put your oxygen mask on before helping others* warning on a flight. Actually, it's not just similar, it's exactly the same thing—take care of you so you can help the one next to you. But in this case, the mask is the investigation or observation of your own behaviors. Once you have that info (oxygen flowing), you can start helping yourself by knowing what type of self-care you need to feel refreshed and nourished. We all tend to operate better on a full tank, whether that's filled with nourishment, accepting help, planning a meal, going for a walk, reading a book, enjoying a friend's company, or simply getting enough rest.

When we think of self-care as a choice, it makes many of the activities more doable. Like if you know you feel better after going on a walk and you remind yourself that you are choosing to invest in your mental and physical wellness, it feels a lot better than a mindset or self-talk like *I should go exercise*.

Here's another example: *I should pack a healthy lunch for tomorrow*. This sure sounds better and more likely to happen: *I'm going to take this leftover burger tomorrow with a side salad because I feel better all afternoon when I have a tasty lunch*. We usually don't get anywhere positive *shouldn' on ourselves*. We laugh, but oh how true.

Over the years, we've collected many self-care strategies our clients have found useful and we want to share them with you. Our clients come from all different walks of life and family situations. You may pick one or two that resonate with you and your needs. That's just fine.

Sample Self-Care Activities for Parents, Caregivers, or any Living Adults

- ❏ I aim for 7 to 8 hours of sleep
- ❏ I get up 15 to 30 minutes early to read, pray, meditate, or journal
- ❏ I walk the dog and enjoy a beautiful day
- ❏ I plan and pack lunch the night before
- ❏ I plan evening meals or get help with planning
- ❏ I make a grocery list at least once a week and shop for groceries at least once a week
- ❏ I meet friends once a week for coffee or happy hour
- ❏ I use deep breathing or meditation exercises when anxious at home or work
- ❏ I ask for help with cooking, cleaning, or running errands
- ❏ I avoid dieting behaviors like skipping meals, restricting my energy intake, tracking my food, or relying on "diet" foods.
- ❏ I let my body be my guide for hunger and fullness
- ❏ I avoid focusing on numbers like calories or weight
- ❏ I ignore or block those who make me second-guess my own body trust (especially on social media)
- ❏ I share the joys and struggles with other parents or friends I trust
- ❏ I call a friend at a scheduled time each week
- ❏ I listen to my favorite playlist or anti-diet podcasts while taking a walk
- ❏ I schedule movement or rest time in my schedule (so it actually exists)
- ❏ I carry a water bottle with me daily to stay hydrated
- ❏ I set my phone alarm for a self-care check-in and ask "How am I doing?" and "What do I need?"
- ❏ I'm aware of negative self-talk (the inner critic) and attempt to change that dialogue. For example, *I'm so awful at this baby-led weaning stuff, my kid deserves better* is the inner critic. *Hang in there, this is new for both of us and we'll catch on soon* is more supportive and useful mental chatter. I can *choose* to change it.
- ❏ I remind myself that unlearning weight-centric and diet culture beliefs take time, but it's worth it for me and my family.
- ❏ I buy foods I really enjoy and plan them into my meals/snacks no matter what diet culture says.

If we're able to help Mom, Dad, or Uncle Joe see the impact their own self-care has on the family, we're making some great progress for everyone. Self-care isn't selfish. Take a moment right now to think about things you need as an individual, a parent, a caregiver, a friend, a coworker, or a nutritional gatekeeper. We hope these examples will get you thinking about your own needs and situation.

"Daring to set boundaries is about having the courage to love ourselves, even when we risk disappointing others."

—Brené Brown

Breaking the Dieting Mold

Many of our adult clients have worried about their own developmental issues around food and eating and how they might overcome the wounds or strongholds of growing up in diet culture. We have the pleasure of working one-on-one with them to move toward a healthier mindset around food and body. If you're one of those people or just want some great help in the direction of body trust, these are some of our favorite recommendations or self-care steps.

These are our favorite resources for adults wanting to regain body trust and buck the diet culture.

❏ *Intuitive Eating: A Revolutionary Anti-Diet Approach* by Evelyn Tribole and Elyse Resch

❏ *Body Kindness: Transform Your Health from the Inside Out—and Never Say Diet Again* by Rebecca Scritchfield

❏ *How to Raise an Intuitive Eater: Raising the Next Generation with Food and Body Confidence* by Sumner Brooks and Amee Severson

❏ *More than a Body: Your Body Is an Instrument, Not an Ornament* by Lexie Kite and Lindsay Kite

❏ *The Body is Not an Apology: The Power of Radical Self-Love* by Sonya Renee Taylor

It starts with slowing down enough and decreasing distractions so we can listen to our own body cues. This means setting boundaries around time so that we have the head space to ask ourselves some questions about what we might need. Am I hungry? Thirsty? Full? We so often just eat by the clock or eat all the items we plugged in on our tracker app. Eating by the time or by a caloric amount doesn't set us up to self-regulate.

It is possible to trust the body again after years of dieting—we've seen it happen time and time again—but it takes patience and trust that the body will do what it's meant to do. The body is capable of giving you physical cues to eat, helping you feel when you're satisfied so that you can stop eating when you've had enough. We're capable of eating both intuitive and intelligently. If we're used to quantifying things and want to know how much to eat if we're not counting something, we can try this.

The hunger and fullness gauge can help us learn our cues if we're not in the habit of paying attention to them or not used to allowing self-regulation. Before we start to eat, we can try to identify where we fall on the hunger side of the scale. As we're eating, and taking our time, we can see how it moves from hungry, to satisfied, to comfortably full. And, sometimes, self-regulating, normal eaters hit the too full mark—like *every* time Leslie goes to a Mexican restaurant—and that's okay. It's also okay to just eat, and we're not always hungry when we have that opportunity. Your body is wise. Don't let diet culture, or the diet industry vultures, tell you any different.

Using Your Own Gauge for Hunger and Fullness

Think of fueling your body like fueling your car. If there's no gas, it goes nowhere. The body is a complex machine that needs to be fueled several times per day to keep you satisfied and moving efficiently. It'd be nice, but the body doesn't have an external gauge posted to show you when to eat or stop eating. We must relearn how to feel our body's internal gauge, or self-regulation, at work. It starts with one question: "Am I physically hungry?"

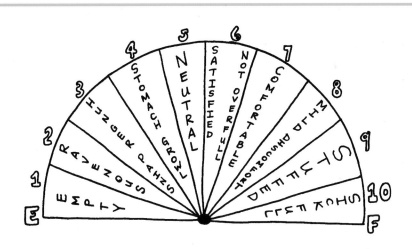

1-2 = Empty to ravenous
3-4 = Hunger pains/stomach growling to subtle hunger feelings
5 = Neutral, neither hungry or full, can't tell if I'm hungry
6-7 = Satisfied but not overfull, comfortable
8 = Full, mild discomfort
9 = Stuffed (like Thanksgiving)
10 = Feeling sick from overfilling (like Thanksgiving after dessert)

At first, you may want to keep a food journal and note how you felt before and after an eating opportunity (meal or snack). You can skip all the numbers, like calories and grams of stuff. That information doesn't help you determine hunger or fullness. First, determine where you fall on the gauge before you eat a meal or snack. Then take a moment during the meal or snack to ask yourself how the food tastes and if your satisfaction level is beginning to change. Do you need a little more or are you starting to feel comfortable and satisfied? When you finish eating, use the scale to determine where you fall after the meal or snack. It could be just right (a 6 to 7), not enough (a 4 to 5), or too much (an 8 to 10). Remember that self-regulating eaters sometimes get too little food (darn, I left my lunch at home and made do) and sometimes get too much (once slice of pizza too many). That's normal from time to time and gives you experience for points of reference. And last but not least, relearning to be a self-regulating and intuitive eater takes practice and patience.

10 Ways *Born to Eat* Parents Can Support Body Trust in *Born to Eat* Kids

1. Talk about listening to and honoring our bodies. For example, if you're hungry, you're honoring your body by eating. If you're full, you're honoring your body by stopping. If you're tired, you're honoring your body by going to bed. If you're eating a food and decide it's not that good, you're honoring your body by not eating something you find isn't satisfying.

2. Compliment each other on things that aren't related to looks or weight. For example, "Miss A, you must really be using your learning skills, your ABCs are great!" Or, "CC you ran so fast in the yard, you must be getting great energy!" It's okay to say a child is cute, pretty, or handsome, but they need to know they're so much more than that—like strong, courageous, smart, caring, capable, etc.

3. Discuss all the amazing things our bodies can do like run, jump, hug, learn, and get energy from the foods we eat.

4. Do not talk negatively about your own body. You are their most amazing example, regardless of how you feel about your body–own it.

5. Do not talk negatively about others' bodies. Ever. Redirect negative talk about others by saying "other people's bodies aren't our business."

>>

6. Celebrate diversity from body shape to food preferences. Some people live in smaller bodies while others live in larger bodies. Some people like asparagus and some people don't.

7. Take care of yourself and have fun. It's the best example a child can have of living a healthy and happy life.

8. Never allow name-calling, especially those referring to one's body, ways of eating, or uniqueness. Stigma around differences in things like weight or looks are learned. They don't have to be.

9. Talk about your own preferences around food and taking care of your body while being open to trying new foods and activities.

10. Make your anti-diet lifestyle a family affair, because once they see diet culture, they can't unsee it! That alone helps us remember and trust that we're Born To Eat our whole lives.

New Parent Stress

There are many joys of being a new parent. We often joke with our friends about all the not-so-joyous stuff that people forgot to tell us. Most of us know that we'll suffer from sleep deprivation, but have no idea what that actually feels like until a month or two after baby is born. In baby's first year, parents will accumulate a 350-hour sleep deficit.[1] That's about two weeks of lost sleep. Lost sleep can cause many other problems like becoming depressed, increased anxiousness, appetite dysregulation, being a sleepy driver, being short tempered (been there), and the list goes on. Sleep deprivation also impacts cognition and disease states and can lead to premature aging. But these are things we might expect.

It's what we don't expect that causes problems. Big ones. The kind that result in neglect. Now we're not suggesting that you would neglect your little one; we're suggesting that, like most parents, you'd neglect yourself to make sure that didn't happen. And we do that, until we can't do it any longer. This is why it's especially important for new parents to make a habit of self-care a priority, whatever that looks like for you.

CHAPTER 10 REFERENCE

1. Karisa Ding. "Sleep Deprivation and New Parents," *HealthDay* (January 20, 2016), accessed September 20, 2016, https://consumer.healthday.com/encyclopedia /parenting-31/parenting-health-news-525/sleep-deprivation-and-new-parents -643886.html.

CHAPTER 11

WHAT YOU CHEW IS UP TO YOU—CHOOSING FOODS FOR YOUR FAMILY

> "Nothing would be more tiresome than eating and drinking if God had not made them a pleasure as well as a necessity."
>
> —Voltaire

CC was just over a year old when she visited Wisconsin for the first time. Leslie and her husband were excited for her to meet friends, relatives, and Aunt Bonnie's cows. CC had been self-feeding for about nine months now. She loved exploring her food and playing with it on her plate before she crammed it into her mouth. This was her first experience seeing food where it began: in the garden and on the farm.

Aunt Bonnie and the cousins were excited to show her the garden. CC went straight for the tomatoes. She picked one right off the vine and shoved into her mouth. At that moment, Leslie realized what an amazing experience this was for her daughter. She got to see a tomato at its freshest moment, not in a package at the grocery store, but right out of the dirt. Just a few miles down the road at Grandma and Grandpa's house, she got to eat an apple right off the tree, along with cucumbers, carrots, rhubarb, and raspberries in the garden. Leslie realized just how important this experience was—not everyone gets to see where their food comes from.

Everyone's an Expert

These days, everyone's an expert. Someone seems to always be telling us what we should do, from where to buy our food, how it should be grown, how to serve it, and what to abstain from. It's exhausting for consumers and infuriating for many nutrition professionals. The misinformation and useless recommendations run rampant. It's hard to know who to believe when it comes to nutrition advice, especially since it seems to change every day. Not only does everyone have an opinion, but they're adamant about it! With social media in the mix, posting real-time food and nutrition information, it can make feeding our little ones confidently a challenge, or at the very least, extremely frustrating.

Even as dietitians, we sometimes find ourselves sifting through the nonsense and evaluating the details to divvy up the facts from the fiction to make informed decisions. Daily, we can get sucked into posts that can make us question foods or certain ingredients. We all want what is best for our children, and social media makes it hard to know what a valid tip is, what a sales pitch is, or what is purely diet propaganda.

It's easy to fall victim to the random, fear-inspiring post. With that said, remember that you can filter out much of that static. Leslie likes to tell her clients to try to insert the *that does not necessarily apply to me* filter in their minds when they see nutrition information pop up on social media or in the mainstream media. It's very possible (and likely probable) that someone's interpretation of said *research* could be just plain wrong, may not even be legitimate (blogs and documentaries are not science), and could send us down a dangerous path.

When you're not sure where to turn for this information, don't sweat it—we've got you covered. We're going to do our best to tackle some of these questions to help you in a quick, practical, and user-friendly way. No matter what, don't forget these seven words: *what you chew is up to you.* You get to make the choice about what you feel is best for you and your family based on the information you choose to absorb from people (or organizations) you choose to trust.

Let us be real with you. We buy a variety of foods from many sources—the only right way is what works for you. We do the best we can with the information and resources we have (time, money, availability, etc.). Food selection can be a great source of concern for parents, but remember this, a fed family is best. Being fed and connected is a much better goal than getting our kids to choke down an organic green bean. With that said, let's break down what all of these labels mean.

Organic, Conventional, or Natural?

Label	Organic Foods	Conventional Foods	Natural
Definition	Can only grow crops using organic-approved chemical pesticides or organic fertilizers, such as manure. Organic foods are non-GMO (genetically modified organisms).	Can use fertilizers, pesticides, and weed killers in the growing of crops. Can use GMO crops.	Currently, no developed definition. Any manufacturer can label their product as natural. It holds no value, nutritionally or otherwise.
Pros	The general ideology of organic farming practices are to conserve and preserve natural resources and reduce pollution. No synthetic pesticides and less overall pesticide residue.	Ability to grow a more consistent, fruitful, and abundant crop annually. Conventional growing meets the demands of an ever-growing population. Tends to be cheaper.	At this point, means nothing, so has no pros.
Cons	Most organic farms are much smaller in scale than their conventional counterparts and require greater efforts to maintain healthy crops. Large-scale operations still use conventional methods that are approved by USDA Organic standards. Organic foods are likely more expensive. Organic foods may have a *health halo*, giving the perception that it is always the healthier choice.	Potentially harms soil with heavy use of pesticides and fungicides. Bugs develop a resistance to chemicals used, making them more difficult to control or manage over time. Possible greater pesticide residue on conventional foods. Cross-contamination into organic farms.	At this point, means nothing, so has no cons. Arsenic (poison) is natural—don't go out of your way to eat it.

Our take on this heated debate is this: picking a side of organic or conventional is like saying there's a good and a bad way to farm. Based on the science, we enjoy, appreciate, and understand both ways of growing food. We recognize it's a growing world, and we want more people to eat fruits and vegetables. Choose foods that fit your budget and environmental practices—it's up to you.

Are You a Gardener?

One of us (not Leslie) is a big gardener. Wendy Jo has had the pleasure of living in many states throughout the United States and living abroad in Germany. While living in Texas and Virginia, Wendy Jo saw the need for products to help keep her crops alive or free from being chewed to death by predators. Whereas in California, she found she had few bugs to compete with and used very little to grow her citrus, pomegranates, figs, and vegetables. While in Germany, she could grow bountiful crops without ever using anything beyond manure (you don't want to eat that, either). Wendy Jo prefers to grow without pesticides and fungicides, and who wouldn't? She also wanted to protect her zucchini in Virginia without standing guard 24/7 to fight off garden invaders.

Wendy Jo's approach has been to grow items that she and her family enjoy that also grow well where she lives. We realize that gardening takes time, and not everyone has time to give to gardening. You don't have to grow it to make it good for your family. Leslie picks much of her produce from a store. She grows just for her family and cannot fathom the efforts it takes to grow and feed a nation as large as the United States.

We love our local farmers and know they're out to earn an honest living, work hard to get food into our grocery stores, and (like the rest of us) want to feed their own families well. If you have the opportunity to meet farmers that live in your area, it can be a great opportunity (like the one CC had at Aunt Bonnie's). Remember, you don't have to be a great gardener or farmer to get food on the table. What you chew is up to you!

Stretching the Food Dollar

It's important to think about our food dollars and how we can make eating a wide variety of foods more feasible for the family budget. There are many foods that are cost-effective and nutritious. Don't forget about dried beans, frozen and canned foods, and weekly sale items. Some discount grocery stores offer produce, dairy items, meats, canned foods, frozen foods, and more for a budget-friendly price. Many farmers' markets accept payments from the Supplemental Nutrition Assistance Program (SNAP), as well.

It's time we forget about the old saying "shop the perimeter of the store for the most nutritious foods." This isn't a helpful or accurate phrase. Great family nutrition can be found on every single aisle.

Local Food Options

Living in Southern California, Wendy Jo does have an advantage when it comes to local growing seasons. Leslie has access to more California-grown foods, but not many things grow well in the Las Vegas heat. Local food options can be very different depending on your geographical area. We get it—local and fresh may seem best, but the reality is that this is not feasible or desirable all year long in many places in the United States. There are items that you can focus on getting locally, like dairy, meats, seasonal produce, and eggs.

Sometimes we can find great blueberries in the grocery or at the market, but other times they don't have a lot of flavor. We love blueberries and so do our families, so it's nice to have them year-round. If you're like us, you can embrace the flavor no matter the season by freezing those regional berries at their peak. Local produce, organic or not, is a great option for produce picked at their prime and delivering peak flavor for that food. Blueberries don't grow everywhere, but when they're fresh, we want them. When we can't get them, we'll head on over to the freezer section and pick up some frozen blueberries. They're pretty tasty dried, as well. This is true for most produce, not just blueberries.

If something is picked in the morning and you buy it at the farmers' market that afternoon, that is *fresh*. This also means that the vegetable or fruit has had the least amount of time to be oxidized, exposed to light, and lose nutrients (slightly, don't worry about it). A farmers' market doesn't just offer great local items; it's also a great experience for kids (and adults) to visit and talk to farmers. If you're unsure about this, check out the USDA's website www.localharvest.org to find nearby Community Supported Agriculture (CSA boxes), farmers' markets, and a great and often economical resource based on what's available in your area.

Seasonal Options

Although we may love strawberries in December, and both of our little ones do, they won't be the sweetest and freshest produce at your local market. Shift gears toward what's in season to maximize the fruit and vegetables nutrition potential, flavor, and cost savings. It doesn't mean we're not going to pick up strawberries in the winter; it just means we're aware of this fact. We love quick-reference guides (we're card-carrying geeks and love it), so here's our handy-dandy seasonal chart.

Born to Eat Seasonal Vegetable Guide		
Spring to Summer	*Fall to Winter*	*Year-Round*
Artichokes	Broccoli	Arugula
Asparagus	Butternut squash	Beets
Bell peppers	Cauliflower	Carrots
Corn	Kale	Chard
Cucumbers	Lettuce	Mushrooms
Eggplant	Pumpkin	Spinach
Green beans	Sweet potatoes	
Peas		
Summer squashes		
Tomatoes		

Born to Eat Seasonal Fruit Guide		
Spring to Summer	*Fall to Winter*	*Year-Round*
Apricots	Apples	Apples
Blackberries	Figs	Avocado
Blueberries	Kiwi	Grapefruit
Cherries	Pears	Lemons
Melons	Plums	Limes
Nectarines	Pomegranates	Oranges
Peaches		
Pineapple		
Raspberries		
Strawberries		

Ways to Make the Most of Each Season

- ❑ Sign Up for a CSA (Community Supported Agriculture) box if available in your area.
- ❑ Find and shop at a local farmers' market when available.
- ❑ Look through grocery store advertisements for seasonal deals on fruits and vegetables.
- ❑ Buy in bulk and freeze or can extras to enjoy all year long.
- ❑ Dry Homemade Fruit Leather (page 216) with your favorite seasonal fruit.
- ❑ Focus on recipes and meal planning that use seasonal produce.
- ❑ Grow your own! Lettuce, tomatoes, kale, and herbs are excellent plants for patio pots or on a windowsill.

Freezing and Buying Seasonal Produce

Whether it is an abundance of berries or a bumper crop of tomatoes, you can make your summer crops or farmers' market finds stretch throughout the year, if you're like Wendy Jo. To freeze berries, wash them and gently pat them dry. Once dry, place a nonstick silicone baking mat or piece of parchment paper down onto a jelly roll pan, then spread the berries out onto the pan in a single layer. If the berries are crowded, they'll stick together, so give them some room and keep it to a single layer. Place the pan into your freezer and freeze for at least four hours. Once frozen, place berries into a freezer-safe storage container, label, and freeze for up to six months or a year in a deep freezer.

Berries and most stone fruits (like peaches, plums, and nectarines) freeze relatively well, whereas vegetables take a bit more effort. But they're well worth the effort! For green beans, carrots, and corn, simply blanch (toss into boiling water and boil for 3 minutes then immerse into an ice bath for 1 minute to halt the cooking) the vegetables then pat dry and freeze in the same manner you did with berries.

Tomatoes are probably one of the best vegetables (okay, yes, it's a fruit, but for the sake of preparation, we will call tomatoes a vegetable) to freeze, because who doesn't love the taste of a vine-ripened tomato? Yum.

First, wash your tomatoes, and with a paring knife mark an X on the bottom of each tomato, gently piercing the skin. Next, pour boiling water over the tomatoes and let them sit for 1 minute. If you let them sit too long, they'll become mushy. Then place the tomatoes into an ice bath for 1 minute. You'll notice the skins are probably starting to peel off the tomatoes, so gently use your fingers to remove the rest of the skin. You can either freeze individually or toss into a freezer-safe bag and freeze in bulk for a tomato sauce or soup later in the winter.

Now, if you're like Leslie, you can pick up all of these in the freezer section of your local grocery—Leslie's definition of local (haha, she likes farmers' markets, too). We believe that frozen and canned fruits and veggies you find in your grocery are a great option that is often overlooked. Frozen foods are picked, prepped, and packaged at peak season so that you can have great nutrition readily available anytime of the year. Speaking of freezing, don't be too quick to overlook the canned goods section of your local market—canned fruits and vegetables are preserved right off the vine, as well. And, they're one of our favorite budget pantry items.

Where Wendy Jo may be the one who actually cans her own bumper crop, you may be more like Leslie and opt for picking up your canned foods at the grocery store. That's just fine. Remember, what you chew is up to you! Check out our favorite freezer and canned staples in chapter 13.

A Hyperfocus on Health Isn't Healthy

There is really no such thing as a perfect diet. Striving for perfection is not only unachievable, but it can lead to a disordering eating pattern. We want to save you from this madness. There are many factors of our overall health; food is a small part.

When we fixate mainly on the food component of health, it can lead to trouble. You may have heard of the term orthorexia. Steven Bratman, MD, first described this unhealthy obsession of superior or righteous eating as orthorexia nervosa. This condition is not yet a clinical diagnosis, but this form of rigid eating can lead to nutrient deficiencies, social isolation, and even a diagnosis of a clinical eating disorder. We think what we eat is important, but let's keep it in check. A drive for "healthy" eating can go too far.

CHAPTER 12

FAMILY MEALS AND MEAL PLANNING

> "Felt safety and connection first. Vegetables later."
>
> —Katja Rowell, MD, and author of *Love Me, Feed Me*

It was the first day of school and it had been a busy day for the whole family. Jane was two years old and had just started preschool and Henry was five and started kindergarten. Elizabeth was exhausted from the last couple of days getting her kids ready for school and working on a project at work. Luckily, she'd remembered to get out the slow cooker over the weekend and planned to make chicken for tacos tonight. They got home and the main part of the meal, the salsa chicken, was done. It was a lifesaver after such a busy day.

It wasn't until they all sat down at dinner that they really had time to talk. Jane had met two new friends and was so excited about her round plate and triangle tortilla chip. Henry dug in and said the tacos were great and he was so hungry. He also mentioned that he was sad that a few of his pre-K buddies ended up in a different class. Elizabeth enjoyed dinner while talking to her kids about friendship and how wonderful it is to have friends—both old and new. The tacos were a hit, but the star of this meal was the felt sense of safety and connection. The family meal is about so much more than food.

Sharing a tasty meal with friends and family is always a treat, but research suggests that engaging in a family meal provides benefits far greater than physical nourishment. Consistently sitting down to family meals may reduce the likelihood of a child engaging in disordered eating behaviors and has been linked to less depressive symptoms.[1] The benefits of the family meal don't stop there. As our kids get older, play sports, and have more homework, the family meal may be one of the few times of connection during a busy week. We may never know that our daughter's feelings got hurt at school if we didn't have that time to talk about it over tacos.

Family Meals are More than Food
Diana Rice, RD of @anti.diet.kids and Tiny Seed Family Nutrition

Our lives change so much when we become parents. Time in the evenings once spent relaxing on the couch becomes time spent washing bottles and doing laundry. And though your obligations will change as your children age, dedicating time to family meals will always take saying no to something else that could occupy that time. So we want to be clear on what we are gaining in return.

The research on family meals tells us that they're associated with nutritious meals and improved academic performance. That they are a chance to model consuming a variety of foods yourself to broaden your child's food acceptance. And that's likely true for some families. But I believe that the real benefits are not items we can measure on a survey.

Dedicating time to family meals shows your children that your family will always make time to carve out a few special moments together wherever you are, sometimes around a table, sometimes in the tailgate of your car.

It creates time for your family to connect and learn what's going on with each other, to share in the joys and struggles of the hours of the day you spent apart.

If there are other adults in your home, it shows your children that you value stopping your busy day to connect with and support them too, even when the eating part of the meal is over and the kids have long since run off to play.

It creates a space for your family to be silly, serious, or supportive together—whatever your family values are—even if some people present don't take a single bite of food.

>>

But most of all, family meals are a chance to show your kids that nourishment comes first. That everyone deserves to eat regularly, especially the adults that they admire most. We eat food that we enjoy, whether homemade, from a drive-through, or from a box in the freezer. All food is good food, all food nourishes.

When our kids see that their grown-ups value regularly eating satisfying food so much so that they will close their emails, leave dishes in the sink, and just come to the table to be nourished and connect with their families, we can have faith that our kids will carry on these values of nourishment and connection for life.

Over the years, we've worked with families that long for a family meal but just don't know how to make it happen within their reality. And, not every family looks the same or has a schedule that allows for consistent family meals. Some realities are just that—reality. Dad may commute an hour to work and not get home until 7:30, but the kids are starving by 6:00. The reality is that they can't wait on Dad for dinner, but Dad is always there making breakfast and sitting down to eat with the kids in the

FAMILY MEALS DON'T HAVE TO LOOK THE SAME FOR EVERYONE

"Sometimes it's not possible to 'just make one meal' for the entire family."
—Naureen Hunani, Dietitian, Feeding Expert, and Founder of RDs for Neurodiversity

Families, just like individuals, are unique. We cannot assume that the dinner table will look the same for everyone. Colleague and feeding expert Naureen Hunani suggests that when we make assumptions like:

• all children have similar sensory needs
• all individuals have the same level of abilities or oral motor skills
• everyone has the same food preferences

We can miss nuances in feeding approaches that could be supportive for many families. If a child only accepts a handful of foods, offering one to two preferred food options may not allow them to get enough food at a meal. It's okay to honor preferences and offer more. It's essential to be responsive. Let's be careful not to assume that eating is easy for everyone.

morning. Another family may have trouble getting all three kids ready for dinner at the same time every night, but they found a way to plan for everyone to secure family meal reservations every Tuesday, Thursday, and Sunday. Although dinner is the most common time for a family meal, there's no rule that says it has to be dinner. A family meal can be any meal (or snack if that's the time you have) during the day with at least one child and one parent (or any loved one) present.

If you and your family aren't in the habit of having family meals, it can be a challenge to get everyone on board at first. We've found these tools and tips helpful in our practices.

- ❏ Have kids help with dinner preparation like chopping or scooping.
- ❏ Have kids help set the table.
- ❏ Have kids decorate the table for the season or make place mats.
- ❏ Place a jar on the table full of conversation starters, like who's your favorite actor, what's your favorite book, or what was the craziest thing you saw today?
- ❏ Go around the table and let everyone tell a joke.
- ❏ Let everyone share the highs and lows of the day. For example, today my high was going on a walk with my mom and my low was that I didn't get to play with my best friend.
- ❏ Go around the table and let everyone talk about one thing they're grateful for that day.
- ❏ Keep dinner talk positive. This is not the time for scolding about a bad grade or bad attitude with the kids. It's also a good idea to keep adult issues like an irritating coworker or financial concerns off the table.
- ❏ Ask each family member to stay at the table until everyone is finished (remember all that conditioning you do with a baby pays off later). If your toddler isn't particularly hungry and becoming a distraction for others, it's okay to let them leave the table as long as they don't disrupt the meal for others. Do what works best for your family.
- ❏ Try serving food family style in bowls on the table. This helps with serving skills and supports a child's autonomy.
- ❏ Avoid pressure to eat more, less, or any of the foods the provided. Remember, you're in charge of what lands on the table. Your child is responsible for what lands in their stomach.
- ❏ When offering new foods, also offer one or two foods you know your child accepts and likes.
- ❏ Remember that the words *you don't have to eat it* can calm a mealtime storm and help redirect with less struggle.

Slowing Down, When Possible

Somewhere along the way, we've found ourselves rushing through meals, eating on the go, or approaching a drive-through window to pick up a quick bite on the way home from sports practice. For Wendy Jo, moving overseas for her husband's job was a bit like going back in time. Where she lived, there was no fast food, most restaurants nearby were closed on Sundays and Mondays, and all grocery stores closed from Saturday at 1:00 p.m. until Monday at 8:00 a.m. If you happen to run out of eggs on Saturday or needed milk for Monday morning, you were out of luck. On the positive side, no one rushed patrons away from their dining table when eating out, bread breaks were a real thing and so were the afternoon cake breaks. Who wouldn't love a cake break?

Needless to say, Wendy Jo found that food isn't a big deal around Europe, meaning it isn't scrutinized, picked over, and served with lite dressing on the side. The food was simply enjoyed.

Wendy Jo will be the first to admit she missed some of the nice conveniences about the United States (especially when the she needed eggs on a Saturday evening). She also began to observe how life seemed to slow down, and food was appreciated. Without this experience, she may not have brushed up on her meal-planning skills as thoroughly. Wendy Jo realized that without meal planning and knowing how to cook the basics, moving abroad, or even living in a more rural area could be frustrating.

Not everyone is a foodie or wants to be a chef, but we're guessing that by reading this book, you want to nourish your baby, and family, the best way you can. We're here to help empower you with kitchen essentials and meal-planning tips. That can include all the ways you choose to get food on the table. You may make most of your food, order take out a couple nights a week, or pop a frozen meal in the oven. It's up to you! In the chapters to follow, we will also touch on basic cooking skills and simple recipes to help support your Born to Eat family. But first, let's get everything in its place.

Everything in Its Place

Our kitchens don't need to be five-star restaurants, but we can learn some great tips from those who've made cooking and serving great food their business. We feel that the French phrase mise en place, which means "everything in its place," can set the stage for an efficient and useful kitchen. In the restaurant world, chefs often refer to mise en place as the art of prepping items prior to starting to cook a dish or meal. In the real world of our home kitchens, this holds true, as well. Recall the times you've started to make cookies and realized you were short an egg. We'll admit it, even Wendy Jo with her culinary training has started mixing up a batch of cookies just to realize she was short that crucial ingredient. There is value to meal planning, grocery shopping accordingly, and prepping items to get ready for the cooking the dish.

There's a reason why companies that deliver mostly prepared meal ingredients accompanied by recipes have become popular in the United States. We like things in their place, and they take on the planning and prepping for us. All we have to do is chop and cook. Having everything in its place or mise en place is helpful for all of us. Let's start with our primary food storage areas.

Dry Goods, or the Pantry

Your dry goods are foods or ingredients that can hang out on the shelf for a bit of time, like canned goods, pasta, rice, grains, beans, spices, dried herbs, vinegars, nuts, nut butters, snacks like trail mix, nut and fruit bars, and whole-grain crackers. These items can be stored in a cabinet or in a pantry.

Cold Storage, or the Fridge

Keep items like whole-fat yogurts, whole milk, butter, cheeses, deli meats, berries, carrots, celery, citrus, nut butters, your favorite condiments, and seasonal greens stored in your fridge. Note: Keep your refrigerator clean and less full than you may think so airflow can deliver cold air to all of your foods, keeping your food safe and at the right temperature (below 40°F).

From the Freezer

Stock your freezer with meats, fish, poultry, nuts, staple vegetables and fruits, premade dinners, and convenience foods that help you out on the nights where dinner is rushed. Similar to the refrigerator, avoid overstuffing your freezer, as your foods won't stay as cold and may suffer from freezer burn when too full. Plus, it's harder to know what you have on hand if you can't quickly see what's stored in the freezer. Keep your freezer below 0°F.

Non-Fridge Perishable Storage, or the Fruit Bowl

Great fruits to keep on hand include apples, pears, bananas, oranges, kiwi, dried fruits, canned fruits, and fruit leather. Buy only what you can enjoy within a week to avoid food waste. Keep bananas separated from your fruit bowl, as the gases emitted from a banana can help ripen your other fruit too quickly. Having a colorful arrangement of fruits available invites everyone to eat them throughout the day. If it's in your eyesight, you'll remember you have it.

In the table below, we're offering ideas of staples to keep on hand. Please be aware that these examples are based on our own preferences, cultural influence, and budgets. Do what works best for you, supports your own preferences, and fits your family's budget.

Born to Eat Staples			
Pantry	**Refrigerator**	**Freezer**	**Snack Basket**
Spices (salt, pepper, garlic powder, cumin, coriander, chili powder, cinnamon, turmeric, vanilla)	Milk	Steaks	Crackers of choice
Dried herbs (thyme, rosemary, parsley, oregano)	Cheese, cheese sticks	Ground meats	Pretzels
Oils (olive, coconut, canola, sesame)	Yogurts	Bacon	Fruit and nut bars
Vinegars (white, apple cider, red wine, balsamic, rice wine)	Deli meats	Whole chicken and chicken breasts	Trail mix
Soy sauce or Bragg's Liquid Aminos	Condiments (ketchup, mayonnaise, mustard, Worcestershire sauce, barbecue sauce, salad dressings, jams, pickles, olives, capers)	Frozen vegetables (broccoli, onion, peppers, corn, green beans, spinach)	Dried fruits with no added sugar like raisins or mango slices

Born to Eat Staples			
Pantry	**Refrigerator**	**Freezer**	**Snack Basket**
Flours	Berries	Frozen fruits (berries, mangos, bananas, peaches, cherries)	
Sugars	Carrots	Premade dinners (lasagna, chicken pot pies, shepherd's pie)	
Leavening agents (baking powder, baking soda)	Celery	Convenience foods (frozen bread dough, pizzas, precut veggie blends, meat sauce)	
Grain or grain alternatives (rice, quinoa, couscous, oatmeal, etc.)	Citrus	Frozen seafood (shrimp, fish)	
Pasta	Apples		
Canned goods (tomatoes, tomato paste, tomato sauce, beans, green beans, corn, etc.)	Nut butters		
Dried beans	Seasonal greens (lettuce, kale, Swiss chard, spinach, arugula)		
Shelf-stable vegetables (onions, shallots, garlic, potatoes, winter squash, sweet potatoes)	Butter		

We recommend keeping a fruit and snack bowl out on the counter. It doesn't hurt to keep veggies out too—it helps us remember to cook them!

Tools of the Trade

- ❏ *Cutlery*—Your knives. We recommend a solidly made eight-inch chef knife, a paring knife, a bread (serrated) knife, and a steak knife set to complete your basic kitchen cutlery needs.
- ❏ *Cutting boards*—Wooden cutting boards are preferred, as they are gentle on your knives; however, they are not dishwasher friendly. For meats, poultry, and fish keep a plastic cutting board on hand that can be placed safely in a dishwasher for sanitizing and cleaning. Although trendy, stone cutting boards are not recommended, as they quickly dull the blades of your knives, and a dull knife is a dangerous knife.
- ❏ *Pots/pans*—We recommend a small and large saucepan, an eight-inch nonstick or stainless steel skillet, a deep dish or Dutch oven cast-iron pan, and a heavy sauté pan.
- ❏ *Storage*—If you want storage to be dishwasher- and microwave-safe, opt for glassware. If you don't mind handwashing, or only serving cold items, plasticware pieces can be used in that fashion. There are excellent bento box–style lunch boxes now available online or at popular retail stores. Our favorites are the lightweight stainless steel boxes that are easily washed in the dishwasher or BPA-free plastic boxes (hand wash and cold storage only). These are also safe to be dropped on hard surfaces. We also like plain glass storage containers with plastic lids for keeping foods fresh on the counter or in the fridge.

Did You Know?

When a nonstick pan gets scratched, it's time to toss the pan. Buy a cheap pan that you won't regret or think twice about tossing when it takes a beating. Avoid using metal or abrasive cleaners, including the dishwasher, on a nonstick pan. As easy as it is to disregard directions on pots and pans, please take the time to read them. All nonstick pans that we've seen come with a warning about heating too hot or on high temperatures. Nonstick materials emit a gas when heated too high—a gas that can kill a bird within an enclosed room.[2] It's best to heat nonstick pans only to a medium heat.

In addition, keep your nonstick pans scratch- and dent-free or use an uncoated stainless steel or cast-iron pan for cooking.

Top 10 Food Safety Tips

Let's face it: getting foodborne illness is not for the faint of heart, but it's particularly dangerous for an infant, pregnant woman, or anyone with a compromised immune system. It's worth it to be safe when handling foods. Although our grandparents or parents did things one way, we now know what science says to keep foods safe. Follow these top 10 tips to keep your family safe.

1. Defrost all meats, poultry, or fish in a refrigerator overnight in cold water or in the microwave (using immediately if you choose this method)—no, not on the counter!
2. Cook all protein foods to the correct internal temperatures. The USDA Recommended Safe Minimum Internal Temperatures of beef, veal, and lamb (steaks and roasts) and fish to 145°F; pork and ground beef to 160°F; poultry to 165°F.
3. Keep your refrigerator below 39°F (every time you open it up, the temperature will go up, and the goal is to always keep cold foods below 40°F, so 39°F helps keep this a reality).
4. Avoid eating raw eggs. Even when tempted to take a taste of cookie dough, be sure to bake first before taking that bite.
5. Always wash your hands with warm, soapy water when handling eggs or raw meats.
6. Be sure to thoroughly wash anything that touched raw meats to avoid cross-contaminating. This includes tongs when cooking. If you use tongs to place food

onto a grill or hot pan, be sure to wash before flipping over, or else raw product will contaminate the cooked surface.

7. Always reheat foods to an internal temperature of 165°F.
8. If a prepared food has been left out at room temperature for more than two hours, it's time to toss it. Keep cold foods cold and hot foods hot to avoid bacteria overgrowth.
9. Wash the surface of all fruits and vegetables before slicing through the skin. Even a cantaloupe or watermelon have things on the surface you don't want to contaminate the edible fruit with when slicing a knife through it.
10. Stay on top of food recalls.

Let's Get Planning

As dietitians and lovers of all things food, we find comfort in planning and preparing a meal. Cooking is one of the things that helps us mentally transition from a busy day to an evening with our families. It's one of our de-stressors, but we realize that cooking and getting a meal on the table isn't that way for everyone. Many times people ask us about cooking, meal planning, and sitting down to dinner. We cook almost every night (especially during pandemic times), and prepping along the way with mise en place makes it a lot less stressful.

Common Barriers to Planning Meals

- ❑ It can feel restrictive or rigid
- ❑ I may not feel like all foods can fit
- ❑ It's hard to be consistent
- ❑ People don't like what I cook
- ❑ I can't cook

One of the main barriers for getting families to enjoy a meal together is meal planning. We can feel like it's just too hard to make a nice meal so forget even trying. Over the years, we've worked with thousands of families to make meal planning doable, all the while getting kids involved in the process. Bringing back the family meal doesn't have to be a cooking show production, but it does require a game plan or strategy. This is how we plan and teach the families we counsel.

Family Meals and Meal Planning

First, set a weekly time to get the whole family involved in a meal-planning meeting. Kids that are involved in cooking, shopping, and planning are often more adventurous eaters. Saying you'll plan and having a specific time for planning are not the same thing. We call this essential step the *plan to plan*. For example, Leslie and her family plan meals on Saturday mornings or Monday evenings, depending on their weekly schedules. We'll set up your family for success by selecting a day and time now.

What day feels right for you and your family?

We use a meal-planning strategy, that we also mentioned in part 2, called the Plate Method. Visualize your plate with half of the plate veggies, and the other half quarters of starchy foods and protein foods. You can even just make it all thirds. This is less about amounts and more about a planning visual. Eat what you like. Sometimes it will have all the components and sometimes it won't. It's up to you. This is just to help you get moving with meal planning creativity. These are the basic components of a complete meal.

1. Protein-rich foods: meats, eggs, sea-food, poultry, cheese, Greek yogurt, beans, etc.
2. Vegetable/fruit side: variety is best. The different colors of vegetables mean you are getting different nutri-ents like dark leafy greens, peppers, Brussels sprouts, cauliflower, carrots, green beans, broccoli, berries, peaches, pears, apples, etc.

3. Starchy side: starchy veggies like peas, corn, potatoes, crackers, rice, quinoa, tortillas, breads, pasta, noodles, etc.
4. Fats: oils, nuts, avocado, butter, dressings, sour cream, etc.

Now you're ready to develop your menu plan using lists of foods that you and your family like in each category. Be as specific as possible. For example, there's more than one way to serve beef, such as sirloin tips, hamburgers, flatiron steak, roast, etc. The same is true for chicken, fish, pork, etc. Get specific and don't forget to add foods you'd like to add to your menu as you're expanding your own variety. These lists gives us more options to work with meals. We'll get you started below with three different ways of serving the same main protein ingredient: chicken breast and ground beef.

Meat/Protein	Veggie/Fruit Side	Starchy Side	Satisfying Fats
Grilled Chicken Breast	Sautéed Broccoli with Parmesan	Wild Rice	Olive Oil on the Rice and Broccoli
Baked Chicken with BBQ Sauce	Baked Cauliflower with Cheddar Cheese	Baked Sweet Potatoes	Butter on the Potatoes and Olive Oil on the Baked Chicken
Slow Cooker Chicken Breast with Salsa	Lettuce, Tomato, and Salsa	Tortillas for Tacos	Sour Cream and Avocado Slices

Meat/Protein	Veggie/Fruit Side	Starchy Side	Satisfying Fats
Ground Beef in Spaghetti Sauce	Side Salad	Pasta noodles	Olive Oil in the Noodles and Salad Dressing
Cheeseburgers	Lettuce/Tomatoes and Fruit Salad	Bun	Mayo, Avocado Slices
Ground Beef in Soup	Tomatoes and Mixed Veggies in Soup	Garlic Bread	Butter on the Garlic Bread

At your first strategy meeting, ask every eating member of your household to help you make a list of ways to cook a meal component expanding beyond the type of protein or veggie. Think of foods that you've enjoyed out to eat or at a friend's house. If you have older kids or other family members, ask them to do the same. If it's just you and baby most of the time, you can make a list of foods you like and would like to try, provide for baby, or cook a new way. This can give you a good amount of options to work with later. Now, have each member of your household plan a few meals. Your extensive meal component list will help you at each meal planning meeting.

We're sharing our favorite meal planning tools with you, but don't forget that we're all human. It doesn't look like this for us every week. Sometimes, we knock it out of the park, sometimes we eat a snack dinner in the park.
The goal isn't to raise a planned meal foodie by four; it's to raise a child who feels safe and secure at the family table, whatever that may look like.

Planning meals together also helps us appreciate other preferences. Meal planning requires a little give-and-take that teaches us to be open to new or different foods while helping us learn to be respectful of others and their food preferences. Remember that it may take several introductions of a food before you develop a preference, like Leslie and asparagus. She always jokes about taking one for the team when it's on the menu. She isn't that fond of it, although she's tried it a gazillion different ways, but she eats it because her family enjoys asparagus.

If you're a part of a family, there will be plenty of preferences to consider. For example, while planning meals, Mom adds a slow-cooker pot roast to the menu. Lucy suggests chicken tenders served with tortellini for one meal while Dad adds cornbread with chili to the menu plan. Each family member contributes their ideas while the menu for the next couple of days is being planned. Here's an example:

Mom's Preferred Meal	Dad's Preferred Meal	Child's Preferred Meal
Slow Cooker Pot Roast	Chili with Ground Beef	Parmesan Chicken Tenders
Carrots, Celery, Onion	Side Salad	Green Beans
Potatoes	Cornbread	Cheese Tortellini
Butter on Potatoes	Dressing on Salad	Olive Oil on the Green Beans and Tortellini

The more you do it, the easier it gets. We promise. Like most habits, getting in a meal-planning groove takes time. And getting kids involved in food prep and cooking early on teaches them valuable life skills like understanding others' preferences while meeting their own needs and planning. We hope that you find meal planning more of an act of self-care than a chore. Don't forget that planning a take-out or snack dinner night can be part of the plan in busy times. The meal you share is less about the food and more about connection. You've got this!

Chapter 12 References

1. Amber J. Hammons and Barbara H. Fiese. "Is frequency of shared family meals related to the nutritional health of children and adolescents," *Pediatrics* 127 (6) (2011): e1565–e1574, DOI: 10.1542/peds.2010-1440.https://dx.doi.org/10.1542%2Fpeds.2010-1440.

2. Katherine A Shuster, Kristie L Brock, Robert C Dysko, Victor J DiRita, and Ingrid L Bergin. "Polytetrafluoroethylene Toxicosis in Recently Hatched Chickens (Gallus domesticus)," *Comparative Medicine* 62 (1) (February 2012): 49–52, Published online February 2012, PMCID: PMC3276392, accessed August 15, 2016 https://www.ncbi.nlm.nih.gov/pmc/articles/PMC3276392/.

CHAPTER 13

THE LEARNING PLATE

> "One cannot think well, love well, sleep well, if one has not dined well."
> —Virginia Woolf

Leslie hated mushrooms for as long as she could remember until she was a senior in high school. She'd tried them several times during her childhood but just didn't like them. Once, while on vacation with a friend, she tried them again and liked them. Even though she didn't think she would, and was just trying to be polite, she enjoyed the flavor and texture. The mushrooms had been sautéed and had a meaty and smooth texture. From then on, Leslie looked for mushrooms cooked that way on every menu. If we're willing to keep trying, tastes and preferences can change.

For every bite we take, there's something new to learn. That learning (or creative process) is even greater for an infant, but truthfully, we never stop learning about food regardless of age. Whether it's a new color (all shades of purple are not the same), a new texture (from a mushroom to a cinnamon stick), or a new flavor (from cilantro to dark chocolate), it's easy to see how our palates evolve. We always have the opportunity to sit down at a learning plate, adults and children alike. Every meal is an opportunity.

Colors and Textures Oh My!

We've all heard the saying that *we eat with our eyes*, and it's the truth. Color is the single best predictor of whether a person will like or dislike a meal.[1] As dietitians, who are also foodies, we think about things like carrots and sweet potatoes being the same color on the plate. We may swap the sweet potato for a roasted potato just to make sure we have variety of color on the plate as well as variety of food. Colors make a difference in meal planning and food acceptance.

Do you find that your meal's colorful or monochromatic? This simple change may improve your family's overall acceptance of a meal and variety.

In addition to color, most of us enjoy a variety of textures. While some textures may downright disgust our senses, others may transport our senses to a more pleasurable place. Our children's reactions are no different. Textures refer to the consistencies of food like hardness, softness, crunchiness, or smoothness. Consider serving as many textures as you can early on to increase oral acceptance of a variety of textures later on in life.[2] Find out what textures excite your little eater, and work to accommodate them while continuing to offer a variety that will challenge them. This may look like offering something slippery, something crunchy, and something smooth in the same meal.

Puréed foods, which we do not consider solids, are all similarly textured in that they're smooth, wet, and easy to swallow. Imagine for a moment that for months, you've only eaten something smooth and then you get a plate with foods that are lumpy, crunchy, or hard. It could be confusing and shocking to the senses. Research suggests early introduction of a variety of textures influences infants' preferences later on in life.[3] If the texture de jour is usually smooth, there's a good chance that a texture transition or acceptance will take longer. This is important because the more flavors and foods you can introduce early on may determine a child's acceptance and willingness to try a variety of foods as they learn and grow.

Some children may take even longer to adjust to a variety of textures, leaving a parent frustrated when trying to serve more foods at home, while dining out, or advancing their little one's skills with eating and using utensils. Providing a variety of textures early on is important, which is why we feel that baby-led weaning provides a great route for a timely oral acceptance of foods in developmentally appropriate infants.[4] On the Academy of American Pediatrics Advocacy and Policy Health Initiatives official website, they also note the importance of exposing babies and children to a wide variety of flavors and textures.

We understand that many babies and toddlers need to be exposed to foods multiple times before they may accept them. Remember, this can be ten, twenty, and even more exposures—don't give up. This goes for adults, too. Parents can be the greatest influence an infant or child can have. While topping a sandwich with a smiley face or cutting things into cute shapes has a place to make food fun, considering the textures and flavors of the foods plays an important role in the development of an infant's palate. Remember, every child progresses at their own pace—just keep offering without pressure.

The Powerful Sense of Taste

Our sense of taste is an important predictor of foods we choose to like and dislike. We have five key taste receptors on our tongue: umami, bitter, salty, sweet, and sour. Babies are born with the ability to taste. Their sensory receptors are so sensitive that they can smell their mother instantly.[5] The only taste babies may not have at birth is for salt; it's estimated that this sense emerges at around four months of age.[6]

As we mentioned in chapter 8, zinc plays an important role in our olfactory nerve, a cranial nerve involved in our sense of smell. If a baby is deficient in zinc, he may have a blunted sense of taste and smell. You can challenge a baby's palate by serving up a juicy slice of steak with a mushroom sauce (umami—the sense that picks up meaty flavors with a velvety texture), a slice of lemon (sour) with a slice of watermelon (sweet), roasted beets or a sliced olive (which are naturally salty), and topped off with a square of dark chocolate (bitter). Voilà, you have just served up a complete meal that challenges and stimulates your family's olfactories!

Beyond Yucky & Yummy

Yummy. Soooo good. Tasty. Yucky. Ewwwww. Although these may be frequent descriptors we choose for foods, they lack in actually describing the complexities of the food. Now, we don't expect you to tell your eight-month-old all about the umami of the tomato sauce, but you can start talking flavor and texture early on with your toddler. These descriptors can help us talk to children about a new food. In turn, it can help your child tell you why they will or won't eat a food. This can be done without pressure to try the new food. For example, you may say "tonight we're having pasta, green beans, and tomato sauce. I like the sweetness and smoothness of the sauce. Put whatever you like on your plate."

There are times you may be met with resistance, and this may be a clue. When children use descriptions for food like yucky or gross, they aren't necessarily being rude or picky. This may be their way of sharing their fear and uncertainty about the food in front of them. Giving additional terms to describe flavor and texture can empower the whole family in identifying foods they like and dislike. This leads to food preferences over time.

Now, we're not saying every single meal is a culinary class. We can talk about new foods when they're offered, and describe what we like about typical foods of the family. Talk about these things when it seems useful for you and your family. Here are a few examples to get you started.

Texture	Flavor
Crispy	Burnt
Crunchy	Fresh
Crusty	Salty
Lumpy	Smoky
Moist	Sour
Slippery	Spicy
Smooth	Stale
Tough	Sugary/sweet

It's a good idea to offer one or two foods you know your child will accept when serving new foods. They may not try the new food the first time it's offered, and that's okay. If they feel safe, and know that there will be foods they like at mealtimes, they're more likely to try new options later on. It's okay if they just eat the dinner roll. Remember, you provide, and they decide.

Don't be discouraged if your little one displays a dislike for a food. It may also be a good idea to avoid rejoicing when they dislike the same ones you do (tempting as it may be). Your little one may pass on your favorite dish or turn up their nose to something you'd otherwise expect them to enjoy. This is part of the preference process. It's also how kids assert their autonomy, and we want to support that!

We've had foods we did not enjoy as kids, but can now tolerate or even like as adults (like Leslie's mushroom story). From broccoli to Brussels sprouts, people generally get over their childhood dislikes of foods the more they try to eat them. Wendy Jo despised chocolate (gasp) until she was in her twenties. She also turned her nose up at onions, peppers, Brussels sprouts, popcorn, and licorice and preferred the spaghetti noodles separate from the meat sauce on her plate. In culinary school, Wendy Jo was challenged when her taste buds were exposed to fresh Brussels sprouts, gently sautéed in olive oil with salty pancetta and finished off with a splash of fresh orange juice (yes, please). She now loves Brussels sprouts and includes them on her holiday menu.

Now, Wendy Jo is total foodie who will eat or try just about everything. She has surpassed her childhood dislikes and moved on. Interestingly, what her parents didn't stop doing was introducing these flavors to her as a child. Her mom still cooked up peppers and onions, snacked frequently on popcorn, and served up mushy Brussels sprouts. Their daughter disliking certain foods wasn't going to stop her parents from enjoying them, nor should it stop you. Wendy Jo's palate soon got past her previous perceptions. Most of ours do! Serve up variety without the "just try it" pressure, and when your child, or young adult, is ready, they'll likely expand their palate.

The Mindful Bites

One of our favorite client experiments is called the the mindful bites activity. This exercise aims to teach us to slow down, tune in, and savor each bite. And, if you find you don't enjoy what you're eating, this can help us realize we don't have to continue eating the food.

The mindful bites activity works great with a piece of dark chocolate and a piece of chocolate-coated candy. You'll either need three pieces of each or plan to take three bites of each. In this activity, focus on the *flavor*, *texture*, and the *overall savor-ability* of the food.

Here goes . . .

Bite 1: Take your piece of chocolate candy. During your first bite, focus just on *flavor*. Close your eyes and ask yourself what words you would use to describe the *flavor* of the candy.

Bite 2: Next, focus on *texture* of the chocolate candy. Is it crunchy? Is it smooth? What *textures* do you pick up?

Bite 3: Take a little bit longer to chew your last bite. Close your eyes and *savor* it all together.

Before giving your final impression, try the same process with a piece of dark chocolate.

One. Two. Three . . .

Now, think back to your overall impressions of both foods. Which satisfied you more? Why? This same principle can be applied to any food and at any meal as long as we slow down long enough to give it our full attention.

Let Go of the Numbers

Throughout the years, our dieting culture has put an emphasis on numbers versus actual satisfaction. Say someone is counting calories and opted for a fat-free, sugar-free bowl of fill-in-the-blank food-like product because of the numbers. There's a perception that lower numbers are better or "healthier." This person may have missed on a more satisfying food because they feared the higher calorie food was a lesser option. We wholeheartedly disagree and suggest that all our clients focus more on the satisfaction of food versus calories of that food. Don't forget that humans lived successfully without those numbers for thousands of years. They ate food that was available to to them. And they likely ate enough of the food to keep them satisfied until their next meal opportunity. Focusing on numbers will keep you hungry and likely underfed. We can model satisfaction and enoughness.

We've both had experiences with clients (and even personally) where we've eaten a food that may be formulated to be *healthier* that removed the satisfying components of the food. We, and our clients, needed to eat more food shortly after because it just wasn't satisfying. The fats that naturally occur in foods or in recipes have a powerful purpose. Fats create a velvety and smooth mouthfeel that so many of us enjoy. The fat also provides a satisfaction that can help us signal the end of an eating experience.

The mindful bites activity can assist *Born to Eat* parents in tuning into what they are eating, tasting, and savoring so you can teach your little one to do the same over time. This also empowers you to choose to step away from a food that really doesn't warrant that third bite. *What you chew is always up to you!* We hope we've given you some quality information to chew on so that you can make the best choice for you and your family.

Making a Plan

In chapter 11, we covered food perceptions and decisions we must make when choosing foods for our families. In chapter 12, we discussed the art of crafting a menu, and now, in chapter 13, we've covered flavor and variety on the plate. Now it's time to pull it all together. While we don't advocate for dieting or following a scripted menu plan, we understand that people like to see what meal planning looks like and have examples.

Before we embark on this menu plan, promise us that you won't feel compelled to follow it to a T or feel guilty if you don't. This is simply our example that we'd want to share with you if you were sitting across from us in our offices. And, if you were, we'd tweak it to work for you and your family specifically. This sample menu plan is simply a way for us to provide you with ideas, show you how we add variety in our daily meals, and highlight how to include a variety of foods to nourish our *Born to Eat* families.

Day/Meal	Protein-Rich Foods	Vegetable/Fruit Side	Starchy Side	Fats
Day 1				
Breakfast	Scrambled eggs	Salsa & strawberries	Toast	Butter
Snack	Cheese stick	Grapes		
Lunch	Grilled chicken (leftover from the night before perhaps)	Salad (lettuce, tomatoes, cucumbers, carrots, kidney beans, canned artichoke hearts)	Croutons	Vinaigrette (olive oil and red wine vinegar)
Snack	Peanut butter	Apple slices		
Dinner	Chicken Enchilada Bake (page 239)	Steamed green beans & sliced tomatoes	Tortillas (used in recipe)	Cheese (used in recipe)
Day 2				
Breakfast	Milk	Grated apple (mixed into oats)	Oatmeal	Peanut butter or chopped nuts (mixed into oats)
Snack	Boiled eggs		Pretzels	
Lunch	Chunk Light Tuna Salad (page 205) or leftovers	Lettuce	Low-ingredient crackers or bread	Mayo
Snack	Yogurt	Berries		
Dinner	Grilled steak	Mushroom sauce (for steak) and side salad	Baked potato	Butter & vinaigrette

Day/Meal	Protein-Rich Foods	Vegetable/Fruit Side	Starchy Side	Fats
Day 3				
Breakfast	Simple & Versatile Frittatas (page 187)	Spinach (inside muffin variation) and banana		Bacon & cheese (inside muffin variation)
Snack			Toast	Peanut butter
Lunch	Steak (leftover)	Quinoa "Pantry" Salad (page 208)	Quinoa (in salad)	Olive oil (drizzled on top of meat with tabbouleh)
Snack	Cheese stick	Watermelon slices		
Dinner	Grilled Salmon (page 177)	Lemon slices, sautéed green beans	Crusty French bread	Butter

It's our hope that you can use the meal-planning, pantry-stocking, and body-trust-supporting tips of this part of the book to become more present and purposeful with food. When we're not overwhelmed with getting food on the table, we can have more mental energy to enjoy a well-thought-out meal. We're not saying every moment or dinner has to be plugged into a spreadsheet, but in our own lives, having a plan makes meals less stressful. We're real people, too, and sometimes even we do the *shovel and run* (gasp). But most of the time, we try our best to plan our meals, particularly dinner.

Being less stressed can allow us to be more present with our meal and our families. It's our hope that you and your *Born to Eat* family will be able to enjoy food, each other's company, and the energy it all provides. Being present with our food and in our family time is a *Born to Eat* value that we feel has lasting benefits. Bon appétit!

CHAPTER 13 REFERENCES

1. Charles Spence, "On the psychological impact of food colour," *Flavour* 4(21) (2015), DOI: 10.1186/s13411-015-0031-3.

2. Dipayan Biswas, Courtney Szocs, Aradhna Krishna, and Donald R. Lehmann. "Something to Chew On: The Effects of Oral Haptics on Mastication, Orosensory

Perception, and Calorie Estimation," *Journal of Consumer Research* 41 (2) (August 2014): 261–273, DOI: 10.1086/675739.

3. Gillian Harris and Helen Coulthard. "Early Eating Behaviours and Food Acceptance Revisited: Breastfeeding and Introduction of Complementary Foods as Predictive of Food Acceptance," *Current Obesity Report* 5 (2016): 113–120, Published online March 8, 2016, DOI: 10.1007/s13679-016-0202-2, PMCID: PMC4796330.

4. Brenda Lundyl, Tiffany Field, Kirsten Carraway, Sybil Harp, Julie Malphurs, Marla Rosenstein, Martha Pelaez-Nogueras, Frances Coletta, Dana Ott, and Maria Hernandez-Reif. "Food Texture Preferences in Infants Versus Toddlers," *Early Child Development and Care* 146 (1998): 69–85, accessed October 5, 2016, http://www2.fiu.edu/~pelaeznm/pdfs/24%20Food%20texture%20preferences.pdf.

5. Shota Nishitani, Tsunetake Miyamura, Masato Tagawa, Muneichiro Sumi, Ryuta Takase, Hirokazu Doi, Hiroyuki Moriuchi, and Kazuyuki Shinohara. "The calming effect of a maternal breast milk odor on the human newborn infant," *Neuroscience Research* 63 (1) (2009): 66–71, DOI: 10.1016/j.neures.2008.10.007.

6. Leslie J. Stein, Beverly J. Cowart, and Gary K. Beauchamp. "The development of salty taste acceptance is related to dietary experience in human infants: a prospective study," *American Journal of Clinical Nutrition* 95 (1) (January 2012): 123–129, DOI: 10.3945/ajcn.111.014282.

PART 4
THE *BORN TO EAT* KITCHEN

The number one request we get when helping clients or friends kick off the *Born to Eat* feeding journey is to dish about our favorite family recipes and how we modify these meals for a baby. We completely understand the frustration and confusion that can come with the start of the eating journey, especially if you're not comfortable in the kitchen. Throughout these final chapters, we will share our favorite first foods, quick and easy breakfasts, lunch box and snacking favorites, and our most frequently served up family dinners. Although Wendy Jo has a knack for elaborate recipe development, we both agreed that the recipes needed to be simple. Most families who have a baby on board aren't up for balancing a thirty-ingredient recipe between loads of laundry, food shopping, menu planning, changing diapers, and actually finding time to sit. We get it.

In addition to the easy recipes, we will break down what it looks like to serve a normal meal for your beginner, novice, and advanced eater. We feel this is one of the most perplexing parts of using a self-feeding approach. Look for Baby Bites, which will break down serving suggestions based on skill levels. If you need a quick refresher on skill levels, jump back to chapters 5 through 9.

We've also added ways to transform many of the recipes into clever carryover meals. If you're really looking for time-saving tips, check out the freezer-friendly guides for many of our favorite meals.

> Did you know that the average family repeats the same twelve meals each year, all year long? You can shake up your favorite meals by simply changing the spices and herbs used in a recipe. Turn a basic meat loaf into a Mexican or Greek-inspired masterpiece just by shifting around the spice profile.

CHAPTER 14

OUR FAVORITE FIRST FOODS

"The purpose of life is to live it, to taste experience to the utmost, to reach out eagerly and without fear for newer and richer experience."

—Eleanor Roosevelt

Beginning the food journey was (in truth) a bit nerve-racking for Wendy Jo. Wendy Jo's husband had just returned from an overseas deployment, and they decided his return marked the perfect time to share their first meal together as a family. Based on challenging communications while he was abroad, Wendy Jo wasn't able to sufficiently prepare her husband for the self-feeding approach, and he had his concerns with veering off the traditional path of baby food. It wasn't until a couple weeks in that he began to relax and really see Miss A advance in her eating skills. Then Wendy Jo's husband was boasting to all of his friends about what a great eater Miss A was and how she could suck all the juices out of a juicy steak or devour an avocado. At the time, Wendy Jo only had the support of her two fellow dietitian friends using this approach (thanks, Leslie and Rebecca) and her

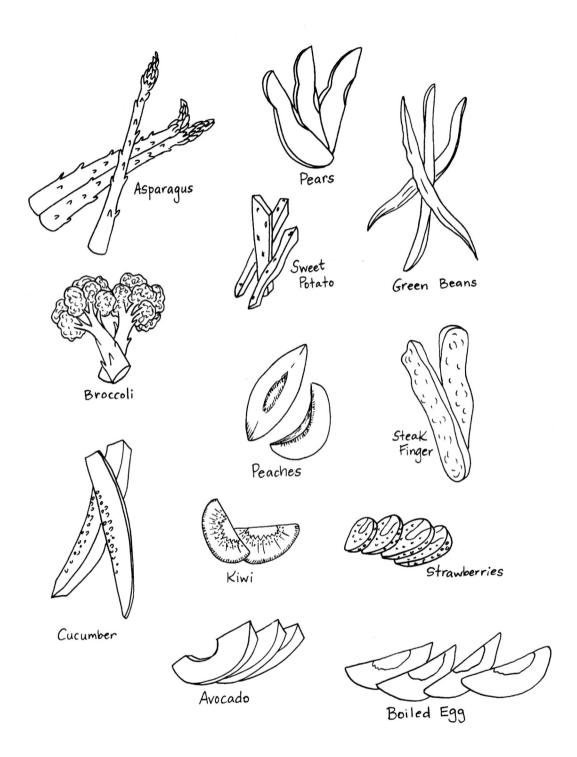

Asparagus

Pears

Sweet Potato

Green Beans

Broccoli

Peaches

Steak Finger

Cucumber

Kiwi

Strawberries

Avocado

Boiled Egg

social media channels. Unfortunately, social media doesn't always provide accurate or safe advice. There are endless questions we all face as we embark on this self-feeding journey about when to progress to solids, what food to start with, how to cook the foods, how to cut the foods, where to serve the foods, etc. The *Born to Eat* team recognized early on how important this chapter, along with chapter 5, would be for all of us embracing this approach with self-feeding babies. We hope you find these recipes and tips useful and easier than expected during those first couple weeks of supporting your self-feeding baby.

This is the exciting, yet scary, start to your baby's eating journey. As we explained back in chapter 5, every baby is different and it's important to tune into what your baby's skill and interest levels are as you progress. Even we get nervous. Miss A took a big ol' bite out of a piece of chicken early on and did gag, leaving Mom a bit unsettled. Needless to say, Wendy Jo stuck with soft veggies, steak, salmon, and chicken salad until she was ready to progress her to chicken slices at eight months. CC had a few gagging episodes, but none that were memorable. Every baby is different, and you know your little one best. Keep trying new things and go with what you feel most comfortable serving. This chapter is not about making baby foods; it's about preparing whole foods that are excellent starters for baby as well as meal components for the whole family.

This chapter includes:

Before we embark on recipes, let's take a look at higher-choking-risk foods and how they can be served safely or avoided to keep your baby safe on this self-feeding journey.

High-Choking-Risk Foods and How to Modify

Let's be real: a baby can choke on anything, and it's up to the parent or caregiver to make a food safe for a baby to gnaw, chew, or swallow. As we've mentioned, the BLISS study created an excellent high-risk-choking foods resource document for their study participants. We also note that study results indicated participants often served their babies high-risk foods. We felt that it was important to share ways high-risk-choking foods can be made safer for your new eater. There's no rush in giving a baby these foods, but when you decide your baby is ready, here are some tips to get you started safely.

High-Choking-Risk Foods	Modifying Risky Foods
Raw Carrots	Grate with a Microplane or finest grater setting, serve mixed into moist foods, such as, yogurt, olive oil, or mashed avocado.
Raw Celery	Grate with a Microplane or finest grater setting, serve mixed into moist foods, such as, yogurt, olive oil, or mashed avocado.
Raw Salad or Leaves (spinach, lettuce, arugula)	Roll up leaves, thinly slice (a.k.a. chiffonade), and sauté or cook.
Raw Apples or Hard Pears	Use a grater and serve in yogurt, oatmeal, or thin slices baked or sautéed to soften to a mash-able texture.
Rice Crackers, Potato Chips, Corn Chips	Avoid; use softer or meltable type crackers if desired.
Whole Nuts	Avoid; however, tiny amounts of nut butters can be added to other moist foods to expose babies to nuts (e.g., yogurt, oatmeal, cooked farina). Finely minced nuts or flour can also be used (e.g., almond meal).
Dried Fruits (raisins, cranberries, apricots, mango)	Soak in hot water for 5 minutes and chop into tiny bites.
Fresh Cherries	Use frozen and defrost, then quarter or chop up cherries.
Grapes	Avoid until a more skilled eater, then quarter (from stem top to bottom cuts, not around the equator), progress to halves (cutting from top to bottom only) as baby skill progresses.

High-Choking-Risk Foods	Modifying Risky Foods
Strawberries	Frozen, defrosted, and sliced or fresh strawberries cut into long, thin strips.
Raspberries	Frozen and defrosted or use very ripe, soft raspberries. Halve berries to serve.
Blackberries	Frozen and defrosted or fresh sliced in quarters.
Cherry Tomatoes	Tomato slices are best or quarter cherry tomatoes.
Cooked Peas	Halve peas, fresh or frozen and defrosted.
Cooked Corn	Serve on the cob or cut kernels in half
Round Sausages or Hot Dogs	Avoid; or slice into rounds and then quarters.
Any hard fruit or vegetable that cannot be squished or mashed with ease using your thumb and index fingers. Tough skins can also make foods risky.	Either avoid or use the techniques mentioned above to make the fruits and vegetables a safe texture or shape for your infant. Remove skins as needed.

Boiled Eggs

Serving size: 1–2 boiled eggs

Prep time: 0 minutes

Cook time: 18–22 minutes

Ingredients:

Raw eggs in shell

Directions:

1. Place eggs in a 4-quart saucepan and cover with cold water.
2. Place pan over high heat and bring to a boil. Once the water begins to boil, immediately cover and remove from heat. Set timer for 12 minutes.
3. Drain off hot water and place under cold running water for 1 minute.
4. Peel and enjoy or refrigerate for later.

Variations:

- If you want your eggs less firm, boil for 10 minutes, or for firmer eggs, set for 14 minutes.

> Older eggs, meaning eggs that have been in your refrigerator for a week or two, will peel easier, so keep an extra dozen on hand just for boiling.

BABY BITES:

Beginner	Novice	Advanced
Serve as a quartered wedge or as egg salad mashed with Greek yogurt or avocado	Serve as a whole egg and let them nibble off bites or in wedges. If a whole egg is challenging to hold, consider rolling in almond meal or slicing in half.	Chopped, whole, or in wedges

Steamed Vegetables

The question of the day (every day) is how long to steam vegetables. This table will help get you started. The times are estimated for a beginner texture. Steaming times will vary based on pots used, how quickly your burner can heat the water, and how thick cut the vegetable is. Remember to test vegetables by gently pressing between your index finger and thumb or by pressing with your tongue to the roof of your mouth. The vegetable should smash with ease for a beginner. For more advanced eaters or for parents, shave off a couple minutes.

Vegetable	Size	Steaming Time (minutes)
Asparagus	Leave whole	13–15
Beets	Whole. Peel off skin and quarter after steaming.	30–50 based on size variances; test with a fork after 30 minutes
Broccoli	2-inch stalks	12–14
Carrots	Baby carrot size	12–14
Cauliflower	2-inch florets	10–14
Green Beans	Leave whole	10–12
Green Peas	Leave whole, and halve for serving	4–6
Sweet Potatoes	Peel and cut into pinky finger–sized pieces	12–16
Zucchini	Finger-sized pieces	5–8

To steam fresh vegetables, use a steamer insert in a saucepan or put 1 inch of water in the bottom of a saucepan, bring to a simmer, cover, and steam vegetables for appropriate times. After steaming, immediately place vegetables into ice water for 1 minute to halt the cooking process and retain bright, vibrant color. Remember, pans and burners influence heat; therefore, test and make adjustments based on your kitchen needs.

If you prefer to use a microwave, be sure to test timing. Every microwave is different and wattage affects cooking time; therefore, we felt it good to mention but not list estimated times for steaming in a microwave. But generally speaking, it takes about half the time spent steaming on the stovetop. To steam in a microwave, you can place frozen vegetables with a tablespoon of water in a bowl, cover with a microwave-safe cover, and

Continued on page 170

then heat. Most microwave steaming can be done in about 5 to 8 minutes. Store-bought frozen vegetable packages give cooking times on the packaging. Be sure to cook longer if a softer texture needs to be achieved, and always check for hot spots in food so not to burn your little one's mouth.

Serving Options:

- We don't eat naked vegetables all the time and we don't think your little one has to either. Steamed veggies taste delicious tossed with items such as olive oil, butter, lemon zest, lemon juice, fresh grated Parmesan, or fresh herbs. The sky's the limit for seasoning steamed vegetables.

Freezer Options:

- To freeze steamed veggies, cool completely, pat dry, and place in a single layer onto a baking sheet lined with parchment paper. Freeze for 4 hours then place into a freezer safe container for 1 to 3 months. To avoid freezer burn and extend freezer shelf life, use a vacuum sealer.

Reality Bite

Most folks consider soft peaches an easy food for most infants. However, Miss A had her best gag reflex responses with cooked peaches. Needless to say, Wendy Jo opted for other fruits for the first couple months until she was ready to try peach slices again later—then Miss A rocked at chewing up the peaches with her new teeth without a gag. It pays to pay attention and not to assume all foods will be the easiest for our little ones. Before too long, they figure out the best way to chew up a food or spit it out. After all, they are *Born to Eat.*

Flatiron Steak

Serving size: 4–5 finger slices

Makes about 5–6 adult servings

Prep time: 15 minutes + 30 minutes to marinade (optional)

Cook time: 20 minutes

Ingredients:

2 (1-pound) flatiron steaks

2 tablespoons extra-virgin olive oil

Salt and pepper to taste, or omit if desired

Directions:

1. Remove flatiron (or sirloin) steaks from packaging and place in a 9 × 13–inch dish.
2. Drizzle the olive oil over the steaks and evenly coat and add salt and pepper to taste.
3. Let the steaks sit at room temperature for about 30 minutes. If you are rushed to get the meal on the table you can skip this step!
4. Heat grill to 400°F (medium-high heat). You can also cook this in a skillet or grill pan at medium-high heat.
5. Grill approximately 6 to 8 minutes per side, turning only once. The thickness of the steak varies, so cook to your desired level of doneness.
6. Allow steak to rest for 5 minutes prior to slicing against the grain.

Variations:

- Dressing up a steak is easy! Top it off with sautéed mushrooms, a slice of compound butter of garlic, rosemary, salt and butter, or an extra drizzle of olive oil.

Carryover Meal Ideas:

- Top off a salad with extra slices of steak
- Chop up steak and add to a burrito or quesadilla
- Reheat or serve cold for a baby or toddler's lunch

Tip: Cut against the grain—look at the direction of the grain of the meat and then use a sharp steak knife to cut the steak at an opposing angle.

Continued on page 172

Baby Bites:

Beginner	Novice	Advanced
Sliced against the grain in a finger shape longer than baby's fist and about as wide as 1 to 2 fingers, whichever is easiest for your baby to hold.	Slice as you would for beginner and then slice in half for two smaller fingers.	Slice steak and then into bite-sized pieces.

Does your beginner baby already have teeth? If so, you could cook their steak medium-well to well done (where the meat is tough to cut through with a knife and a baby's teeth couldn't break off a piece) and serve a two finger-width piece so they don't bite off a piece just yet. The initial goal is for them to suck on the steak, gaining nutrition from the juices, and gum the meat as they learn the process of chewing.

Slow-Cooker Whole Roasted Chicken

Serving size: 3–5 ounces

Makes about 4–6 adult servings

Prep time: 15 minutes

Cook time: 6–8 hours

Ingredients:

5 carrots, scrubbed and cut into 3-inch pieces

5 celery stalks, washed and cut into 3-inch pieces

1 onion, sliced into rings

10 new potatoes, scrubbed

1 tablespoon salt (omit if desired)

1 teaspoon paprika

1 teaspoon dried thyme

1 teaspoon ground coriander

3½–4½ pound whole chicken

1 lemon

Directions:

1. Place cut vegetables in the bottom of a slow cooker.
2. Mix together salt, paprika, thyme, and coriander in a small bowl.
3. Remove the innards bag (often found in neck cavity). Rinse and pat chicken dry (be sure to clean sink after). Rub dried chicken with spice mixture, getting into all the crevices to include the inside cavity.
4. Slice lemon into quarters. Place two wedges in chicken cavity and place the other two on top of the vegetables.
5. Place chicken on top of vegetables, cover with lid, and cook on low for 8 hours or on high for 4 to 6 hours. Baste (pour pan drippings or juices over the chicken) chicken with juices every hour if possible, although not necessary.
6. Remove the chicken carefully, as it will be very tender and falling off the bone. Dark meat is tender and moist, which is great for a beginner. They can eat white or dark meat as long as it's soft and moist. Discard skin and any bones or cartilage.

Variations:

- Spice mixtures can change the flavor profile, from Mexican (cumin, coriander, chili powder, and an orange) to Greek (oregano, coriander, cumin, and olives) or Indian (curry, lime, and finely chopped cashews).

Continued on page 174

Freezer Options:

- Whatever you don't finish can be chopped and frozen to use in a variety of dishes like enchiladas, chicken salad, or chicken pot pie later.

BABY BITES:

Beginner	Novice	Advanced
A fingerlike piece of dark or white meat or chopped and mashed with a little Greek yogurt, olive oil, or mayonnaise for a chicken salad. Vegetables will be very tender. Place 1 finger piece each of carrot and celery and chop up potato without skin.	Cut chicken into small, bite-sized pieces. Serve vegetables whole or chopped.	Let them enjoy a drumstick, modeling how to eat it, or chop up any part of the chicken. Serve vegetables in bite-sized pieces.

Tips:

- Add pan drippings or olive oil to the meat if it's too dry for your little one.
- Leftover chicken makes for perfect chicken salad, chicken quesadillas, chicken enchiladas, or chicken pot pie . . . or any other recipe calling for cooked chicken.

Hamburgers and Hamburger Fingers

Serving size: 3–5-ounces

Makes about 4 adult servings

Prep time: 10 minutes

Cook time: 20 minutes

Ingredients:

1 pound ground beef

⅛ teaspoon ground black pepper

⅛ teaspoon salt, omit if desired

1 tomato, sliced

1 avocado, sliced

4 leaves green lettuce

1 onion, thinly sliced

4 hamburger buns

Directions:

1. In a mixing bowl, combine ground beef with salt and pepper, as desired. Using your hands, mix lightly but thoroughly. Lightly shape into four (½-inch thick) patties and 1 to 2 beef finger-shaped pieces.

2. On a preheated gas grill over medium heat, grill the patties, covered, for 7 to 9 minutes or until instant-read thermometer inserted horizontally into center registers 160°F, turning occasionally. If you prefer stovetop cooking, heat a dry, heavy skillet over medium-high heat. Place burgers and fingers in pan (avoid overcrowding skillet) and cover. Cook covered for 7 minutes, flip burgers, and cook for an additional 3 to 5 minutes or until a meat thermometer reads 160°F.

3. Place each burger on a bun and top with lettuce, tomato, avocado, and onion slices.

Variations (note: omit salt from infant portion if desired):

- Barbecue: mix beef with Worcestershire sauce, salt, and pepper and serve with barbecue sauce, fried onions, and pickles

Continued on page 176

- Mexican: mix beef with taco seasoning and serve with salsa, cheddar, and shredded lettuce
- Italian: mix beef with salt and pepper and serve with fresh mozzarella, tomato, and basil
- Greek: mix beef with salt, pepper, dried oregano, coriander, and crumbled feta and serve with cucumber slices, spinach, and roasted red bell peppers

Tips: If you're nervous about your baby working with a burger finger, you can try chopping and mashing with an avocado and then place pieces of this on a tray for baby. Go with your comfort level!

BABY BITES:

Beginner	Novice	Advanced
Serve a cooled hamburger finger with sliced tomato and avocado wedge all separate from one another.	Same as beginner	Make a tiny hamburger patty and serve as a mini burger or slider, just as you would enjoy it or with toppings on the side.

Grilled Salmon

Serving size: 3–5 ounces

Prep time: 10 minutes

Cook time: 16 minutes

Ingredients:

1½ pounds salmon fillets

1 lemon, zested and cut into wedges

1 tablespoon fresh dill, chopped, or
   1 teaspoon dried dill

2 cloves garlic, minced

2 tablespoons olive oil

½ teaspoon sea salt (adult portions
   only)

Directions:

1. On a baking sheet lined with parchment paper or foil, lay out salmon fillets. In a small bowl, mix together lemon zest, dill, garlic, and olive oil. Drizzle mixture evenly over salmon fillets on both sides. Season adult fillets with sea salt.

2. Heat a grill over medium-high heat.

3. Once the grill is heated to 400°F, cook fillets for 6 to 8 minutes on each side or until cooked to desired texture. Serve with lemon wedges.

4. If indoor is preferred, heat an oven to 400°F and bake salmon for 20 minutes or until desired doneness.

Variations:

*   Asian-inspired with hoisin sauce and sprinkle with sesame seeds, serve with fresh lime wedges

Carryover:

*   To make salmon patties: Mix together leftover cooked salmon (2 cups) with ¼ cup bread crumbs, ½ medium onion (chopped up finely), ¼ cup mayonnaise, 1 egg, a squirt of mustard, and a couple pinches of chopped fresh herbs (parsley, dill, thyme, or basil). Now, form mixture into patties and place on a baking sheet. Spray patties with olive oil spray and bake for 20 minutes. This recipe is incredible served up with plain Greek yogurt mixed with chopped garlic, lemon zest, and lemon juice. If you want to kick up the parents' version, add a squirt of sriracha into the mix.

Continued on page 178

Canned salmon can easily be mixed into scrambled eggs, served on a salad, or made into patties. Don't dismiss the goodness in the can!

BABY BITES:

Beginner	Novice	Advanced
1 or 2 tablespoons of cooked, flaked salmon or 1 finger patty of carryover recipe	3 to 4 tablespoons of cooked, flaked salmon or 1 small patty cut into bite-sized pieces of carryover recipe with sauce	¼ cup to ⅓ cup of cooked, flaked salmon or 1 small patty cut into bite-sized pieces of carryover recipe with sauce

Roasted Pork Loin with Dijon Apricot Glaze

Serving size: 3–5 ounces

Prep time: 5 minutes

Cook time: 60 minutes

Ingredients:

1 (2–2½ pounds) pork loin roast

1 (12-oz) jar apricot or peach preserves

2 tablespoons Dijon mustard

1 tablespoon olive oil

Salt and pepper to taste, omit if desired

Directions:

1. Preheat oven to 350°F.
2. Place roast in a small roasting pan or jellyroll pan.
3. In a small bowl, mix together preserves, mustard, and olive oil. Spread half the preserves mixture on the roast and place the roast in the oven for about 60 minutes or until juices run clear, cooked to an internal temperature of 145°F to 160°F.
4. Once cooked, allow roast to cool for 10 minutes before slicing. Discard cooked sauce and juices. Use remaining uncooked sauce to drizzle over sliced pork roast. Season adult portions with salt and pepper to taste based on preference.

Variations:

This recipe also works well with applesauce instead of preserves. Unsweetened applesauce can be served to a beginner eater. It was one of CC's favorite flavor combos.

Baby Bites:

Beginner	Novice	Advanced
Serve in a pinky finger–sized slice without additional sauce.	Serve in bite-sized pieces with sauce on the side or drizzled over a couple pieces.	Serve in bite-sized pieces with sauce over top or on the side based on toddler preference.

Nutty Banana Parfaits

Serving size: 1¼ cup

Servings: 1 adult and 1 infant

Prep time: 5 minutes

Cook time: 0 minutes

Ingredients:

1 cup whole-fat, plain Greek yogurt

1–2 tablespoons peanut or almond butter

1 banana, thinly sliced

1 tablespoon chia seeds (optional)

Directions:

1. In a small mixing bowl, whisk together Greek yogurt and almond butter until well blended (about 1 minute).
2. Next, layer yogurt mixture, bananas, then chia seeds, and repeat in a serving bowl and enjoy.

Variations:

- Frozen/defrosted mangos (chopped small) + plain, unflavored coconut yogurt + cashew butter
- Chopped frozen cherries + plain Greek yogurt + almond butter
- Frozen/defrosted strawberries (chopped) + plain Greek yogurt + sunflower butter
- Add a thin layer of oats, crushed graham crackers, or minced nuts for added textures (based on skill level)

Freezer Options:

- To make a teething popsicle, pour and layer mixture into a tiny (2-ounce) cup, insert straw into center, and freeze for 4 hours or overnight before serving.

Tip: Frozen fruits are usually frozen without any sweeteners, but be sure to check the labels prior to purchasing. They make for an excellent texture for beginner eaters. If your little one is teething, gnawing on a frozen and slightly thawed piece of fruit may help ease gum discomfort.

You know your little one the best. Trust yourself to make the best and safest food decisions for your little self-feeder. If a food makes you feel uncomfortable, there's no reason to push it or question your intuition. Skip it and come back to it when you feel your little one can handle the food. Give them time to learn with safe foods, then progress as you see your self-feeder is mastering skills to move up to the next skill level of eating.

Baby Bites:

Beginner	Novice	Advanced
Serve 2 to 4 tablespoons just as you would for yourself, but consider a smock bib and something under the high chair and then let the painting—errrr, eating begin!	Serve just as described, 2 to 4 tablespoons. Smock may be helpful for easy cleanups.	Serve just as described; fruits can be in bigger pieces or chopped small.

Spinach Muffins

Serving size: 1 muffin

Makes about: 6

Prep time: 3 minutes

Cook time: 14 minutes

Ingredients:

- Coconut oil or cooking spray
- 1 banana
- 1 egg
- ½ cup frozen spinach

Directions:

1. Preheat oven to 350F° and grease a muffin pan (6 muffins) with coconut oil or cooking spray.
2. Toss banana, egg, and spinach into a blender and blend for 15 seconds.
3. Pour mix into muffin wells.
4. Bake for 12 to 14 minutes or until slightly firm to touch.

Note: Using frozen spinach adds more liquid, which is great for a beginner texture. If you want these to be a bit firmer, opt to defrost and squeeze dry the spinach to remove excess water.

BABY BITES:

Beginner	Novice	Advanced
Serve ½ muffin cut into fingers	Serve 1 muffin and consider serving with a yogurt dip for a fun activity	Serve 1–2 muffins with yogurt dip and/or syrup

Tex-Mex Carne Guisada

Serving size: ¾ cup shredded meat

Makes about: 6 servings

Prep time: 10 minutes

Cook time: 8 hours

Ingredients:

2 pounds cubed stew meat

½ cup flour

1 tablespoon salt

1 tablespoon black pepper

¼ cup extra-virgin olive oil

1 large onion, thinly sliced

2 cloves garlic, coarsely chopped

1 cup beef stock

1 can chopped tomatoes

2 teaspoons ground cumin

Directions:

1. In a mixing bowl, toss together stew meat, flour, salt, and pepper. Remove meat and dust off excess flour. Discard flour and seasonings.

2. In a large skillet, heat olive oil over medium-high heat. Brown meat in small batches for 2 to 3 minutes, then transfer to a slow cooker.

3. Once meat is browned, add the onion to the skillet and sauté for 5 minutes. Add the garlic and sauté for 1 minute. Transfer onions and garlic to slow cooker.

4. Deglaze the pan with beef stock and transfer to slow cooker.

5. Add in tomatoes and cumin and cook for 6 to 8 hours on low heat or 4 hours on high.

Continued on page 184

Simple Grain Bowl Ideas

Quinoa, chopped cilantro, red onion, pinto beans, sliced avocado, and grated carrots

or

Rice, shredded lettuce, baby corn or canned corn, black beans, sliced avocado, cheddar cheese, cilantro

BABY BITES:

Beginner	Novice	Advanced
Finely chop meat and serve mixed with rice or quinoa + steamed carrots (mix with minced cilantro & olive oil) + avocado	Serve in little bites + avocado wedges + mashed beans + raw finely grated carrot (mix with minced cilantro & olive oil)	Serve chopped and as you would serve your family or deconstructed per toddler's preference

CHAPTER 15

BREAKFAST

> "The shared meal elevates eating from a mechanical process of fueling the body to a ritual of family and community, from the mere animal biology to an act of culture."
>
> —Michael Pollan, bestselling author, journalist, and professor at UC Berkeley

Spaghetti for breakfast anyone? For the first two months of Miss A's eating journey, Wendy Jo served up dinner for breakfast and breakfast for dinner. Miss A was a morning girl from the start who was most sharp, skilled, and ready to learn at 7:00 a.m. Knowing Miss A needed excellent iron and protein sources at breakfast, Wendy Jo often flipped the meals. Breakfast is an excellent time for beginners to eat and work on skills, because babies are often well rested, alert, and ready to learn in the mornings. Wendy Jo often opted for dinner foods for breakfast to help Miss A master her skills. Our dear friend and fellow dietitian Jane Gray found herself getting frustrated with her toddler, as he would eat everything at breakfast and lunch but struggled at dinnertime. She decided to flip her meals, too. There are no rules as to what time you eat and what foods you choose at a particular mealtime, so go with what works best for your family at whatever time that may be.

In this chapter, we've included some of our favorite savory and (subtly) sweet breakfast dishes that are perfect at any meal but especially when breaking the fast.

This chapter includes:

Do not offer or use foods with honey to children under one year due to *Clostridium botulinum* (severe food poisoning) risks. Just a reminder: no honey means not even in baked foods. If a recipe you find calls for honey, opt for maple syrup or molasses instead.

Simple & Versatile Frittatas

Serving size: ⅛ of frittata

Serves 8 adult portions

Prep time: varies based on vegetables used; basic recipe is 10 minutes

Cook time: 23 minutes

Ingredients:

Cooking spray
2 tablespoons olive oil
8 large eggs
½ cup milk or cream
¼ cup thinly sliced scallions
1 cup fresh spinach (see notes below)
½ cup finely grated cheddar cheese

Directions:

1. Preheat oven to 350°F. Coat 8-inch oven-safe skillet with cooking spray.
2. In a skillet over medium, heat the olive oil.
3. Whisk together eggs, milk, scallions, and spinach. Pour egg mixture into heated skillet and stir occasionally for 5 minutes. Stir in cheddar cheese and remove from heat.
4. Place skillet in the oven and bake for 18 minutes or until set in the center.
5. Remove from the oven. Run a knife around the edge of the frittata, slightly lifting edges to help frittata loosen from pan. You can either dish it up right from the pan (Leslie's method) or remove the frittata from the skillet to serve (Wendy Jo's method). If you prefer the latter, place a plate over the top and, using two hands (and pot holders), flip frittata onto the plate. Do not remove skillet from plate. Allow frittata to rest in this position for 5 minutes before removing skillet. Slice into appropriate serving sizes based on eating skills.

Continued on page 188

Variations:

- Thinly sliced parboiled potatoes
- Quartered cherry tomatoes
- Thinly sliced zucchini slices
- Thinly sliced asparagus spears
- Fresh herbs
- Chopped smoked salmon
- Minced ham
- Crumbled bacon
- Broccoli florets

BABY BITES:

Beginner	Novice	Advanced
Chiffonade (tightly roll and thinly slice) spinach	Chop spinach	Spinach may be left whole or chopped
Serve as ½-inch to 1-inch x 3-inch finger slices of frittata (only 1 at a time to avoid overwhelming infant).	Serve as a finger or in ¼-inch bites based on infant's preference and pincer grasp.	Serve in bite-sized (½-inch) pieces and encourage use of fork or spoon.
Only use vegetables you can mush with your tongue to the roof of your mouth with ease. Only use the flower portion of the broccoli florets.	Vegetables still need to be tender and in small or thinly sliced pieces (e.g., quartered cherry tomatoes, blanched and thinly sliced zucchini, blanched and chopped broccoli floret, and thinly sliced parboiled potatoes).	Vegetables still need to be tender, but raw vegetables such as zucchini, broccoli florets, and tomatoes can be used as chewing skills improve.
Parboil or steam vegetables used in frittata to help make them safe for infant to gum.		

Tips:

- When inverting a dish onto a plate, it's useful if the plate is larger than the skillet. A cutting board is also a great item to use if you do not have a plate large enough for the frittata.
- Nonstick skillets are not a good choice for baking in an oven, as they may get too hot, which is not safe for the pan. Stainless steel pans are great for frittatas.
- A pizza cutter or pie cutter simplifies slicing of frittata.
- Frittatas may also be baked in muffin cups and frozen for later enjoyment. Freeze in airtight containers for 1 month. To reheat, wrap in damp paper towel and microwave for 30 seconds, flip, and microwave for an additional 30 seconds or until heated thoroughly (times may vary based on microwave wattage).

Cast-iron skillets heat evenly and are great moving from stovetop to oven. Be sure your cast-iron pan is well seasoned and oiled before using. If you're worried about iron or whether your baby is taking in enough iron, be sure to use a cast-iron skillet!

Overnight Oats with Jam & Dates

Serving size: ¼ recipe

Servings: 4 adult portions

Prep time: 5 minutes

Cook time: 0 minutes

Ingredients:

2 cups rolled oats (not instant or steel-cut)

2 cups whole milk

2 teaspoons vanilla extract

½ cup dried dates or raisins, finely chopped

¼ cup 100% fruit preserves (any flavor)

Instructions:

1. In a large mixing bowl, stir the first three ingredients together. Next, stir in dates and preserves, then mix until thoroughly combined. Store in covered bowl.
2. Refrigerate bowl overnight and for up to 3 days.
3. Overnight oats can be eaten hot or cold. Leslie reheats her serving for about 30 to 60 seconds in the microwave. Test the temperature before serving to your little one.

Variations:

- Add in 1 tablespoon chia seeds
- Replace fruit jam with fresh, chopped berries, or soft cooked apples or applesauce
- Stir in 1 to 2 tablespoon nut butters to your mix

Mixes for the Win:

- Wendy Jo's favorite mix is cherry jam, sliced bananas, chia seeds, and almond butter.
- Leslie's favorite blend is applesauce and cinnamon.

Steel-cut oats aren't a good substitute for rolled oats in this recipe. Steel-cut oats are the whole oat that has been coarsely chopped, whereas rolled oats have been steamed, pressed, steamed again, and toasted in their flat shape (a processed yet great food). There is little nutritional difference between the two products. Choose what works best for you and your family and the preferred texture.

BABY BITES:

Beginner	Novice	Advanced
Place 1 to 2 tablespoons on a plate for baby (try different temperatures to see which they prefer and to expose them to flavor changes that occur with heating). A loaded spoon can be introduced here, as well.	2 tablespoons to ¼ cup of oats, serve as warm, cold, or both.	¼ cup to ½ cup oats served warm or cold based on toddler's preference.

Orange Cottage Cheese Muffins

Serving size: 1–2 muffins

Prep time: 15 minutes

Cook time: 22 minutes

Ingredients:

2 cups flour

½ teaspoon baking powder

½ teaspoon baking soda

¼ teaspoon salt

¼ cup granulated sugar (omit for babies under 1 year)

1 orange, zested

1 cup whole-fat small-curd cottage cheese

1 stick (½ cup) unsalted butter, softened

1 large egg

1 teaspoon vanilla extract

100% fruit orange marmalade,
    for the glaze

Directions:

1. Preheat oven to 350°F and line 12 muffin cups with foil liners (or paper liners gently sprayed with cooking spray to help muffins come out of wrapper).
2. In a large bowl, whisk together the flour, baking powder, baking soda, and salt.
3. In a small bowl, mix together the sugar, orange zest, cottage cheese, softened butter, egg, and vanilla extract.
4. Make a well in the dry ingredients and pour the wet ingredients into the well. Stir until all flour is mixed in, about 1 minute. Avoid overmixing batter.
5. Scoop ¼ cup of batter into each muffin liner or until evenly divided.
6. Bake muffins for 22 minutes or until golden on top and set in the center.
7. While muffins are baking, slightly heat orange marmalade in a microwave-safe bowl for 30 seconds.
8. Immediately after removing muffins from oven, drizzle orange glaze over the top to allow the glaze to soak into the muffins. If necessary, poke small holes in the surface of the muffins to help the syrup soak in. Serve immediately. Recommend storing leftovers in the refrigerator.

Variations:

- Add in chopped pecans or dark chocolate chips for advanced eaters.
- Dried cranberries or blueberries make great additions, too. Soak in boiling water for 5 minutes before using for beginner eaters.

Freezer Options:

- Muffins can be frozen for up to 1 month in an airtight container. They can be defrosted in the refrigerator or microwave (without foil wrapper) for 20 seconds.

Have extra ricotta on hand after making lasagna? Ricotta and cottage cheese can be used interchangeably. Yum!

BABY BITES:

Beginner	Novice	Advanced
Omit orange glaze, serve as ¼ muffin wedge	Cut muffin into small, bite-sized pieces and serve glaze on side	Cut muffin into quarters (to avoid waste) or serve them muffin as a whole with glaze

Pumpkin Bites

Serving size: 1 muffin

Servings: 36 bites or 12 muffins

Prep time: 10 minutes

Cook time: 8 minutes

Ingredients:

¼ cup boiling water

½ cup chopped dates

2¼ cups rolled oats

1 cup pumpkin purée

2 eggs

1 tablespoon vanilla extract

¼ cup peanut butter or almond butter

¼ cup whole milk

1 teaspoon baking powder

½ teaspoon baking soda

½ teaspoon salt

1 teaspoon cinnamon

Directions:

1. Preheat the oven to 350°F.
2. In a heat-safe bowl, pour ¼ cup boiling water over chopped dates and allow to sit for 5 minutes.
3. Line a baking sheet with parchment paper.
4. Place all the ingredients, including dates with water, into a blender or a food processor and blend for about 1 minute or until smooth.
5. Using a tablespoon, make 36 mounds on parchment paper, slightly spaced. Bake for 8 minutes or until golden brown.

Variations:

- Add in ½ cup chopped nuts or dark chocolate chips for advanced eaters. Nuts can be softened in boiling water, too, for novice eaters.
- Prefer muffins? You can bake these as muffins; simply adjust baking time to 22 minutes.

Freezer Options:

- These bites are perfect for the freezer and make for an easy, on-the-go snack later on. Once pan is cooled, place in freezer for 1 hour. Place frozen bites in a freezer-safe container and freeze up to 3 months.

BABY BITES:

Beginner	Novice	Advanced
Bake in small finger shapes for easy gripping; serve 1 to 2 bites at a time.	Serve 2 to 4 bites.	Serve 3 to 6 bites.

Egg Pancake Fingers

Serving size: 8–12 finger slices

Prep time: 5 minutes

Cook time: 10 minutes

Ingredients:

2 eggs
1 large, ripe banana
¼ cup flour, oats, or almond flour
⅛ teaspoon cinnamon
2 tablespoons coconut oil or butter

Directions:

1. In a medium mixing bowl, mash together eggs and banana for 2 to 3 minutes or until most large lumps are gone. Stir in flour of choice and cinnamon.
2. Heat a large nonstick skillet or cast-iron pan over medium heat. Add in 1 tablespoon coconut oil (or butter). Once coconut oil (or butter) is melted, make fingers of batter in the pan and cook until bubbles rise to the surface of the finger, about 3 minutes. Turn and cook until golden, approximately another minutes.
3. Melt remaining coconut oil (or butter) and cook up the rest of the batter.

BABY BITES:

Beginner	Novice	Advanced
1 to 3 pancake fingers served with 2 tablespoons of Greek yogurt mixed with 1 teaspoon of nut butter.	3 to 5 pancake fingers served with ¼ cup Greek yogurt mixed with 1 tablespoon nut butter.	Serve as you would any pancakes.

Beefy Breakfast Sausage

Serving size: 1–2 tablespoons or 1 finger (infant), ½ cup or 1–2 patties (adult)

Serving: ~3½ cups of crumbled sausage or 8 patties

Prep time: 5 minutes

Cook time: 12 minutes

Ingredients:

1 pound ground beef	1 teaspoon cumin powder
1 teaspoon dried oregano	½ teaspoon coriander powder
1 teaspoon garlic powder	½ teaspoon salt

Directions:

1. Combine ground beef and seasonings in large bowl, mixing lightly but thoroughly.
2. To make patties or fingers, lightly shape sausage mixture into four (½-inch-thick) patties. Heat large nonstick skillet over medium until hot. Add patties; cook 10 to 12 minutes or until instant-read thermometer inserted horizontally into center registers 160°F, turning occasionally.
3. To prepare as ground sausage, heat large nonstick skillet over medium until hot. Add sausage mixture and cook 8 to 10 minutes. Break into bite-sized pieces while stirring occasionally until cooked through.

Freezer Options:

- Leftover fully cooked sausage can be frozen for 3 to 4 months. To use, heat large nonstick skillet over medium until hot. Add frozen crumbled sausage, and cook 6 to 9 minutes or until ground sausage reach 165°F, stirring occasionally

BABY BITES:

Beginner	Novice	Advanced
1 to 2 tablespoons of ground sausage or 1 finger patty.	2 to 4 tablespoons of ground sausage or 1 finger patty.	⅓ cup ground sausage or 2 finger patties.

Wild Blueberry Muffins

Serving size: 1 muffin

Makes about: 8 servings

Prep time: About 10 minutes

Cook time: 22 minutes

Ingredients

1¼ cups all-purpose flour

2 teaspoons baking powder

¼ cup sugar

½ cup milk

⅓ cup melted butter or coconut oil

1 egg

½ teaspoon salt

1 cup frozen wild blueberries

3 tablespoons cold butter

¼ cup rolled oats

¼ cup brown sugar

Directions

1. Preheat the oven to 350°F. Place muffin cup liners into 12 muffin cups or use a nonstick spray in the muffin cups.

2. In a medium bowl, stir together the flour, baking powder, and sugar.

3. In another bowl, whisk together the milk, butter, egg, and salt.

4. Make a well in the center of the dry ingredients and pour the wet ingredients into the center. Stir just until combined; the batter will still be lumpy. Gently fold in the frozen berries until combined. Divide the muffin batter between the 12 muffin cups.

5. In a small bowl, use your fingers to mix the butter, rolled oats, and brown sugar. Sprinkle the mixture over the top of the muffins. The topping is optional; skip for the infant's portion if you prefer.

6. Bake for 20 to 25 minutes or until set in the center.

Baby Bites:

Beginner	Novice	Advanced
Cut muffin into small finger sizes. The bread can be further softened with breast milk or formula.	Cut the muffin in half and serve.	Serve the muffin.

Morning Glory Quinoa Porridge

Serving size: ½ cup

Makes about: 8 servings

Prep time: About 5 minutes

Cook time: 20 minutes

Ingredients

2 cups quinoa

2 cups milk or milk alternative

2 cups water

1 teaspoon cinnamon

1 carrot, grated

¼ cup raisins

¼ teaspoon salt

2 tablespoons almond butter

Directions

1. Rinse the quinoa under cold, running water for 3 minutes in a sieve before cooking. Drain and shake off excess water.

2. In a medium saucepan, stir together the rinsed quinoa, 2 cups of the milk, water, cinnamon, grated carrot, raisins, and salt. Heat over medium-high heat until the mixture begins to bubble; then cover, reduce the heat to low, and continue to simmer until thickened. Stop cooking after 20 minutes and remove from the heat. Stir in almond butter and sweeten if desired.

BABY BITES:

Beginner	Novice	Advanced
Cut any raisins in half and serve mixture on a loaded spoon or allow infant to palm and self-feed. Chill mixture in a square pan and cut into thin fingers. Serve with breast milk or formula over the top, if desired.	Continue to cut any raisins, serve with a spoon or in fingers as described above. Serve with breast milk or formula over the top, if desired.	Serve porridge with a spoon with milk on top, as desired.

Cookie
Baby Corn
Granola
Roasted Potatoes
Peas
Crackers
Tortilla
Bread

Avocado
Cookie
Dark Chocolate
Nuts/seeds
Nutella
Ranch

Starch

Fats and Others

Sliced chicken and steak

Boiled Eggs

Protein

Nut Butters
Yogurt
Cottage Cheese
Beans

Apples
Mangoes
Carrot Sticks
Broccoli

Fruits and Vegetables

Banana
Pears
Cherry Tomatoes
Berries

CHAPTER 16

LUNCH BOX

> "One cannot think well, love well, sleep well, if one has not dined well."
> –Virginia Woolf

Let's be real here: any food can be considered lunch food. Whether it's carryovers from last night's dinner or you're craving breakfast foods at noon, all foods are a go. Bless the folks who create these adorable bento box lunches with shapes and styles—they really are adorable. To throw these ideas together, you don't need to be an artist or even crafty: simply place them in a container and call it a meal. In this chapter, we break down some of our favorite go-to lunches and family-friendly snacks. Keep it simple, sweetie! No need to stress over a lunch box. Follow this bento box guide on ways to pair up food without having to buy an overly processed cracker and lunch meat box at the grocery store. These are just as easy and much healthier!

This chapter includes:

Avocado Chicken Salad

Serving size: ½ cup

Serves: 2 adults

Prep Time: 5 minutes

Cook Time: 0 minutes

Ingredients:

1 cup cooked, shredded/finely chopped chicken breast, packed

1 ripe avocado, sliced and scored

2 tablespoons Greek yogurt or mayonnaise

Salt and pepper to taste, or omit if desired

Directions:

In a medium bowl, mix all ingredients together, making sure to mash in the avocado. You can leave chunks as desired for advanced eaters.

Variation:

- Add a pinch of curry powder, grated apples, finely grated carrot, grated or minced celery, finely chopped nuts (as small as you can get them for beginner and novice eaters), or all of the above for a fancier version of curried chicken salad.

Don't Freak Out!

There's a decent amount of fat in this recipe. Fat is an important part of a healthy diet. It also helps maintain satiety to get your little one (or you) through a high-energy day.

Tips: If you have a stand mixer, you can place baked or roasted chicken breast right into the bowl with the paddle attachment on low. It will shred it right up for you! Then just toss in the rest of your ingredients. Crunched for time? You can use leftover roasted or rotisserie chicken to get this mixed up in a flash.

Baby Bites:

Beginner	Novice	Advanced
Chop up chicken finely and mix the salad (omitting salt) and serve as 1 to 2 clumps on their tray for easy grabbing.	Chop chicken finely and serve 3 to 5 spoonfuls on their tray, with soft crackers or wrapped in a tortilla (like a pinwheel sandwich).	Serve just as you would or as preferred by toddler.

Greek Yogurt Egg Salad

Serving size: 1 egg

Serves 1 adult

Prep time: 5 minutes

Cook time: 0 minutes

Ingredients:

1 hard-boiled egg, peeled
1 tablespoon whole-fat Greek yogurt (or mayonnaise)
Salt and pepper to taste, omit if desired

Directions:

1. In a small bowl, use a fork to mash up egg. Add in Greek yogurt and blend together with a couple strokes of the fork.

Variations:

- Avocados make a great swap for the yogurt and are an excellent dairy-free alternative.

BABY BITES:

Beginner	Novice	Advanced
Serve as 1 tablespoon or 3 teaspoons on their platter. A loaded spoon can be introduced here, as well.	Serve 1 to 2 tablespoons on a spoon or served with a cracker.	Serve on crackers, as a sandwich (cut into strips), or as the toddler prefers.

Chunk Light Tuna Salad

Canned chunk light tuna salad is a convenient protein product that is safe for infants. This recipe boosts the nutrition and flavors with grated carrots, onions, and Greek yogurt.

Serving size: ½ cup

Prep time: 5 minutes

Cook time: 0 minutes

Ingredients:

1 small carrot, finely grated

¼ small onion, finely grated

¼ cup whole-fat Greek yogurt
(or mayonnaise)

1 (6-oz) can chunk light tuna in water,
drained

Salt and pepper to taste, omit if desired

Directions:

1. In a small mixing bowl, fork mix together finely grated carrots, onion, and Greek yogurt.
2. Next, add in the chunk light tuna and stir. Refrigerate for 1 hour before serving for the best flavor or serve immediately if you're in a rush! Season adult portion and enjoy.

> Serving a little salmon or tuna to our infants is a good thing! They can enjoy 2 to 3 age-appropriate servings per week.

BABY BITES:

Beginner	Novice	Advanced
Serve 1 to 2 tablespoons on loaded spoons or on tray for them to grab.	Serve with small spoon.	Serve rolled in a tortilla, on crackers, or as a sandwich cut into finger strips or wedges.

Dissected Salad

Serving size: ½ recipe

Serves: 2 adults

Prep time: 10 minutes

Cook time: 0 minutes

Ingredients:

4 cups romaine lettuce, chopped

2 hard-boiled eggs, chopped

6 cherry tomatoes, quartered

1 cup chopped meats (canned or fresh roasted chicken, canned chunk light tuna, or fresh roasted turkey)

½ avocado, chopped

1 small carrot, grated

¼ cup cheddar cheese, grated

½ cup cottage cheese

¼ cup sunflower seeds

¼ cup canned corn, drained and rinsed

½ cup canned kidney beans, drained and rinsed

⅓ cup extra-virgin olive oil

¼ cup red wine vinegar

½ teaspoon dried oregano

⅛ teaspoon garlic powder

1 teaspoon prepared mustard

Salt and pepper to taste, omit if desired

Directions:

1. On a platter or two large plates, place lettuce as base for salad.
2. Next, down on the center of the lettuce, place crumbled eggs. On either side of eggs, place tomatoes, then meats, avocado, carrot, and then cheeses. Sprinkle sunflower seeds, corn, and kidney beans over the top of salads.
3. In a small bowl, whisk together olive oil, red wine vinegar, dried oregano, garlic powder, and mustard. Drizzle salads with desired dressings and season adult portions with salt.

Tips: If you see your little one gagging on a food, simply remove it from the tray once your baby releases it. Avoid reacting and continue to watch them learn and explore a variety of textures.

Baby Bites:

Beginner	Novice	Advanced
Serve salad completely dissected in little mounds: 1 tablespoon cottage cheese mixed with ½ teaspoon finely grated carrot; 1 tablespoon finely chopped meat mixed with mashed avocado; 3 mashed or halved kidney beans. Omit dressing or drizzle with olive oil only.	1 tablespoon cottage cheese mixed with 1 teaspoon finely grated carrot and sunflower seeds; 1 to 2 tomato slices with a drizzle of dressing; 1 avocado spear; 4 mashed or halved kidney beans; 1 to 2 tablespoons chopped meat.	Any combination based on toddler preferences: 1 cherry tomato, quartered or chopped; 1 avocado spear; 4 halved kidney beans; 2 to 4 tablespoons chopped meat; 1 tablespoon cottage cheese mixed with sliced corn, sunflower seeds, cheddar cheese, and finely grated carrots.

*Avoid placing too much on their plates—too much food on plates can overstimulate new eaters. Don't forget to offer seconds and even thirds if needed. Enjoy your complex salad and keep it simple for the little ones.

Quinoa "Pantry" Salad

Serving size: ½ cup

Serves: 10–12 adult portions

Prep Time: 10 minutes

Cook Time: 15 minutes

Chill Time: 2 hours

Ingredients:

2 cups dried quinoa

4 cups no-salt-added chicken stock or vegetable stock or water

1 tablespoon dried oregano

1 (3.5–4-ounce) jar roasted red peppers, drained and chopped

1 (14-ounce) can artichoke hearts, drained and chopped

¼ cup drained and rinsed capers or olives

1 (4-ounce) package feta cheese crumbles

⅓ cup extra-virgin olive oil (more as desired)

⅓–½ cup parsley leaves, washed, dried, and chopped fresh

Salt and fresh cracked pepper to taste (omit for babies under 1 year)

Directions:

1. Prepare quinoa as directed using stock as your liquid (instead of water to add more protein and flavor). Once cooked, place in large mixing bowl and refrigerate for at least 1 hour.

2. Once cooled, you can mix in all the tasty stuff! Feel free to leave out anything you dislike, but the olive oil is nonnegotiable. Mix preferred ingredients and chill for 1 additional hour. Enjoy for several days. Salad can be served warm or cold and topped with any protein source you have around.

Time-saver

Once this salad is prepared, you have ample options for carryover meals. One idea could be to toss in grilled chicken or steak for an easy lunch. This salad is great warm or cold, so it's perfect for trips to the park or play groups. Miss A had a knack for tossing the little grains everywhere; therefore, Wendy Jo got smart and started mixing any small grains (like quinoa, rice, or bulgur) with hummus or mashed beans to help hold the grains together and make clean up a bit easier.

Quesadillas

Serving size: 1 quesadilla

Serves 1 adult

Prep time: 5 minutes

Cook time: 8 minutes

Ingredients:

Cooking spray

2 small corn or flour tortillas

2 tablespoons mashed black or pinto beans or refried beans

⅓ cup grated cheddar, Monterey Jack, or Colby cheese

Directions:

1. Spray an 8- or 9-inch skillet with cooking spray.
2. Spread mashed beans on one side of a tortilla.
3. Heat the skillet over medium-high. Place the other tortilla in the skillet and cook for 1 minute on one side then flip to the other side for 30 seconds. Top with grated cheese and place other tortilla on top to make a sandwich. Flip tortilla to heat the unheated side until cheese has melted inside. If needed, turn down the heat so tortillas don't get crispy.
4. Allow quesadilla to cool and cut according to eater's skill.

Variations:

- Have cooked sweet potato or pumpkin on hand? Mash up and spread thinly onto one side the tortilla.
- Cooked ground beef or turkey can be mixed into the mashed beans or melted cheese to help boost protein and iron sources.

Tips:

- This is a great food to introduce fun dips for little ones. Start off with a guacamole, mild salsa, or bean dip.
- This is also a great way to use leftover protein sources and veggies. Just add thinly sliced meat, shredded cheese, and chopped veggies to your tortilla and heat in the microwave. Slice into triangles or fingerlike strips and serve.
- Time-saver: Fold quesadilla in half with ingredients on bottom half and microwave for about 30 to 45 seconds, depending on your microwave. Let cool and slice.

BABY BITES:

Beginner	Novice	Advanced
Serve 1 pinky finger–sized slice.	Serve 1 to 2 finger slices.	Quarter quesadilla and serve 1 to 2 wedges.

Fruit Kebabs

Serves 4

Prep time: 5 minutes

Cook time: 0 minutes

Ingredients:

2 cups seasonal fruit (see chart below)
straws

Directions:

1. Wash fruits and pat dry.
2. Using hard, flexible, or stainless-steel straws (your preference) gently skewer the fruit, trying not to break up the pieces.

Tips:

- If you're struggling or worried about breaking the fruit with the straw, you can pre-poke holes using a chopstick—save them next time you order takeout!
- Check out our seasonal list of fruits in chapter 11.
- When cutting grapes for little ones, remember to cut from pole to pole, not around the equator.
- Even fruits with a rind should be washed. As you cut through the rind, the knife will contaminate the fruit unless it's washed.

Baby Bites:

Beginner	Novice	Advanced
Skip the straw kebab and stick with beginner fruits below.	Straw (easier to hold and creates a bigger hole in center to break fruit up).	Straw (continues to be best for little ones). Use a chopstick to create a hole for harder fruits.
Blueberries; strawberries; raspberries; bananas (½-inch slices); canned or frozen cherries (be sure there are no pits).	All beginner fruits + watermelon (1-inch cubes); peach wedges (½-inch slices, skins removed); plums (½-inch slices, without peel).	All beginner & novice fruits + cantaloupe (1-inch cubes); mangos (1-inch cubes); pears (½-inch slices); grapes (halved); plums (with or without peel).
Be sure fruits are ripe enough that a baby can easily gum the fruit.	Fruits should still be ripe and soft; however, your baby has more skill and knowledge on how to maneuver fruits in their mouth. At this stage, babies will spit out pieces of foods they don't want to chew.	Your skilled baby can now gum, chew, and grind up harder fruits.

Apple Cinnamon Greek Yogurt Dip

Serve: ⅔ cup

Serves 4 as a dip or 2 adult servings

Prep Time: <5 minutes

Cook Time: 0 minutes

Ingredients:

1 cup plain Greek yogurt

¼ cup applesauce

⅛ teaspoon ground cinnamon

Directions:

1. In a small bowl, thoroughly mix all ingredients.
2. Refrigerate until ready to use. Serve with fresh fruit, pancakes, or on its own.

> Time-saver:
>
> Have four small reusable containers ready. Fill each cup evenly and pop in the refrigerator for easy-to-grab portions.

Tip: This recipe makes for a perfect popsicle. Fill up a small paper cup with yogurt mix, place a straw in the center, and freeze until solid (about 4 to 6 hours). Once frozen, peel off the outer paper cup, enjoy, or store in a freezer-safe container for up to a week. They are perfect for a teething infant. There are tiny (2-ounce) paper cups, ideal for beginner eaters.

Baby Bites:

Beginner	Novice	Advanced
Perfect for all levels. Yes, this food gets messy. Load up a spoon and allow your infant to self-feed. If your baby is struggling, you can also freeze as a popsicle and let them enjoy it frozen—great for teething, too.	Appropriate for all levels.	Perfect for all levels.

Homemade Fruit Leather

Serving size: 4–5 finger slices

Servings: 2 sheet pans (~12 long rolls)

Prep time: 10 minutes

Cook time: 6–8 hours

Ingredients:

3 cups strawberries

½ cup applesauce

2 teaspoons lemon or lime juice

Directions:

1. Preheat oven to the lowest heat setting (140–170°F), best with a conventional oven setting over a convection setting, as the convection oven may dry out the mixture too fast.
2. Use a silicone baking mat or parchment paper sprayed with cooking spray on a baking sheet.
3. In a blender, blend ripe strawberries (see variations on page 217) with applesauce and lemon juice. Check for desired sweetness. Pour a thin layer onto baking pan lined with silicone or parchment paper, leaving edges free of fruit purée.
4. Bake for 6 to 8 hours or until center is no longer moist and is set.
5. Place parchment paper or plastic wrap on a cutting board. Gently, starting from the edges, lift off fruit leather and place on a fresh piece of parchment paper or plastic wrap. Using a sharp knife or pizza cutter, cut into long strips, about 6 per pan. Cut into desired serving sizes, roll up the fruit leathers, and store in an airtight container for up to 3 weeks.

Variations:

- 2 cups strawberries + 1 cup peaches + ½ cup applesauce + 2 teaspoons lemon juice
- 2 cups blackberries + 1 cup applesauce + 2 teaspoons lime juice
- 2 cups raspberries + 1½ cup pears + 2 teaspoons lemon juice

BABY BITES:

Beginner	Novice	Advanced
Avoid with beginners.	Serve 2 to 3 finger pieces.	Serve 3 to 5 finger pieces.

Greek-Inspired Salad

Serving size: 1¼ cups

Serves: 4

Prep time: 10 minutes

Cook time: 0 minutes

Dressing

¼ cup olive oil

3 tablespoons red wine vinegar

¼ teaspoon Dijon mustard

½ teaspoon dry oregano

1 small garlic clove, minced (optional)

Pinch salt and pepper

To serve

Dry oregano

Mint leaves

Plenty of fresh crusty bread

Salad

4 medium tomatoes, cut into bite-sized
    pieces

1 medium cucumber, cut into bite-
    sized pieces

½ cup kalamata olives, pitted

½ red onion, thinly slices

3 ounces feta cheese, cubed

Directions

1. Add all the dressing ingredients to a mason jar. Feel free to add less garlic or avoid altogether. Ask your child to do the shaking part and watch the ingredients to mix.

2. Add the tomatoes, cucumber, olives, and onion to a salad bowl, mix together, then add the feta cheese and the dressing, before giving it one extra stir.

3. Ask the kids to add extra oregano or mint to their bowls. Don't forget to mop the juices with bread.

4. The salad makes a fantastic deconstructed dish for the whole family. You can serve all the ingredients separately on a chopping board, with the dressing on the side, and invite everyone to build their own plate.

Baby Bites:

Beginner	Novice	Advanced
Make the dressing and grate the raw vegetables with a Microplane. This provides the flavors of raw vegetables without the risk of choking while they explore the raw vegetables.	Serve the tomatoes and olives quartered. Finely dice cucumber or grate cucumber into salad. Serve with thin slices of toasted baguette.	Serve salad mixed or allow child to select which items they want on their plate. Continue to ensure the vegetables are age-appropriate bite sizes.

Recipe contributed by Natalia Stasenko, RD, Feeding Expert, and Founder of the Easy Bites App.

Iron-Rich Lentil Salad

Serving size: ¾ cup

Serves: 4–6

Prep time: 15 minutes

Cook time: 20 minutes

Ingredients

¾ cups dry or 2 cups cooked French (or Puy) lentils

1 small red onion, sliced very thinly

Juice of ½ lemon

Zest of ½ lemon

2 tablespoons olive oil

¼ teaspoon salt

1 garlic clove, minced

1 cup cherry tomatoes, halved

3 ounces feta cheese, crumbled

2 tablespoons cilantro, chopped

Directions

1. If starting with dry lentils, cook them according to the package instructions. Drain and cool until slightly warm to the touch.

2. Meanwhile, place the sliced red onion into a small bowl and pour the lemon juice over it. Leave to marinate for 10 to 15 minutes.

3. Add the lemon zest, olive oil, salt, and garlic to the onion and mix everything together. Pour the mixture over the lentils when they are still warm and stir to combine.

4. The salad can be prepped to this point and kept in the refrigerator up to 5 days. Make sure to bring it to room temperature before mixing in the rest of the ingredients and serving.

5. Add the tomatoes, feta cheese, and cilantro to the lentils, mix well, and serve.

6. To deconstruct, serve the lentils with the dressing in a salad bowl and the rest of the ingredients on a chopping board. Ask everyone to assemble their own salad on their plates.

Baby Bites:

Beginner	Novice	Advanced
Grate the onion and tomatoes with a Microplane. Serve on a loaded spoon.	Quarter tomatoes. Finely dice cucumber or grate cucumber into salad. Serve thin slices of toasted baguette.	Serve family-style and allow child to indicate which foods they want and have them serve themselves with assistance.

Recipe contributed by Natalia Stasenko, RD, Feeding Expert, and Founder of the Easy Bites App.

Deconstructed Taco Salad

Serving size: 2 cups

Servings: 4

Prep time: 10 minutes

Cook time: 10 minutes

Ingredients

1 pound ground beef

1 teaspoon cumin powder

1 teaspoon dried oregano

1 teaspoon garlic powder

½ teaspoon onion powder

2 tablespoons chili powder

½ teaspoon salt

8 cups chopped or torn romaine lettuce

2 cups broken tortilla or corn chips

1 cup shredded red cabbage

1 can black beans, drained and rinsed

1 Hass avocado, diced

1 cup cherry or grape tomatoes, halved

½ red onion, thinly sliced

2 cups shredded cheddar cheese or Monterey Jack

1 lime, juiced

2 tablespoons extra-virgin olive oil

½ cup Greek yogurt or sour cream

4 tablespoons hot sauce, optional

Directions

1. In a large skillet, cook the ground beef over medium-high for 5 minutes. Add cumin, garlic powder, dried oregano, onion powder, chili powder, and salt to the cooking meat. Then continue cooking until the meat mixture is browned and fully cooked, about 5 more minutes.

2. The salad can be served as a layered salad or served at the table family-style, allowing family members to serve themselves and create their own desired version. To serve the salad as a layered salad, place the lettuce at the base of a salad bowl. Top with the tortilla chips, cabbage, black beans, avocado, tomatoes, onion, and shredded cheese. Place the cooked meat on top of the salad. See Baby Bites below for notes about chips and infants.

3. In a small bowl, make the dressing. Whisk together the lime juice, olive oil, Greek yogurt or sour cream, and hot sauce. Drizzle the dressing over the top or allow people to dress their own salad as desired.

Tips: Save time by purchasing preshredded lettuce, cabbage and cheese.

Note: Chips pose a choking hazard for infants and small children. Finely crush chips and stir into meat mixture to soften tortilla chips or serve a finger piece of a corn tortilla instead.

Baby Bites:

Beginner	Novice	Advanced
Serve 1 teaspoon ground beef with a mashed bean, finely chopped cabbage, an avocado finger (make sure this avocado is easy to smash before serving), and top with 1 teaspoon dressing. Allow infant to palm food and look for cues that your infant wants more.	Serve 1 tablespoon ground beef along with 1 avocado finger (ensuring it is easy to mash), 1 tablespoon mashable beans, quartered cherry or grape tomatoes, grated cheese, and top with dressing.	Serve family-style and allow child to indicate which foods they want and have them serve themselves with assistance.

French-Inspired Canned Tuna Salad

Serving size: 2 cups

Serves: 4

Prep time: 15 minutes

Cook time: 30 minutes

Ingredients

6 small new potatoes, quartered

3 teaspoons sea salt, divided

2 cups green beans, trimmed

1 lemon, juiced

3 tablespoons white wine vinegar

1 tablespoon Dijon mustard

½ cup extra-virgin olive oil

½ teaspoon pepper

6 cups torn romaine lettuce

1 cup grape tomatoes, halved or quartered

½ English cucumber, sliced thinly

4 hardboiled eggs, grated or thinly sliced

1 cup mixed, pitted olives, chopped

1 (16-ounce) can or package chunk light tuna, drained

Directions

1. In a medium saucepan, place the cut potatoes and fill with water, just to cover the potatoes. Season the water with 1 teaspoon of the sea salt. Place the pot over high heat and bring to a boil. Then cover the potatoes and reduce the heat to a simmer. Simmer until the potatoes are fork-tender, about 15 to 20 minutes. Drain and set aside.

2. In a medium saucepan, bring 4 cups of water with 1 teaspoon of the salt to a boil. Add the green beans, and parboil for 5 to 10 minutes, based on desired texture. Drain and immediately submerge the green beans in ice water for 1 minute. Drain and set aside.

3. Make the lemon vinaigrette. In a small bowl, whisk together the lemon juice, vinegar, mustard, olive oil, the remaining 1 teaspoon of sea salt, and pepper. Add potatoes and green beans to the dressing and toss to coat.

4. Serve family-style or to assemble the salad, place the lettuce on a large serving platter. Top with the potatoes, green beans, tomatoes, cucumbers, grated eggs, olives, and tuna. Drizzle remaining lemon vinaigrette over the top.

Baby Bites:

Beginner	Novice	Advanced
Fork-mash potato wedge with dressing and add grated egg and tuna on top. Serve with a very soft green bean and tomato wedge with dressing over the top, as well.	Serve a finely chopped potato wedge with dressing and add grated egg and tuna on top. Serve with a very soft green bean, cucumber spear, and tomato wedge with dressing over the top, as well. Finely dice softened vegetables if infant is doing well with pincer grasp.	Allow child to indicate which foods they want and have them serve themselves. Cut into small, bite-sized pieces and serve with dressing over the top. Chiffonade lettuce for easy serving.

Beefy Korean Bowls

Serving size: 2 cups

Servings: 4

Prep time: 10 minutes

Cook time: 20 minutes

Ingredients

2 cups water

1 cup basmati or jasmine rice, rinsed

1 pound ground beef

2 teaspoons brown sugar

2 tablespoons low-sodium soy sauce

2 garlic cloves, minced

¼ teaspoon ground ginger

3 tablespoons sesame seeds

2 carrots, grated

1 English cucumber, thinly sliced

2 scallions, thinly sliced

2 cups finely grated cabbage

½ cup Greek yogurt

1 lime, zested and juiced

Sriracha to taste (optional)

Directions

1. In a medium saucepan, bring the water to a boil over high heat. Stir in the rice, cover, and reduce the heat to a simmer until cooked, about 15 to 20 minutes.

2. Meanwhile, in a large skillet, add the ground beef, brown sugar, soy sauce, garlic, and ginger. Cook over medium heat until browned and completely cooked, about 10 minutes. Stir in the sesame seeds and remove from heat.

3. To assemble, divide the rice among 4 bowls. Divide the ground meat and sauce on top of the rice. Top with grated carrots, cucumbers, scallions, and grated cabbage.

4. In a small bowl, whisk together, Greek yogurt, lime zest, lime juice, and sriracha based on taste preference. Drizzle creamy sauce over the top and serve.

BABY BITES:

Beginner	Novice	Advanced
Serve 1 to 2 teaspoons of rice mixed with ground beef, grated carrot, and grated raw cucumber. Drizzle the sauce over the top, if desired.	Serve rice with beef, grated carrots, finely shredded cabbage, and thin spears of cucumbers with sauce to dip or for on top.	Allow child to indicate which foods they want in their beef bowl and have them serve themselves with assistance. Continue to grate carrots and cut raw vegetables into small, bite-sized pieces with sauce on the side for dipping or on top.

CHAPTER 17

FAMILY DINNERS

> "When the joy goes out of eating, nutrition suffers."
>
> —Ellyn Satter, MS, RDN, MSSW

If people sit and think about what their family meal looked like growing up, and not just the food, a variety of memories come flooding back. They remember slipping food to the dog, fighting with their sister at the dinner table, eating on the way to soccer practice, or the family's favorite meal. Whether we sat at the kitchen table, in the back seat of the car, in front of the television, or in front of fancy menu items we couldn't pronounce, the memory of whatever the family meal was creates a lasting impression.

The family dinner table isn't the place for food battles or stressful conversations. It's about sharing memories of the day, giving thanks for the food on the plate, and savoring one of the few precious moments of calm in a day. Wendy Jo grew up with a strict dinner regimen that involved finishing the plate (or sitting there all night until you did), setting a proper place setting, asking to be excused, using cloth napkins, using utensils correctly, and so forth. Needless to say, there are aspects of the family dinner table we choose to keep and those we choose to lose. Her fondest memories included using cloth napkins, saying grace, and hearing about the exciting things her sisters had done throughout the day, and, of course, her mom's fried chicken or spaghetti with meat sauce.

We remember what dinner was like in our families decades later. Leslie remembers sitting down at the kitchen table with her family (and dog) most nights of the week. She remembers favorite dinners of chili, spaghetti with a side salad, beef Stroganoff, and chicken pot pies. While her parents cooked a couple nights a week, there were many evenings when brinner (breakfast for dinner) or leftovers hit the table. Luckily, besides the food, one of her fondest memories include her dad's jokes. Sometimes they were so ridiculously not funny, she couldn't help but laugh.

We thought long and hard about this chapter. We wanted to come up with simple meals for busy families. This chapter is packed with easy carryover main dishes, combo meals that are freezer friendly, simple sides, and a helpful vegetable roasting guide.

This chapter includes:

Main Dishes

Rotisserie Four Ways

No formal recipe is needed with a rotisserie chicken. Just pick up a rotisserie chicken at your local market and toss these meals together. If you're not feeling like a rotisserie bird (some come "naked" with little to no seasoning), don't forget the slow-cooker roasted chicken recipe we have in chapter 14. We've got you covered.

BABY BITES:

Beginner	Novice	Advanced
Deconstruct meal by placing meat separate from grain and vegetables. Ensure vegetables are mash-able and chicken is shredded into tiny bites. Tender pasta is okay at this stage.	You can deconstruct or keep meal whole based on skill readiness. Cut items into tiny, bite-sized pieces.	Serve as you would for the whole family, and cut into bite-sized pieces.

Continued on page 232

How We Dish It	Lemon Chicken & Veggie Penne Pasta	BBQ Chicken Pizza	Chicken & Veggie Stir-Fry	Basic Chicken Noodle Soup
What You Need	¼ cup olive oil 1 medium zucchini 1 small onion 8 ounces mushrooms 8 ounces cooked penne pasta 1 lemon Parmesan, to taste Salt and pepper, to taste	½ cup BBQ sauce 2 pita breads ¼ bell peppers, sliced ¼ onion, sliced ½ cup shredded mozzarella cheese	2 teaspoons sesame oil 1 teaspoon canola oil 1 (12-oz.) bag frozen stir-fry vegetables 1 teaspoon soy sauce 2 teaspoons sesame seeds (optional) 2 cups cooked rice or quinoa	6 cups chicken stock or broth 12–16 ounce bag of mixed veggies 6 ounces small, dried pasta ½ teaspoon ground black pepper 1 tablespoon dried parsley Fresh grated Parmesan (optional)
Simple Directions	Sauté zucchini, onion, and mushrooms in olive oil. Add the juice of one lemon. Mix all ingredients together and add grated Parmesan and salt and pepper to taste.	Preheat your oven to 425°F. Chop up your chicken meat. Mix with your preferred BBQ sauce. Place on top of a tortilla or pita. Top with shredded cheese and sliced bell peppers. Pop in the oven for 8 to 10 minutes until crisp.	Heat a medium skillet with oils over high heat, then add in stir-fry vegetables and chicken, and cook for 5 to 8 minutes or until cooked through. Season with soy sauce and sesame seeds and serve over cooked rice or quinoa.	Place stock, vegetables, and pasta into a large stockpot. Bring mixture to a boil over high heat and cook until pasta is tender (see package for times). Once the pasta is ready, reduce heat to low and throw in some chicken, ground black pepper, and dried parsley. Serve with grated Parmesan cheese.

Porcupine Meatballs

Serving size: 8–10 meatballs

Serves: 4 adult portions

Prep time: 10 minutes

Cook time: 40 minutes

Ingredients:

1 pound ground beef

½ cup leftover cooked rice (or leftover cooked quinoa)

½ small onion, finely chopped

1 small carrot, grated

1 small zucchini, grated

1 teaspoon salt, or omit if desired

2 garlic cloves, minced

1 egg

2 cups tomato juice

½ teaspoon cinnamon

½ teaspoon coriander

2 tablespoons sugar

2 tablespoons Worcestershire sauce

Directions:

1. In a large bowl, combine the meat, rice, onion, carrot, zucchini, salt, garlic, and egg. Shape the mixture into small balls, about 1 inch wide.
2. In a deep skillet over medium-high heat, whisk together the tomato juice, cinnamon, coriander, sugar, and Worcestershire sauce.
3. Add meatballs to skillet and simmer for 30 to 40 minutes until meatballs are cooked through. Flip meatballs occasionally and braise with liquid.

Variations:

- The meatball mixture is perfect to make into meat loaf muffin cups, too! Ditch the sauce and instead make up the meat mixture, divide into 12 muffin cups, and top with a squirt of ketchup before baking. Bake for 25 minutes or until meat is cooked thoroughly, 160°F.

Continued on page 234

Freezer Options:

- These are perfect for the freezer, too! Make a batch, cool completely after cooking, and then put into a freezer-safe container for up to 2 months. To reheat, place frozen contents in a skillet, cover, and cook over medium heat until meatball temperatures reach 165°F, about 25 minutes. Add water if the sauce gets too thick.

Baby Bites:

Beginner	Novice	Advanced
Mash up a meatball with ample sauce.	Serve 2 to 3 meatballs chopped up into bite-sized pieces with sauce.	Serve 3 to 5 meatballs with sauce, cut in half or quartered.

Easy Chili

Serving size: ~2 cups

Serves: 12 adult portions

Prep time: 10 minutes

Cook time: 45 minutes or 6–8 hours with a slow cooker

Ingredients:

2 pounds ground beef

2–4 tablespoons chili powder, based on preference

1 tablespoon garlic powder

2 teaspoons onion powder (or ½ medium onion, chopped)

1 teaspoon cumin powder

2 (14½-ounce) cans pinto beans, drained and rinsed

2 (14½-ounce) cans kidney beans, drained and rinsed

2 (14½-ounce) cans diced tomatoes

Fun Toppings:

Sour cream

Shredded cheese

Scallions

Directions:

1. In a large stockpot or Dutch oven, brown meat over medium-high heat until completely cooked, about 12 minutes. Once the meat is cooked through, add seasonings to meat and cook for 1 minute.

2. If you want to use the slow cooker, transfer the meat now, add remaining ingredients, and cook on low heat for 6 to 8 hours. Otherwise, just add it all in the pot. Open all of your cans—chili beans, kidney beans, and tomatoes. Don't forget to drain and rinse beans. Dump beans and tomatoes into pot. Bring pot to a low boil over medium-high heat, then drop temperature to low and simmer for at least 45 minutes.

3. Serve chili with or without toppings.

Continued on page 236

Freezer Options:

- Chili is perfect for the freezer. Allow chili to cool completely then place into freezer-safe containers and freeze up to 3 months. Reheat mixture on the stove top until chili reheats to 165°F or in the microwave (time based on your microwave power).

BABY BITES:

Beginner	Novice	Advanced
Mash beans and cut up ground beef into tiny bites. Be sure to check tomatoes for tenderness. Help infant by loading a spoon.	Cut beans in half and cut up ground beef into small bites. Be sure to check tomatoes, too, for tenderness. Help infant by loading a spoon.	Cut beans in half and ensure ground beef is in bite-sized pieces. Serve chili with a spoon.

Single-Crust Chicken Pot Pie

Serving size: ¹⁄₆ pot pie

Serves: 6 adult portions

Prep time: 10 minutes

Cook time: 1 hour

Ingredients:

1 refrigerator-ready piecrust dough

1 pound boneless, skinless chicken breast

6 medium new potatoes, chopped

2 medium carrots, sliced in half lengthwise and thinly sliced into half-moons

1 large celery stalk, chopped small

1 tablespoon chicken stock base plus 4 cups cold water or 4 cups chicken stock

¼ cup unsalted butter

¼ cup onion, chopped

¼ cup all-purpose flour

1 teaspoon salt

¼ teaspoon black pepper

½ teaspoon dried thyme

½ teaspoon garlic powder

1 cup frozen peas

⅔ cup whole milk

Directions:

1. Spray a 9-inch-deep dish pie pan or round casserole dish with cooking spray.
2. In a 4-quart stockpot, combine chicken, potatoes, carrots, and celery. Pour 4 cups cold water over chicken and veggies and stir in chicken base (don't worry about dissolving, it will). Turn burner on high heat. Once mixture comes to a boil, turn down to low, cover, and simmer for 12 minutes.
3. Preheat oven to 425°F.
4. Strain chicken and vegetables, reserving 1¾ cups of the stock (this will be used in the gravy sauce). Chop chicken into bite-sized pieces.
5. Next, in a large skillet, melt butter over medium heat then sauté onion for 3 minutes. Using a whisk, add in the flour to make the roux. Let the mixture cook over medium-low heat for 3 minutes or until golden brown in color. Using reserved liquid, whisk in stock to make a gravy. Add in chopped chicken and vegetables

Continued on page 238

and stir. Add in seasonings (salt, pepper, thyme, and garlic powder). Stir in frozen peas and milk. Heat mixture for 3 minutes.

6. Pour gravy into prepared dish and top with premade pie crust. Crimp the edges and cut 5 slit marks on the top as vents for the steam while baking.

7. Cover the pan with foil and bake for 15 minutes. Remove foil and continue baking for 20 minutes or until crust is golden.

Freezer Options:

- Double this recipe and make two! One to eat now and one for the freezer. Consider using a disposable pan for the freezer pie. Once pot pie has cooled completely, cover in plastic wrap and then foil, and freeze up to 2 months. To bake, pull out of freezer and bake at 375°F for 1 hour or until internal temperature reaches 165°F. If crust gets to golden before inside is heated, simply cover with foil and continue baking.

BABY BITES:

Beginner	Novice	Advanced
Cut peas in half, chop or mash potatoes in gravy, and shred any chicken cubes. Ensure carrots and celery are tender. Place 2 to 3 tablespoons on tray. Omit crust so baby fills up on higher protein and nutrient-dense foods first.	Cut peas in half, chop potatoes in bite-sized pieces, shred chicken in gravy, and ensure carrots and celery are tender. Place ¼ cup on tray and help infant with loaded spoons. Crust or no crust, parent discretion.	Cut peas in half, chop potatoes in bite-sized pieces, and cover small chunks of chicken in gravy. Ensure carrots and celery are tender. Serve in a bowl with spoon.

Chicken Enchilada Bake

Serving size: ⅛ of pan

Servings: 8 adult portions

Prep time: 10 minutes

Cook time: 40 minutes

Ingredients:

3 pounds boneless, skinless chicken breast, cubed

2 tablespoons extra-virgin olive oil

12 taco-sized corn tortillas

1 (8-ounce) package cream cheese

1 cup sour cream

4 Roma tomatoes, chopped

Salt

Pepper

1 tablespoon taco seasoning

1 (15½-ounce) can enchilada sauce

8 ounces cheese of choice (Colby Jack, cheddar or Monterey Jack), shredded

1 (4-ounce) can sliced black olives, drained and rinsed (optional)

½ cup fresh cilantro, chopped (optional)

Directions:

1. Preheat oven to 350°F.

2. In a large skillet, heat olive oil over medium heat. Next, add the cubed chicken and cook completely, about 8 to 10 minutes. While the chicken is cooking, spray a 9 x 13-inch dish with nonstick spray. Using a pizza cutter, cut tortillas in half and then in half again. They should be quartered. Use half the tortillas to cover the bottom of the pan. When the chicken is cooked, remove from heat and add cream cheese, sour cream, salt, pepper, chopped tomatoes, and taco seasoning into the warm skillet. Stir thoroughly until the cream cheese and sour cream have been completely mixed. Pour the chicken mixture over the tortillas. Use the remaining tortillas to layer over the chicken mixture.

3. Pour all of the enchilada sauce evenly over the top. Cover with shredded cheese then garnish with olives if desired.

4. Bake casserole uncovered for 25 to 30 minutes. Remove from oven and let it set for 5 to 10 minutes. Top casserole with fresh chopped cilantro (optional) and serve with a heaping plate of vegetables.

Continued on page 240

Variations:

- Ground beef or leftover roasted turkey can be used instead of chicken in this recipe.

Freezer Options:

- Allow casserole to cool. Cover casserole with plastic wrap and foil to avoid freezer burn. Casserole can be frozen up to 3 months. To reheat, bake casserole at 400°F for 45 to 60 minutes right out of freezer or until sauce is bubbling. Internal temperature should measure 165°F for serving.

Baby Bites:

Beginner	Novice	Advanced
Pull out chicken pieces and shred finely with a little gravy or a dollop of Greek yogurt. Serve with an avocado wedge and thin tomato slices.	Chop up casserole into tiny bites and serve with a loaded spoon. Serve with an avocado wedge and tomato slices.	Chop up casserole into small bites and serve with a spoon or fork. Serve with a side of vegetables.

Simple Shepherd's Pie

Serving size: 1½ cups

Servings: 4 adult portions

Prep time: 10 minutes

Cook time: 55 minutes

Ingredients:

2 medium potatoes or 6 new potatoes, scrubbed

4 ounces cream cheese

¼ cup whole milk

Salt and pepper, to taste

1 tablespoon olive oil

½ medium onion, chopped small

2 medium carrots, chopped small

1 pound ground beef or lamb

1 tablespoon Worcestershire sauce

1 tablespoon tomato paste or ketchup

1 cup frozen peas

1 cup frozen cut green beans

½ teaspoon salt, or omit if desired

½ teaspoon ground black pepper

Directions:

1. Preheat oven to 400°F.
2. Cut potatoes into large chunks or leave new potatoes whole. In a large stockpot, cover potatoes with cold water and bring to a boil over high heat. Once at a boil, turn heat down to low, cover, and simmer for 12 to 14 minutes or until fork-tender. Drain potatoes and mash with cream cheese and milk. Season with salt and pepper to taste.
3. Next, in a Dutch oven or large skillet, heat olive oil over medium-high heat. Add in onion and carrots and sauté for 3 minutes. Add in ground meat and cook until done, about 12 minutes. Add in Worcestershire sauce, tomato paste, frozen vegetables, salt, and pepper. Cook mixture for 5 minutes over medium heat.
4. Place cooked meat into a 9x9-inch casserole dish. Top meat mixture with potato mixture evenly. Bake shepherd's pie for 25 minutes.

Variations:

- Top off the potato mixture with grated cheddar cheese for a cheesy version.
- Skip the tomato paste and Worcestershire sauce and replace with 1 cup salsa for a quick Mexican-style shepherd's pie.

Continued on page 242

Freezer Options:

- To freeze, bake in disposable bread pans or double the batch depending on your family size. No need to bake the one going into the freezer! Simply assemble, cool completely, and cover with plastic wrap before freezing. Shepherd's pie can be frozen for up to 2 months. When you are ready to bake, remove plastic wrap, heat your oven to 350°F, and bake for 1 hour or until heated thoroughly through to a 165°F internal temperature.

Baby Bites:

Beginner	Novice	Advanced
Dissect shepherd's pie into potatoes, sliced peas, mashed green beans, and saucy meat mixture. Ensure all vegetables are easy to mash.	Dissect or keep as a casserole. Ensure peas are split and green beans are in tiny, bite-sized pieces. Serve with a loaded spoon.	Split peas in half and cut vegetables into bite-sized pieces before serving with a spoon.

Poblano Chicken and Zucchini

Serving size: 2 cups

Servings: 6

Prep time: About 15 minutes

Cook time: 20 minutes

Ingredients

2 medium sweet potatoes, peeled

4 boneless, skinless chicken breasts, cut
  into 3-inch strips

2 poblano peppers

2 cloves garlic

3 medium zucchini

½ teaspoon ground cumin

½ teaspoon paprika

½ teaspoon ground coriander

1½ teaspoons sea salt, divided

½ teaspoon black pepper

2 tablespoons extra-virgin olive oil

2 tablespoons butter

2 tablespoons all-purpose flour

1 cup sour cream or plain Greek yogurt

¼ cup cilantro or parsley

1 lime, zested and juiced

Directions

1. Preheat the oven to 450°F. Line a baking sheet with parchment paper.

2. Cut the sweet potatoes in 3-inch finger-length pieces. Place potatoes in a micro-wave-safe bowl and cover with water. Microwave on high for 6 minutes. Drain the sweet potatoes with a strainer and set aside.

3. Meanwhile, place the cut chicken breasts on half of the parchment paper. In the center, place the peppers (whole) and the garlic.

4. Slice the zucchini in half lengthwise, and then cut into 2-inch pieces. Place the zucchini on the other side of the parchment paper. Place the sweet potatoes on the sheet pan with the zucchini.

5. In a small bowl, mix the paprika, cumin powder, coriander, 1 teaspoon of the salt, and the pepper. Sprinkle the food with the spice mixture, and drizzle with the olive oil. Give the food a little stir to fully coat with oil and spices. Bake for 20 minutes. After 10 minutes, place a piece of foil over the vegetables to steam roast, creating a more tender vegetable with roasted flavors.

Continued on page 244

6. Next, in a small saucepan or skillet, heat the butter and flour over medium heat until lightly golden, about 3 minutes, stirring occasionally. While stirring, add the sour cream and allow the mixture to bubble for 1 minute. Then remove from the heat.

7. Remove the pan from the oven. Place the chicken, sweet potatoes, and zucchini on a serving platter.

8. Remove the stems from the poblano peppers. Place the peppers, garlic, the remaining ½ teaspoon of salt, the pan drippings from the sheet pan (chicken broth juices), and the thickened cream in a blender; pulse until smooth. Add the cilantro, lime zest, and lime juice, and blend for 30 seconds or until smooth. Serve the sauce over the chicken and vegetables or on the side for dipping.

BABY BITES:

Beginner	Novice	Advanced
Shred the chicken and mix with mashed sweet potato and the sauce. Serve on a loaded spoon or allow infant to palm feed. Check that zucchini is easy to mash and serve as finger-sized pieces for easy handling. Serve with sauce over the food.	Cut into pincer-appropriate pieces for easy handling. Serve 1 to 3 pieces of chicken and 1 finger of each vegetable with sauce over the top or on the side for dipping. Replenish as infant indicates a desire for more food. Shred chicken and serve in sauce if infant struggles with chewing meat.	Skip the steam roasting step, as an advanced eater can handle chewier pieces of vegetables. Serve family-style and allow child to indicate which foods they want and have them serve themselves with assistance. Cut into small, bite-sized pieces with sauce over the top or on the side for dipping.

Curried Mini Meat Loaves with Cauliflower

Serving size: 2 cups

Servings: 6

Prep time: About 10 minutes

Cook time: 25 minutes

Ingredients

1½ pounds ground beef

2 eggs, whisked

½ cup whole wheat panko bread crumbs

3 teaspoons curry powder, divided

1 teaspoon sea salt, divided

½ cup ketchup

½ head cauliflower, cut into bite-sized pieces

1 teaspoon ground cumin

¼ cup red wine vinegar

1 teaspoon black pepper

½ teaspoon turmeric

3 tablespoons extra-virgin olive oil

Directions

1. Preheat the oven to 400°F. Line a baking sheet with parchment paper.

2. In a large bowl, mix the ground beef, eggs, bread crumbs, 2 teaspoons of curry powder, and ½ teaspoon of salt. Form into 12 rounds or use a muffin pan for baking. In a small bowl, whisk together ketchup and ½ teaspoon curry powder. Top each loaf with curried ketchup.

3. In another bowl, mix the cauliflower, the remaining ½ teaspoon of curry powder, cumin, red wine vinegar, pepper, turmeric, and olive oil. Place the cauliflower on the sheet pan. Place both pans into the oven.

4. Bake until the meat reaches an internal temperature of 160°F, about 20 to 25 minutes. After about 10 minutes of baking, cover the cauliflower with a sheet of foil to steam roast for the remaining time. The cauliflower should be golden and toasted, but not blackened. The cauliflower should be fork-tender.

Continued on page 246

Baby Bites:

Beginner	Novice	Advanced
Crumble small pieces of the meatloaves and top with ketchup for a sauce. Check that cauliflower can be mashed with ease or mash with the meat loaf and load on a spoon for an infant to self-feed.	Cut meat loaf into finger pieces or small, bite-sized crumbles. Serve with ketchup on top or on the side for dipping. Serve 2 to 3 pieces of cauliflower cut into small, bite-sized pieces—still easy to mash.	Skip the steam roasting step, as an advanced eater can handle chewier pieces of vegetables. Serve family-style and allow child to indicate which foods they want and have them serve themselves with assistance. Cut into small, bite-sized pieces with ketchup over the top or on the side for dipping.

Butter Chicken

Serving size: 1½ cups

Servings: 6

Prep time: 10 minutes

Cook time: 25 minutes–6 hours

Ingredients

6 (about 1½ pounds) boneless, skinless chicken thighs, cut into bite-sized pieces

1 cup tomato sauce

3 cloves garlic, chopped

1 teaspoon ground ginger

1 teaspoon ground turmeric

1 teaspoon ground cumin

1 teaspoon paprika

1 teaspoon garam masala

1 teaspoon sea salt

½ teaspoon black pepper

1 cup chicken broth

1 cup full-fat plain yogurt (4–5% fat)

¼ cup cubed unsalted butter

½ cup chopped cilantro or parsley (optional)

Directions

1. Place the chicken, tomato sauce, garlic, ginger, turmeric, cumin, paprika, garam masala, salt, and pepper into the base of a multicooker or slow cooker. Add chicken broth into the insert of a multicooker or slow cooker.

2. In a pressure cooker, select high pressure for 10 minutes and naturally release for 10 minutes. Stir in yogurt and butter and top with cilantro before serving. In a slow cooker, cook for 6 to 8 hours on low, then stir in yogurt, butter, and cilantro before serving.

3. Serve with steamed rice, sautéed spinach, and flatbread.

Baby Bites:

Beginner	Novice	Advanced
Shred pieces of chicken and serve on a loaded spoon. Serve with steamed rice formed into fingers and finely minced, cooked spinach.	Cut chicken into small, bite-sized pieces with sauce. Serve sauce over rice and cut cooked spinach.	Serve family-style, allowing the child to select which items they want and serve sauce for dipping or over the top.

Creamy Peanut Chicken

Serving sizes: 1½ cups

Servings: 6

Prep time: About 5 minutes

Cook time: 20 minutes–6 hours

Ingredients

4 boneless, skinless chicken breasts or chicken thighs

1 cup coconut milk

½ cup creamy peanut butter

1 teaspoon garlic powder

1 tablespoon soy sauce

1 teaspoon ground ginger

1 cup chicken broth

3 tablespoons cornstarch

3 tablespoons cold water

½ lime, juiced, or 1 tablespoon rice wine vinegar

1 cup finely chopped peanuts

Directions

1. **If using a pressure cooker,** add the chicken, coconut milk, peanut butter, garlic powder, soy sauce, ginger, and broth. Stir to mix the ingredients together, working to break up the peanut butter. Secure the lid. Pressure cook on high for 10 minutes. Allow the pot to naturally release for at least 10 minutes. **If using a slow cooker,** place the chicken, coconut milk, peanut butter, garlic powder, soy sauce, ginger, and broth into slow cooker. Secure the lid and cook on low for 6 hours.

2. In a small bowl, stir together the cornstarch and water; stir into the sauce, along with the lime juice or vinegar. Top with the chopped peanuts. Serve immediately or hold warm until ready to serve.

Note: Use full-fat coconut milk from a can, not from a refrigerated carton, as these are very different products.

Tip: Serve with steamed rice and steamed vegetables.

BABY BITES:

Beginner	Novice	Advanced
Shred a teaspoon of chicken with sauce and serve on a loaded spoon with a piece of steamed or mashed vegetables and rice.	Mix steamed rice, shredded chicken, and peanut sauce and serve 1 to 2 tablespoons at a time, reading your infant's cues if they want more food. Serve steamed soft vegetables in small, bite-sized pieces.	Serve family-style and allow child to indicate which foods they want and have them serve themselves with assistance. Cut the chicken into small, bite-sized pieces with rice and vegetables in bite-sized pieces.

Chicken Cacciatore

Serving size: 2 cups

Servings: 8

Prep time: About 10 minutes

Cook time: 25 minutes–6 hours

Ingredients

6 skinless, boneless chicken breasts, cubed

½ teaspoon salt

½ teaspoon black pepper

1 tablespoon dried oregano

2 tablespoons extra-virgin olive oil

2 large bell peppers, chopped (any color)

1 onion, chopped

6 cloves garlic, chopped

¼ cup capers, drained and rinsed

½ cup white wine

1 teaspoon paprika

1 (28-ounce) can diced tomatoes

1 cup chicken broth

½ cup chopped, fresh parsley or basil

½ cup grated Parmesan cheese

Directions

1. In a gallon-sized freezer bag, place the chicken, salt, pepper, oregano, olive oil, bell peppers, onion, garlic, capers, white wine, paprika, and tomatoes. If you'll be using a pressure cooker, place the bag in a bowl that will fit in your cooker, and then place the bowl in the freezer. If you'll be using a slow cooker, you can freeze the bag flat. Freeze up to 3 months.

2. If using a pressure cooker, place the chicken, salt, pepper, oregano, olive oil, bell peppers, onion, garlic, capers, white wine, tomatoes, paprika, chicken broth in the cooker. Secure the lid and set pressure cooker to cook on high for 12 minutes. Allow the pressure to release naturally for at least 10 minutes, then do a quick release. If using a slow cooker, Place the chicken, salt, pepper, oregano, olive oil,

bell peppers, onion, garlic, capers, white wine, tomatoes, and chicken broth in the slow cooker and secure the lid. Set slow cooker for 6 hours on low.

3. Top with the chopped parsley or basil. Serve immediately with the grated Parmesan.

Tip: Serve with pasta or mashed potatoes.

Baby Bites:

Beginner	Novice	Advanced
Shred a teaspoon of chicken with sauce and peppers and serve on a loaded spoon with a strand of pasta or thinned mashed potatoes. Stir sauce into mashed potatoes to thin the consistency. Thick mashed potatoes can be a choking risk. Allow infant to palm and scoop mashed potatoes.	Serve tiny, bite-sized pieces of chicken with sauce and saucy mashed potatoes or pasta.	Serve family-style and allow child to indicate which foods they want and have them serve themselves with assistance. Cut chicken into small, bite-sized pieces with sauce and pasta or mashed potatoes.

Cream of Turkey with Biscuits

Serving size: 2 cups

Servings: 4–6

Prep time: 5 minutes

Cook time: 20 minutes

Ingredients

1 (16-ounce) can biscuits or 8 frozen biscuits

1 tablespoon extra-virgin olive oil

2 tablespoons butter

½ small onion, minced

1 celery stalk, finely diced

1 green bell pepper, finely diced or grated

⅓ cup flour

2½ cups turkey or chicken broth

½ cup heavy cream or half-and-half

3 cups chopped, cooked turkey (or chicken)

Salt to taste

Pepper to taste

Directions

1. Preheat the oven and bake the biscuits according to package directions.

2. In a heavy skillet or Dutch oven, heat the olive oil and butter over medium-high heat. Add the onion, celery, and bell pepper. Cook for 5 minutes, stirring frequently.

3. Add in the flour, stirring to toast or lightly brown the flour for 2 to 3 minutes.

4. Whisk in the broth and cream and reduce the heat to simmer for 10 minutes until sauce thickens. For picky eaters or beginner infants, consider blending the sauce with a stick blender or in a traditional blender.

5. Stir in the chopped turkey and season with salt and pepper.

6. Cut the biscuits in half to open them; then ladle the cream of turkey over the top to serve.

Tip: Save your sanity by using time-saving convenience foods like premade biscuits. If you prefer a homemade biscuit, they can absolutely be used, too!

BABY BITES:

Beginner	Novice	Advanced
Blend sauce before adding in turkey. Finely chop cream of turkey and serve on a loaded spoon. Serve biscuit fingers, if desired, but not necessary at this skill level or age.	Serve biscuits cut into fingerlike strips with cream of turkey over the top. Check to see that vegetables and turkey are easy to mash with a fork.	Allow child to indicate how they'd like to be served the dish, either to dip the biscuit into the sauce or with the biscuit smothered. Cut into small, bite-sized pieces.

Old-Fashioned Chicken Dumplings

Serving size: 2 cups

Serves: 6

Prep time: 10 minutes

Cook time: 25 minutes

Ingredients

2 cups all-purpose flour

1 tablespoon baking powder

1 teaspoon dried thyme or dried rosemary

¼ cup cold salted butter, grated

¾ cup milk

2 tablespoons unsalted butter

1 tablespoon extra-virgin olive oil

1 small onion, finely diced

1 carrot, grated

1 celery stalk, finely diced

3 tablespoons flour

4 cups chicken broth

½ cup whipping cream

3 cups chopped, cooked chicken

1 cup frozen peas or green beans

Salt to taste

Pepper to taste

Directions

1. In a medium bowl, mix together the flour, baking powder, and thyme or rosemary. Cut in the salted butter until pea-sized crumbs are formed. Stir in the milk to form a wet dough. Set aside.

2. In a Dutch oven or large, heavy saucepan, heat the unsalted butter and olive oil over medium-high heat until melted, about 1 minute. Add the onion, carrots, and celery, and sauté for 2 minutes. Whisk in the flour until lightly golden brown, about 2 minutes. Add the broth, and stir for 3 minutes. Add the whipping cream, chicken, and peas. Stir and reduce the heat to medium.

3. Add a heaping tablespoon of the wet dough onto the surface of the liquid, ladling the soup over the dumplings. Lower the temperature to a low simmer, cover, and cook until the dumplings are cooked through, about 12 to 15 minutes. The smaller the dumplings, the quicker they'll cook.

4. Season with salt and pepper and serve warm.

Baby Bites:

Beginner	Novice	Advanced
Serve mashed dumpling with saucy shredded chicken and mashed peas on a loaded spoon.	Check peas to ensure they mash with ease, and serve a finger of a dumpling with sauce, chicken, and vegetables over the top. Load spoon as needed.	Allow child to indicate how much they want and have them serve themselves with assistance

Indian Spiced Cauliflower and Garbanzo Beans

Serving size: ½ cup

Servings: 4

Prep time: 10 minutes

Cook time: 30 minutes

Ingredients

1 cup whole-fat plain yogurt (4–5% fat)

1 tablespoon curry powder

1½ teaspoons sea salt

1 teaspoon paprika

1 tablespoon tomato paste

¼ cup extra-virgin olive oil, divided

1 (14.5-ounce) can garbanzo beans, drained and rinsed

1 head cauliflower, cut into bite-sized pieces

1 lemon, juiced

4 flatbreads or pita

¼ cup chopped parsley or cilantro

Directions

1. Preheat the oven to 400°F. Line a baking sheet with parchment paper.

2. In a large mixing bowl, mix together the yogurt, curry powder, salt, paprika, tomato paste, and 3 tablespoons of the olive oil. Add in garbanzo beans and cauliflower and stir to coat.

3. Spoon out beans and cauliflower onto the prepared baking sheet. Place remaining yogurt sauce in the refrigerator. Place baking sheet in the oven and roast for 30 minutes. Cover with foil after 15 minutes to steam roast, according to infant skill level.

4. Meanwhile, with the remaining sauce, whisk in the remaining 1 tablespoon of olive oil and the lemon juice.

5. Place the flatbread or pita in the oven the final 3 minutes of baking to heat through.

6. Drizzle the sauce over the roasted vegetables and top with chopped parsley or cilantro. Serve with the toasted flatbread or pita bread.

Note: Broccoli, sweet potatoes, or butternut squash can be added or used in place of cauliflower in this dish.

Baby Bites:

Beginner	Novice	Advanced
Steam roast the beans and cauliflower. Gently mash beans and cauliflower and stir in yogurt sauce and serve on a loaded spoon or allow infant to palm feed.	Make sure that cauliflower mashes easily with a fork, along with beans or gently squash them with a fork and mix with yogurt sauce and a finger piece of flatbread.	Skip the steam roasting step, as an advanced eater can handle chewier pieces of vegetables. Allow child to indicate which foods they want and have them serve themselves. Cut into small, bite-sized pieces with sauce over the top or on the side for dipping.

Skewer-Free Chicken Kebabs

Serving size: 2 cups

Servings: 6

Prep time: 8 hours (marinating)

Cook time: 20 minutes

Ingredients

1 pound small red or gold potatoes

1½ pounds chicken breasts or thighs, cubed

1 (15-ounce) bottle Italian dressing, divided

2 red, yellow, or orange bell peppers, cut into bite-sized pieces

1 (6-ounce) package cremini or baby bella or button mushrooms, cleaned

1 sweet onion, cut into bite-sized pieces

Directions

1. In a large, microwave-safe bowl, add in the small potatoes and cover with water. Microwave on high for 5 minutes, which will start the cooking process for the potatoes. Drain and set aside the potatoes. The potatoes will not be soft at this point but will fully cook later.

2. Place the chicken in an airtight container or bag and pour in half the bottle of Italian dressing.

3. Place the bell peppers, mushrooms, onions, and potatoes in another container or bag and pour the remaining Italian dressing over the top. Shake to fully coat. Refrigerate for at least 8 hours or up to 48 hours before cooking.

4. Preheat the oven to 425°F. Line two baking sheets with parchment paper.

5. Drain the marinade and discard. Place half the veggie mix onto one baking sheet and the other half of the veggie mix on the other baking sheet. Divide the chicken between the two sheets.

6. Bake for 20 minutes, stirring halfway through the baking time and covering with foil to steam roast. Serve immediately.

Tip: Serve with basmati rice and flatbread.

BABY BITES:

Beginner	Novice	Advanced
Mash potato and bell peppers with a fork and finely chop the chicken to mix with the mashed potato. Add olive oil if you need to make this less thick. Serve on a loaded spoon.	Cut chicken and vegetables into tiny, bite-sized pieces and serve on a loaded spoon or allow infant to practice pincer grasp to pick up pieces. Ensure all vegetables are easy to mash with a fork. Top with olive oil if needed to make this juicier.	Skip the steam roasting step, as an advanced eater can handle chewier pieces of vegetables. Allow child to indicate which foods they want and have them serve themselves. Cut into small, bite-sized pieces before serving.

Loaded Baked Potatoes

Serving size: 1 potato

Servings: 4

Prep time: 5 minutes

Cook time: 10 minutes

Ingredients

4 large russet potatoes

6 slices raw bacon

½ cup finely chopped broccoli, cooked

1 cup sour cream or plain Greek yogurt

1 cup shredded cheddar cheese

2 scallions, chopped

Directions

1. Wash the potato skins well. Using a fork, poke holes on all sides of the potatoes, including the ends.

2. If using a microwave, cook on high for 4 minutes, turn the potatoes, and continue cooking for about 2 to 4 minutes, checking every minute for doneness. Check the firmness. The potatoes should give with gentle squeezing; if necessary, microwave longer (time may vary based on your microwave and the size of the potatoes). If using an oven, preheat to 425°F. Wash potatoes and rub outside with olive oil and season with salt and pepper. Place potatoes directly on the oven rack and bake for 35 to 45 minutes or until the potatoes are easy to squeeze.

3. Place 2 pieces of paper towel on a heat-safe plate. Place the bacon slices on 1 piece of paper towel and cover with the other piece of paper towel. Microwave the bacon for 3 minutes and check for doneness; continue baking, to desired doneness, about 2 minutes. (Times vary based on microwaves.) Chop the cooked bacon for crumbling into the potatoes.

4. Cut the baked potatoes open lengthwise. Squeeze the potatoes to break up the inside. Add 2 tablespoons cooked broccoli and ¼ cup sour cream and cheese to each potato and stir to mix with the potato. Top with scallions and serve immediately.

Tip: The sky is the limit when it comes to toppings. Baked potatoes are a great way to honor autonomy in eating. Allow all family members to choose their own toppings and explore the various flavor combinations. Here are some of our favorites: olives; tomatoes; salsa; avocado or guacamole; sausage; chives; sour cream or plain yogurt; broccoli and cheese soup; chili; or creamed spinach or spinach and artichoke dip.

Baby Bites:

Beginner	Novice	Advanced
Mix together soft broccoli, potato pieces, and Greek yogurt. Serve on a loaded spoon or allow infant to palm the mixture and self-feed. Remember, the broccoli should be so soft that it easily mashes.	Scoop out potato from skin and mix in soft broccoli, Greek yogurt, cheese, and finely minced bacon pieces. Serve with a spoon and see how your infant self-feeds.	Serve the baked potato as you would for yourself. Allow your baby to select their preferred toppings and self-feed with a spoon or their hands.

Mediterranean White Bean Soup

Serving size: 1 cup

Servings: 8

Prep time: about 10 minutes

Cook time: 40 minutes–8 hours

Ingredients

1 onion, finely chopped

2 celery stalks, thinly sliced

2 carrots, grated

2 cloves garlic, chopped

1 teaspoon dried thyme

1 bay leaf

2 (14.5-ounce) cans cannellini beans, drained and rinsed

5 cups chicken or vegetable broth

1 lemon, zested and juiced

1 cup chopped fresh parsley

Salt to taste

Pepper to taste

½ cup grated Parmesan

Directions

1. If using a pressure cooker, place the onion, celery, carrots, garlic, thyme, bay leaf, cannellini beans, and broth into pot. Secure the lid and select Pressure Cook for 5 minutes. After cooking has completed, hold warm until you're ready to serve or do a Quick Release. If using a slow cooker, place the onion, celery, carrots, garlic, thyme, bay leaf, cannellini beans, and broth into pot. Place the lid on top, select the low heat setting, and cook for 6 to 8 hours.

2. Stir in the lemon zest, lemon juice, and parsley. Season with salt and pepper. Remove bay leaf.

3. Top with Parmesan, and serve.

Tip: Add in ground sausage, cubed chicken, or bacon for a meatier version. Serve with crusty French bread or garlic bread.

Baby Bites:

Beginner	Novice	Advanced
Strain the liquid and mash the beans and vegetables together and load on a spoon or allow infant to palm and self-feed the strained soup. Check beans for tenderness, if tough gently mash.	Serve soup with a spoon and a wedge of crusty bread for them to dip and eat.	Serve the soup and allow them to sprinkle the cheese on top. Serve bread on the side.

Thai Coconut, Chicken, and Edamame Soup

Serving size: 1 cup

Servings: 8

Prep time: About 10 minutes

Cook time: 30 minutes–6 hours

Ingredients

1 tablespoon coconut oil

2 chicken breasts, cut into bite-sized cubes

1 onion, thinly sliced

1 carrot, grated

2 cups thinly sliced mushrooms

1-inch piece fresh ginger, peeled and grated

1 teaspoon curry powder

1 tablespoon soy sauce

1 cup frozen edamame beans, shelled

5 cups vegetable broth

1 (13.5-ounce) can coconut milk

1 lime, zested and juiced

½ cup chopped cilantro

Salt to taste

Directions

1. If using a pressure cooker, sauté coconut oil, chicken breasts, onion, and carrot for 4 minutes. Next, add in mushrooms, ginger, and curry and sauté for 2 minutes. Next, add soy sauce, edamame, vegetable broth, and coconut milk into the pot. Secure the lid and select Pressure Cook for 5 minutes. After cooking has completed, you can choose to hold warm until you're ready to serve or do a quick release. If using a slow cooker, first use a skillet to sauté chicken, onion, and carrot in coconut oil for 4 minutes over medium high heat. Next, place chicken mixture, mushrooms, ginger, curry, soy sauce, edamame, and vegetable broth into a slow cooker. Place the lid on top, select the low heat setting, and cook for 4 to 6 hours. After 3 hours, stir in the coconut milk.

2. Before serving, stir in lime juice, zest, and cilantro. Adjust seasoning with salt, as desired.

BABY BITES:

Beginner	Novice	Advanced
Strain the soup and serve on a plate. Edamame can be a firm bean; gently mash the beans. Finely chop the chicken. Serve about 1 to 2 tablespoons of vegetables and just a little broth over the top. Allow infant to self-feed with their palms and serve loaded spoons.	Slightly strain soup and continue to check texture of vegetables and beans. Serve chicken in small, bite-sized pieces. Serve with a spoon but recognize that infant will most likely use their hands.	Serve the soup, checking bean texture and mashing hard beans and cutting chicken into small, bite-sized pieces.

Simple Sides

Dipping can be fun! Adding in sauces or dressings for dipping can make trying new foods a more enjoyable experience for little ones.

Leslie's Easy-Peasy Roasted Potatoes

Serving size: 4–8 fingerling potatoes

Serves: 4–6 adults

Prep time: 10 minutes

Cook time: 30 minutes

Ingredients:

1 (1½-pound) bag of small or fingerling potatoes
2 tablespoons olive oil
½ teaspoon crushed black pepper
1 teaspoon dried oregano
½ teaspoon salt, or omit if desired

Directions:

1. Preheat oven to 400°F.
2. Wash and dry your potatoes. Using a cutting board, slice your fingerling or small potatoes in half lengthwise. Place in a mixing bowl and add olive oil, pepper, and oregano. Toss to coat evenly and pour onto your baking sheet. Space out on the pan. Pop in the oven for 25 to 30 minutes, stirring halfway.

Variations:

- Potatoes are very versatile. You can make a variety of spice blends (Mexican—cumin, oregano, coriander; Greek—garlic powder, rosemary; Indian—curry powder) or try a low-sodium version by roasting potatoes with just olive oil and before serving toss with fresh lemon juice and the zest of a lemon.

- Want *more* variety? Replace potatoes with carrots, rutabagas, turnips, or any hard squash.

> If the skin is tough on the potato, try peeling it to make it easier for baby to enjoy. Fingerlings have a very thin skin, whereas russet potatoes have a thicker skin.

BABY BITES:

Beginner	Novice	Advanced
Remove skin, if desired. Check the texture to ensure potato wedges smashes with ease. Serve 1 to 2 wedges at a time.	Serve 2 wedges cut into small, bite-sized pieces.	Serve 3 to 4 as wedges or chop into bite-sized pieces.

Zucchini Fries

Serving size: 4–5 finger slices

Prep time: 20 minutes

Cook time: 20–25 minutes

Ingredients:

2–3 large zucchini

1 cup flour

3 teaspoons salt, divided

2 large eggs, beaten

¼ cup whole milk

2 cups panko or plain bread crumbs

½ cup flour

½ teaspoon ground cumin

½ teaspoon paprika

½ teaspoon garlic powder

Olive oil cooking spray

Directions:

1. Preheat oven to 425°F. Line two baking sheets with parchment paper or foil.
2. Slice and ready your vegetables (zucchini in ½-inch slices, cauliflower sliced in ½-inch pieces or florets, green beans are done whole).
3. Prepare your breading area with 1 large plate for flour and 1 teaspoon salt, 1 large bowl for the eggs, milk, and 1 teaspoon salt, and 1 large plate for the panko, flour, and seasonings to include 1 teaspoon salt.
4. Working in batches, first dredge each piece of vegetables into flour, then dunk them into the egg mixture (letting excess drip off), and last dip into the panko mixture. Transfer breaded zucchini fries to prepared baking sheet and spray them liberally with cooking spray.
5. Bake vegetables for 20 to 25 minutes or until golden and tender.

Variations:

- Add grated Parmesan cheese and serve with a marinara dipping sauce for a fun twist!

Baby Bites:

Beginner	Novice	Advanced
Consider blanching vegetables first by putting them in boiling water for 1 to 3 minutes and then immediately into an ice bath to ensure that the veggies are mash-able once baked.	Serve 1 to 3 fries, ensuring texture is tender for a bite.	Serve 1 to 3 fries.

Parmesan Roasted Cauliflower or Broccoli

Serving size: 4–5 finger slices

Prep time: 5 minutes

Cook time: 20 minutes

Ingredients:

1 head cauliflower or broccoli

½ cup Parmesan cheese, grated

½ teaspoon lemon pepper

½ teaspoon dried oregano or thyme

cooking spray

Salt, to taste

Directions:

1. Preheat oven to 400°F and line two baking sheets with parchment paper or foil.
2. Remove fibrous core of cauliflower or dense stalk of broccoli. Next, cut vegetables into ¼-inch slices (yes, slices). Lay vegetables onto baking sheet. Sprinkle vegetables with Parmesan cheese, lemon pepper, and dried oregano evenly. Spray vegetables evenly with cooking spray.
3. Bake for 15 to 20 minutes or until cheese becomes golden in color and vegetables are tender with slightly browned edges. Season with salt as desired and serve.

Variations:

- Out of Parmesan? Mix grated cheddar with bread crumbs and crumble over the top. Omit lemon pepper and use thyme to season.

Before you toss out the thick broccoli stalks, consider peeling away the thick, fibrous part to expose the tender stalk.

Baby Bites:

Beginner	Novice	Advanced
Serve 1 to 2 cauliflower slices, ensuring texture is tender enough to mash.	Serve 2 to 3 cauliflower slices.	Serve 2 to 5 cauliflower slices

Roasted Vegetable Guide

1. Fully preheat and roast at 425°F.
2. Give the vegetables some space instead of overcrowding the pan.
3. Roast vegetables of similar texture together with similar cooking time like carrots and potatoes.
4. Be liberal with the oil (you can always use the oil in salads later).
5. How small or large you dice or cut up vegetables will influence the time you need to roast. Try to keep size uniform.
6. Look for toasted edges and check for tenderness to determine doneness.

Now that you have the basics, let's break down a timetable for most vegetables:

Vegetables	Cut	Roasting Time
Potatoes, sweet potatoes, carrots, beets, or hard squashes	Cut into finger-sized pieces or large cubes	25–45 minutes
Asparagus, green beans, bell peppers, or zucchini	Whole or in strips	10–20 minutes
Broccoli, cauliflower, cabbage, or Brussels sprouts	Trim or peel off fibrous stems and cut in half or quarter	15–20 minutes
Tomatoes	Cut in half or quarter	20–25 minutes
Onions	Cut into ½-inch slices or rings	30 minutes

Tips: Any time you bake or roast foods you want the food pieces to be uniform in size to ensure even cooking.

CONCLUSION

As you kick off this journey of creating a *Born to Eat* family, we hope you will frequently pull out this book as a guidebook. We hope you've found *Born to Eat* a wonderful resource that will help you and your little one for years to come. Every bite of food has the potential to nourish a *Born to Eat* baby and family. Remember the key values behind the *Born to Eat* philosophy:

1. Eat whole food as often as possible, from the developmentally appropriate infant through adulthood
2. Honor and support self-regulation of body nourishment
3. When possible, eat as a family
4. Be present and purposeful with food
5. Support a healthy body through body confidence, trust, and gratitude

The self-feeding and baby-led feeding approaches are gaining support worldwide, so don't ever feel as though you are alone. Social media, albeit overwhelming, has fabulous support groups or pages on a variety of social media channels. We have a list on our website to get you started.

It is our hope that the *Born to Eat* philosophy has ignited a spark in you that helps foster self-regulation and body trust in your whole family. Because we are all *Born to Eat*.

ABOUT THE AUTHORS

Photo by Grace Geri Goodale

Leslie Schilling

Leslie Schilling, MA, RDN, CSCS, CEDS-S, owns a Las Vegas-based practice specializing in nutrition counseling for families, people with disordered eating concerns, professional athletes, and performers. Leslie has served as a performance nutrition consultant for Cirque du Soleil® and the NBA and an expert contributor to *U.S. News & World Report*. With her warm, compassionate, and entertaining personality, Leslie has been featured in media outlets like *Health*, *Women's Health*, *Self*, *Pregnancy Magazine*, *Yoga Journal*, *Bicycling*, *BuzzFeed*, the *Huffington Post*, and on HGTV. As a registered dietitian certified as an eating disorder specialist and supervisor, Leslie spends much of her time supporting professionals across the nation through supervision. When she's not hiking or playing board games with her family, you can find her sharing non-diet messages on her social media and speaking platforms. Leslie is passionate about educating ministry, military, health, medical, and fitness professionals about the harms of diet culture.

Photo by Grace Geri Goodale

Wendy Jo Peterson

Wendy Jo Peterson, MS, RDN is a non-diet dietitian and culinary nutritionist. She is the author of eight books, including *Bread Making For Dummies* and *Meal Prep Cookbook For Dummies*. As with all military spouses, she wears many hats, but her favorite is her role as a mama. You can find Wendy Jo in her garden, walking the beach, in her camper van, or providing culinary education across the globe. She splits her time between Austin, Texas; San Diego, California; and Europe.

ACKNOWLEDGMENTS

> "Feeling gratitude and not expressing it is like wrapping a present and not giving it."
>
> —William Arthur Ward

To Jani Moore: If it weren't for you and Chris, we wouldn't even know about this amazing and incredibly logical way to feed our kids. You and Chris gave us courage to be bold and bring our voices to light.

To our editor, Nicole Frail: Thank you for answering our endless questions, giving us great feedback, and helping *Born to Eat* come to life.

To our agent, Matt Wagner, at Fresh Books, Inc.: Thank you for you for supporting us and tirelessly hunting for the right home for *Born to Eat*.

To our amazing expert reviewers who selflessly gave their time to improve our book. Gill Rapley, PhD: without you we would have never known about baby-led weaning. You are a pioneer and your reviews truly made *Born to Eat* great! To Katja Rowell, MD: Your support and revisions helped us make *Born to Eat* a great resource for all new parents. We are honored to use resources from your amazing books in *Born to Eat*. To Jacqueline Henry, SLP: You helped us see through the eyes of a different discipline and gave us great pointers to make the book easier for parents to use. Thank you all for being early reviewers of *Born to Eat*. Our editor thanks you, too!

To our publisher, Skyhorse: We are so grateful you took a chance on us. We appreciate all you've done to make *Born to Eat* what we really wanted it to be.

Acknowledgments

To our cover designer, Jenny Zemanek: You took so many random details from us to make a beautiful and happy cover that is exactly what we wanted. Thank you!

To our illustrator, Holly Kennedy: Your drawings brought our words to life, and created whimsical, loveable images to share our visions. We appreciate your time with the whole process and love that you too are a *Born to Eat* mom.

To our friends and colleagues who contributed stories, tested recipes, reviewed the manuscript, and supported our process: Rebecca Scritchfield, Janet Borland, Blair Mize, Julie Hight, Jane Gray Bledsoe, Katie Ferraro, Sidney Fry, Lindsay Stenovec, Lindsay Livingston, Kristen Cook, Heather Wosoogh, Mimi Powell, and Courtney Hansen. We love that you all added to our knowledge base, shared fears and experiences of self-feeding babies, tested recipes, and trusted us with *Born to Eat* approach. You are a powerful and strong group of moms.

To our research adviser (Leslie's brilliantly sweet husband), Brian Schilling, PhD: Your research prowess and scientific writing knowledge was tremendously helpful and so very appreciated.

To our families: You've always pushed us, loved us, and supported us even when you had no idea what we were up to. We thank you for that!

To our girls: You have changed our lives and our worlds in the most beautiful ways. You've shown us just how big our brave is.

INDEX

CONVERSION CHARTS

METRIC AND IMPERIAL CONVERSIONS

(These conversions are rounded for convenience)

Ingredient	Cups/Tablespoons/Teaspoons	Ounces	Grams/Milliliters
Butter	1 cup/ 16 tablespoons/ 2 sticks	8 ounces	230 grams
Cheese, shredded	1 cup	4 ounces	110 grams
Cornstarch	1 tablespoon	0.3 ounce	8 grams
Cream cheese	1 tablespoon	0.5 ounce	14.5 grams
Flour, all-purpose	1 cup/1 tablespoon	4.5 ounces/0.3 ounce	125 grams/8 grams
Flour, whole wheat	1 cup	4 ounces	120 grams
Fruits or veggies, chopped	1 cup	5 to 7 ounces	145 to 200 grams
Fruit, dried	1 cup	4 ounces	120 grams
Fruits or veggies, puréed	1 cup	8.5 ounces	245 grams
Honey, maple syrup, or corn syrup	1 tablespoon	0.75 ounce	20 grams
Liquids: cream, milk, water, or juice	1 cup	8 fluid ounces	240 milliliters
Oats	1 cup	5.5 ounces	150 grams
Salt	1 teaspoon	0.2 ounce	6 grams
Spices: cinnamon, cloves, ginger, or nutmeg (ground)	1 teaspoon	0.2 ounce	5 milliliters
Sugar, brown, firmly packed	1 cup	7 ounces	200 grams
Sugar, white	1 cup/1 tablespoon	7 ounces/0.5 ounce	200 grams/12.5 grams
Vanilla extract	1 teaspoon	0.2 ounce	4 grams

OVEN TEMPERATURES

Fahrenheit	Celsius	Gas Mark
225°	110°	¼
250°	120°	½
275°	140°	1
300°	150°	2
325°	160°	3
350°	180°	4
375°	190°	5
400°	200°	6
425°	220°	7
450°	230°	8

BORN TO EAT BASICS
HANDOUT

Developmental signs of feeding readiness can include:

- Independently sitting up

- Absence of tongue thrust

- Grasping items with more hand control

- Putting toys to his or her mouth

- Demonstrating an interest in table foods

Safety Checklist

- We have taken Infant CPR

- We understand the difference between a gagging infant versus a choking infant

- We are present and eating with our baby

- Baby is in a secure, upright seat during mealtime

- We have tested the temperature and texture of each food offered

- We are allowing baby to self-feed and not putting our fingers into their mouth

Check out chapters 5-9 for feeding stages, checklists, and food progressions.

Division of Responsibility

- <u>Baby Decides:</u> What & How Much

- <u>You Decide:</u> When, Where & What Is Offered

Check Your Expectations

- Be patient with every bite and every mealtime
- Adjust mealtimes to support a happy and alert baby
- New foods can take multiple trials before a baby accepts a new food, so don't give up
- There's no such thing as a perfect food, a perfect meal, or a perfect eater
- Don't worry about how much baby is eating; every child is different, so instead look for cues of hunger/fullness and let your child be the guide

Things to Avoid

- Suggesting one more bite or encouraging a child to eat more
- Foods that can pose a choking risk, such as, whole grapes, nuts, spoonfuls of nut butters, hard vegetables or fruits, or dried fruits, see pages 166 and 167 for an extensive list of choking hazards and how to create a safer bite for your baby.

Building the Baby Plate

High Iron/Protein + High Energy + Fruit/Veggies

½ Boiled Egg
3 Raspberries
2 Soft Steamed Green Beans

2 Tbsp. Lentils
2 Frozen Strawberries
1 Raw Broccoli Stalk and Floret

1 oz. Sirloin Steak
1 Kiwi Wedge
1 Sweet Potato Finger

Please refer to Chapter 14 of *Born to Eat* for appropriate food preparations and serving suggestions.